J U N G

O N   C H R I S T I A N I T Y

ENCOUNTERING

JUNG

ENCOUNTERING

J U N G

ON CHRISTIANITY

SELECTED AND INTRODUCED BY MURRAY STEIN

PRINCETON UNIVERSITY PRESS · PRINCETON, NEW JERSEY

This book is composed of texts selected from the following volumes of the Collected
Works of C. G. Jung: *The Zofingia Lectures*, Supplementary Volume A © 1983 by Princeton
University Press; *The Symbolic Life*, Volume 18, © 1958 by Bollingen Foundation, © re-
newed 1986 by Princeton University Press; *Aion*, Volume 9ii, © 1959 by Bollingen Foun-
dation, 2nd ed. © 1969 by Princeton University Press, © renewed 1987 by Princeton
University Press; *Psychology and Religion: West and East*, Volume 11, © 1958 by Bollingen
Foundation, 2nd ed. © 1969 by Princeton University Press, © renewed 1986 by Princeton
University Press; *Psychology and Alchemy*, Volume 12, © 1953 by Bollingen Foundation, ©
renewed 1981 by Princeton University Press; *Alchemical Studies*, Volume 13, © 1967 by
Bollingen Foundation; and *Dream Analysis*, © 1984 by Princeton University Press. Other
excerpts are taken from *The Collected Letters of C. G. Jung*, Volumes 2, © 1953, 1955, 1961,
1963, 1968, 1971, 1972, 1974, 1975 by Princeton University Press; *Memories, Dreams,
Reflections*, © 1961, 1962, 1963, and renewed 1989, 1990, 1991 by Random House, Inc.
(reprinted here by arrangement with Pantheon Books, a division of Random House,
Inc.).

Jung, C. G. (Carl Gustav), 1875–1961.
On Christianity / selected and introduced by Murray Stein.
p.   cm. — (Encountering Jung)
Includes bibliographical references and index.
ISBN 0-691-00697-0 (pbk. : alk. paper)
1. Christianity—Psychology.   I. Stein, Murray, 1943–
II. Title.   III. Series: Jung, C. G. (Carl Gustav), 1875–1961.
Selections. English. 1995.
BR110.J84   1999
230—dc21   99-28902

http://pup.princeton.edu

Printed in the United States of America

10   9   8   7   6   5   4   3   2   1

CONTENTS

JUNG

ON CHRISTIANITY

INTRODUCTION

> The arcane substance [of alchemy] corresponds to the Christian
> dominant, which was originally alive and present in consciousness
> but then sank into the unconscious and must now be
> restored in renewed form.
>
> C. G. Jung (CW *14, par. 466*)

In the passage quoted above, taken from the late work *Mysterium Coniunctionis*, Jung speaks as a religious man (a *homo religiosus*), and also as one for whom the central images of Christianity are a psychic reality that carries significant meaning. Often he writes about Christian themes in this way. He cares deeply about their value and importance, and he even proposes several important theological and practical revisions for Christianity. He speaks, however, as a psychologist and not as a Christian theologian or believer. This combination of factors, which characterizes Jung's approach to Christianity, has led to several general misunderstandings.

One major misinterpretation is that Jung was a Christian apologist, i.e., a defender of Christian truths within a contemporary setting using modern concepts and language. By some he has even been looked upon as a possible savior of Christianity in a time when its spiritual message is going unheard for want of persuasive images and concepts. His writings are taken at times as the words of a modern prophet. He is seen as a kind of evangelist in the garb of a medical psychologist.

Clearly this kind of evangelical persuasion was not Jung's intention, even if some of his writings give this impression. When he states (as above) that the Christian message "must now be restored in renewed form," one might imagine him speaking in the voice of the Protestant Reformation but, given Jung's overall perspective and psychological program, this is a misreading. Unlike his Swiss countrymen, Karl Barth and Emil Brunner, two Protestant contemporaries who did consider the revitalization of Christian theology to be their mission, Jung does

3

not place himself within the Christian theological circle. This would be presumptuous. He was trained as a medical doctor, not as a theologian. He was not out to serve the church, nor, like Paul Tillich, to correlate Christian "answers" to modern culture's "questions." It is true that he expresses grave concern about a perceived lack of vitality in contemporary Christianity, but his focus lies not so much on the church as on modern people who are spiritually adrift and need living symbols to find meaning and direction in their lives. Also, unlike the theologians, Jung does not look to the Bible or to Christian tradition for authority or inspiration. Instead, he turns to the psyche and most particularly to the unconscious. This brings a wholly different dimension into play. To date, Christian theologians have not paid serious attention to the unconscious.

A second major misinterpretation—precisely the opposite of the first—is that Jung was anti-Christian and out to destroy Christianity or to supplant it with his own psychological theory, analytical psychology. This is as erroneous as it is to view him as a modern evangelist of Christianity. Jung's attachment to Christianity was indeed profound, and it ran stronger than a mere nod to Swiss conventionality. His commitment became increasingly evident in the latter years of his life. After his taxing journey to India in 1938 at the age of sixty-eight, Jung turned almost exclusively in his thinking and writing about religious matters to Western—specifically to Christian—themes. He writes eloquently and with great sensitivity about religious rituals like the Roman Catholic mass ("Transformation Symbolism in the Mass") and about Christian doctrines like the Holy Trinity ("A Psychological Approach to Dogma of the Trinity"). He also dwells deeply on the symbol of Christ and considers the meaning of Christianity for Western culture and humankind (*Aion*). In *Answer to Job*, he offers a stunning and highly controversial interpretation of the Bible. In all of these late texts, he speaks as a concerned psychologist. While he confesses ignorance of formal theology, he shows great awareness of theological issues and tackles some of the thorniest theological doctrines known to Christendom. These are not attacks upon Christian belief and practice, nor do they foresee their demise or suggest their replacement by analytical psychology. Clearly, Christianity meant a great deal to Jung. I believe that in later life it became for him something like an "ultimate concern," to use Paul Tillich's phrase for the religious attitude.

Christianity's past and future were close to Jung's heart. He advocated the transformation of Christianity. This is significantly different from seeking to revitalize and reform it on the one hand or from abandoning or destroying it and supplanting it with psychology on the other.

Jung's relationship to Christianity was complex, though it is not impenetrable. "Was Jung a Christian?" This is a question many people have asked. There are many levels to consider in addressing this sensitive issue. If one uses the term Christian in a cultural sense and not in a more rigorous fashion that requires accepted denominational practices of belief and piety, the answer is yes. Officially Carl Jung was a Christian by virtue of his baptism, and he died a Christian, his remains being interred in the Swiss Protestant cemetery in the village of Küsnacht where he lived. In fact he was steeped in Protestantism. His grandfather, his father, and six of his uncles were pastors in the Swiss Reformed Church, and he grew up in a parsonage. He attended church as a child and received communion at the appropriate age. Habits of mind and attitude were importantly shaped by Swiss Protestant Christianity. Even as a youth, however, he showed tendencies toward freethinking, and he could not accept the standard catechism answers to his theological questions. As an adult he did not attend church services regularly. His intellectual interests in religion ranged all over the map— from the Upanishads to Buddhist teachings, from Chinese Taoism to North American Indian nature worship—and he respected them all. With some justice, he has been seen as a harbinger of New Age spirituality, which also blends Eastern and Western (and other) traditions into numerous individual religious practices and notions. Yet he was highly critical of people who sever themselves from their historical religious roots and try to become practicing members of exotic foreign belief systems. Jung was a cultural conservative, if also a highly adventuresome and far-reaching intellectual explorer. He was a spiritually sensitive man who never left his native Christianity for another religion.

In the excerpts from Jung's works that are included in this anthology, one finds the writings of a man who, though untrained formally in Christian theology, is surprisingly steeped in its history. One must keep in mind, however, that theology and Church doctrine are not absolutes for Jung. He reckons with them as a psychologist, reading them as statements made by people who were in touch with the symbolic dimension of the psyche and who experienced numinous images of the collective unconscious. He does not regard Christian belief and doctrine (or "dogma") as the definitive words about spiritual reality in any sense. Nor does he understand the Biblical account of God as a final and complete revelation. For Jung, individual experience is the ultimate arbiter and final authority in religious matters. There is no higher judge. The religious life has, for him, little to do with church and traditional piety, or with following received teachings and established rituals. Its home is in the psychic world of the individual. It is a life that befalls a person unbidden and often unwelcomed.

← this is most certainly true

THE NATURE OF RELIGIOUS EXPERIENCE

Jung's most frequent definition of God is "the name by which I designate all things which cross my wilful path violently and recklessly, all things which upset my subjective views, plans, and intentions and change the course of my life for better or worse" (*Letters*, 2, p. 525); ". . . it is always the overwhelming psychic factor that is called 'God' " (*CW* 11, par. 137). There are many stories in the Bible that suggest this view of God and the religious life. Jung's favorite was the story of Job. Jung does read the Bible as a testament to authentic, original religious experience, but he does not regard it as a privileged document that lies outside the range of comparison and criticism. The Scriptures of other religious traditions are similarly rich with authentic accounts of genuine religious experience, and in fact equally genuine experiences of God could just as well befall people today as they drive to work in comfortable sedans. Visions and revelations of what we call God happen to people in every time and place and are not limited to one privileged historical epoch. The theologizing based on such contemporary experiences, moreover, is as valid as the words of the Apostles about their experiences.

The essence of the religious life is, for Jung, religious experience, not piety or correct belief or faithfulness to tradition. To understand specifically what he means by this term, it is helpful to note three paradigmatic instances of it described in his writings.

The first of these is an experience from his own childhood. He reports in his autobiography, *Memories, Dreams, Reflections* (pp. 36–41), that as a schoolboy in Basel he had a "religious experience" that remained with him for the rest of his life. It happened that one fine summer's day, as he came out of school and stood in the courtyard in front of the impressive Basel cathedral, he entertained an image of God sitting on His throne high above the scene before him. The twin towers and checkered tile roof of the Cathedral were bathed in brilliant sunlight. It is a massive brick structure, and on that day it seemed to him exceptionally solid and weighty. Jung's maternal grandfather had been the pastor of this fortress of Swiss Reformed Protestantism, and the boy must have felt some pleasure in recognizing a degree of kinship to God Almighty Himself. Suddenly, however, he had an unexpected urge to unleash a blasphemous fantasy. Given the majestic sanctity of the mighty Cathedral before him and its solemn, somewhat threatening, towering presence, this so frightened him that he ran home and consciously suppressed the fantasy with all his might. For three days he struggled against a looming thought that would not be denied. Finally he could no longer resist it, and with fear and trembling he let himself return mentally to the scene of the Cathedral. Once again he stood in the courtyard and looked up to the heavens where Almighty God sat on his golden throne. With a courageous gesture he released his impertinent mind, and the following sequence of images welled up in him: a trapdoor opened underneath God's throne, and a gigantic turd fell down and smashed the Cathedral to bits. When all was said and done, he did not feel guilty but rather experienced a rush of relief and grace. A big thought had been released in his mind.

Perhaps more remarkable than this fantasy itself is Jung's way of understanding it. For him this kind of explosive outburst of unexpected, unwelcome and unconventional mental content—image and thought—became a touchstone for the authenticity of religious experience. The experience of God is the experience of being overwhelmed, terrorized, even humiliated by His awful and contrary Will. In religious experience, Jung postulates, one's conscious mind is usurped by a superior inner force and becomes possessed by alien images and thoughts from the unconscious. Responsibility for this—both for the phenomenon of the mind's state of possession and for the unconscious contents that flow into it—belongs to God, that "overwhelming psychic factor." God is the force behind the unconscious images that break their way through the ego's defenses and inundate the conscious mind. Jung testifies eloquently to the Protestant sense of the individual's direct, unmediated experience of the Divine.

It was this kind of foundational experience of God in his own life that allowed Jung to recognize a similar moment in the canonized life of his fellow countryman, Brother Klaus, the patron saint of Switzerland. Blessed Nicholas of Flüe was a religious figure of the fifteenth century who apparently was frightened into a life of sanctity by a series of mostly terrifying visions. In one, he saw "the head of a human figure with a terrifying face, full of wrath and threats" (Jung, *CW* 11, par. 478), which to him was not commensurate with the orthodox image of the loving God he had been taught about in church. Afterwards he reported that he had seen "a piercing light resembling a human face" (ibid.). This vision (and presumably others) drove him into a life of seclusion in a tiny hermit's cell within walking distance of his home and considerable family. The frightening, unbidden, unorthodox nature of these images from the unconscious is what most impressed Jung. Brother Klaus eventually rationalized his visions into conventional theology and squared them with images of the Trinity—doing this, Jung felt, in order to preserve his sanity. The life of the religiously gifted is not a comfortable one.

The third classic example of religious experience for Jung is Biblical. It is the story of Job. Like Jung and Brother Klaus, Job is utterly overcome by the awesome display of God's power. He, too, is reduced to silence when presented with a vision of God's dreadful might and terrifying magnitude. In Jung's interpretation, Job is completely innocent. He is a scrupulously pious man who follows all the religious conventions, and for most of his life he is blessed with good fortune. This is the expected outcome for a just man in a rationally ordered universe. But then God goes to work on him, tests him with misfortune, reduces him to misery, and finally overwhelms him with questions and images of divine majesty and power. Job is silenced, and he realizes his inferior position vis-à-vis the Almighty. But he also retains his personal integrity, and this so impresses God that He is forced to take stock of Himself. Perhaps He is not so righteous after all! And out of this astonishing self-reflection, induced in God by Job's stubborn righteousness, He, the Almighty, is pushed into a process of transformation that leads eventually to His incarnation as Jesus. God develops empathy and love through his confrontation with Job, and out of it a new relationship between God and humankind is born. This is the kernel of Jung's interpretation of the Book of Job and its position in the Bible.

THE EVOLUTION OF THE GOD IMAGE

Jung was severely taken to task by many of his theological readers and religious friends (notably by Fr. Victor White) for his psychological interpretation of The Book of Job and the Bible. White expressed surprise and consternation that Jung would actually publish such a controversial and heterodox text. He felt such thoughts are better kept to oneself or perhaps shared with a few close confidants. Within the greater context of Jung's life and work as a whole, however, one must acknowledge that his audacious reflections on The Book of Job contribute to his overall program. The fundamental idea behind *Answer to*

Job is that the God image evolves according to basic archetypal patterns ("archetypes") and that the Biblical tradition, including Christianity, shows evidence of such developments. While Jung was not a faithful son of the Christian church, he was profoundly engaged by the dilemma of what he saw in it as an ailing religious tradition. As I have argued at length in my book, *Jung's Treatment of Christianity*, Jung actually diagnosed and set out to treat Christianity much as he would a patient in his analytic practice. He saw modern Christianity as having entered a cul de sac and as being endangered by stagnation and slow death. He wanted to help Christianity get back on the track of its potential internal development.

According to Jung's understanding, Christianity was initially born out of a historical psychological development within Judaism, which is reflected in the Hebrew Bible. The inner logic in the emergence of Christianity from Judaism has to do with the evolution of the God image, and this process continues to the present time. The God image of a people is not static; it evolves through time. That is to say, the ultimate God image, which is embedded in the collective unconscious, gradually emerges into consciousness over the course of millennia. The historic changes in the God image can be studied in the texts handed down by tradition, texts like the Bible and the writings of commentators, theologians, the Church Fathers, and the various heretics (e.g., the Gnostics and alchemists). The development of the God image is a result of interplay between the images and definitions presented by tradition and the human protagonists who carry that tradition forward. This dynamic—as demonstrated in the Book of Job and its aftermath in the following centuries—leads to the manifestation of a more complete God image, in this case an image that is less one-sidedly Patriarchal and more inclusive of the Feminine. In Christianity, this evolution is still underway. The image is not complete. There is still more to come, and the blocks to its manifestation need to be cleared away. This is the task of psychology.

It is this view of doctrine as evolving and the ambition for psychology's part in the theological enterprise that make Jung's work on Christianity so controversial, and for many theologians so completely unacceptable.

The religiously gifted (or perhaps "cursed" would be a better term, given Jung's views on the nature of religious experience) contribute to this ongoing development of the God image. They do this by raising into collective awareness those aspects of the full image that have either been left out of the picture or have never before been revealed. In the time of Job, it was God's love and wisdom (Sophia) that had been lost or repressed in the disappearance of the feminine from the God image in the Patriarchal religion of Jahwism. This needed to be recalled. This aspect of God came to the fore in the Gospels of the New Testament and in the testimony of Christianity that God is love. In the heterodox visions of Brother Klaus, Jung felt, one sees the emergence of further aspects of the Divine—its feminine aspect as God the Mother, and the combination of Father and Mother as "the androgyny of the divine Ground" (Jung, *CW* 11, par. 486). Through Br. Klaus's visions this becomes available to consciousness, but in a form so terrifying that it nearly drove the man insane. However, this vision is a contribution to the ongoing transformation and emergence of the full God image. In Jung's own case—we can say it though Jung would not have been quite so bold as to suggest it himself—his inner experiences, his visions, and his writings based on them portray an image of God that is more whole and complete than the Biblical Christian image. Jung's proposed revision of the God image is presented not as a vision but at the level of theory (the "Quaternity" instead of the "Trinity") and conscious reflection made available by psychological terminology and concepts. Experientially, however, the source of it was primitive and at times terrifying.

While Jung does not stand within the theological circle so adequately defined and maintained by his Swiss Reformed countrymen, Barth and Brunner, he does make a strong positive contribution to the potential further development of the Christian God image and to the evolution of Christian tradition.

JUNG'S PERSONAL RELATIONSHIP TO CHRISTIANITY

On a personal level, as one can see from the selection of readings included in Part I of this anthology, Jung did not consider himself to be a committed member of a Christian denomination. He grew up in a parsonage, but his early experience of Swiss Reformed Protestantism left him cold. To him it seemed like a lifeless institution without either much intellectual honesty or spiritual vitality. While he maintained a correct relation with the Reformed church throughout his life—being baptized, married and buried in it, having his children do likewise, etc.—he did not seek or find any further spiritual benefits from this source. Yet his mind was occupied with theological questions and problems from early on and until the end of his life. Even as a lad he questioned his father about such doctrines as the Holy Trinity, and as a medical student in Basel he took the time to read philosophy and theology (see below, his Zofingia lecture "Thoughts on the Interpretation of Christianity, with reference to the Theory of Albrecht Ritschl"). Always his critique was that the modern church lacked spiritual depth and intellectual rigor.

It has been speculated that Jung's attitude toward the contemporary church and Christian tradition would have been different had he grown up in another cultural setting. But this is hard to imagine. Perhaps a different parson father would have been a greater positive influence on him. The Swiss Protestant church that Jung confronted was not atypical of mainstream Protestant denominations. Always politically and theologically correct, it had nevertheless lost its savor, and in Jung's view the Holy Spirit had left for other parts. "God is dead," Nietzsche, another denizen of Basel, announced in the late nineteenth century, and it would take the likes of Karl Barth, writing during World War I on the book of Romans, to awaken European Protestants from their comfortable (or uncomfortable) slumbers.

The life and work of Karl Barth, only a few years Jung's junior, forms an instructive contrast to Jung's. It demonstrates that someone could grow up in the same cultural and religious milieu and still take a lively interest in the Christian church. Also the son of a Swiss Reformed clergyman and theologian, Barth entered the theological circle early in life and stayed there. His too was a highly creative life, only with a compass turned unwaveringly to the heart of the Christian theological tradition and its source, the Bible. From there he drew the inspiration that fueled the writing of his massive *Church Dogmatics* and anchored him intellectually and spiritually in a time of frightening social and political upheaval in Europe. While Barth began his career with a strong appreciation of religious experience and the personal feeling side of religious life, he became suspicious of their seductions and later rooted himself instead in more objective matters, namely in the Bible and in the received teaching of the Church. Interestingly, his emphasis on the utter freedom of God from human control somewhat parallels Jung's view of God as an overwhelming force that does not conform to the ego's plans or notions. God is autonomous and free for both men, but for Barth the Biblical revelation is final and complete. For Jung, ever the psychologist, much of the God image is still unconscious and will be further revealed as time goes on.

11

It would have made for an exciting intellectual event to have had Jung and Barth face one another and discuss matters theological and religious, but sadly this never happened. Both were inspiring and witty public speakers, and both loved the homely metaphors and rough guttural language of their native Swiss culture. There was, however, no contact between them. Even with Brunner, who lived in Zurich and taught at the university, only a stone's throw from Jung's chair at the Federal Polytechnic Institute (ETH), there was no communication. Jung complained that Protestant theologians ignored him despite his repeated signals of interest in their subject matter, and in Switzerland at least this was largely true. Unhappily, these giants lived side by side but did not manage to bridge the abyss between their academic faculties.

VICTOR WHITE, O.P.

Jung's efforts at building a bridge between psychology and Christian theology met with better results from another quarter, from Roman Catholic clergy, and perhaps never with more promise than in the case of the Dominican theologian and expert on Thomas Aquinas, Fr. Victor White. White had discovered Jung's works in the 1930s and had studied them carefully, with an eye to opening a dialogue between theology and science. He wrote Jung a brief letter of introduction and a birthday greeting upon the occasion of Jung's seventieth birthday in the summer of 1945. Jung responded with enthusiasm, seeing in White the possibility for fruitful collaboration with a first-class theological mind. These were the years in Jung's life—beginning in the late 1930s and extending into the 1950s—when he most energetically and consistently turned his attention to Christian themes. The writings in Parts II and III of this anthology all date from this period. In Victor White, whom he jokingly named his "white raven" (*Letters*, Vol. 1, p. 383), Jung thought he had finally found the promise of *terra firma* in Christian theological territory. White taught dogmatic theology at Blackfriars in Oxford, and from his letters he was obviously enthusiastic about collaborating in a dialogue between psychology and theology (see Lammers for the complete account).

Jung's writings had attracted White because he saw them as offering a firm basis in contemporary psychological science in which to anchor the truth of Christian revelation. In Jung's work, White thought, he had discovered a foothold for theology within the realm of modern science. If a scientist like Jung, working completely outside the theological enterprise, could produce evidence for a God image in the human soul—an *imago Dei*—would this not lend credibility to the claims of medieval Thomistic theology that there is no contradiction between natural science and divine science (theology)? White thought that in Jung's discovery of the archetype he had located the key for a new synthesis similar to the one St. Thomas had achieved between Aristotelian science and Christian teaching in the thirteenth century.

The level of excitement is palpable in their correspondence, which begins in 1945 and continues vigorously through the decade and then tapers off in the early 1950s. The two men met for the first time in 1946, when they spent two weeks together at Jung's Bollingen retreat house. Here they became personally acquainted in the domestic environment of a primitive stone house on Lake Zurich. The place lacked electricity and running water, meals were prepared by one or the other of them over an open hearth (White had warned Jung before he arrived that he did not know how to cook!), and whatever wood was burned for fuel had to be chopped by hand. Jung loved to sail on the alpine lake in front of the tower, and many of their theological discussions doubtless took place in his small sailing vessel as the old man adjusted sheet and rudder to suit the shifting winds. For White this was a far cry from a theological seminar in Oxford. It must have been quite an impressive experience for an introverted person like White—who was not known to engage in small talk or inconsequential chatter or to laugh a great deal—to find himself in the constant presence of a man as electrifyingly alive as C.G. Jung.

Each man had his own agenda, and in the end both were gravely disappointed. White came to despair of ever reaching a fundamental understanding with Jung because, as he said in a letter, they had grown up in such different philosophical climates. White was a Thomist, which entails a conviction that truth can be reached by careful thinking in the light of divine revelation. Jung was a Kantian, which meant that the most he could ever hope to arrive at were more or less plausible hypotheses about the nature of reality. While White thought he could achieve certainty, Jung remained skeptical, restlessly exploring, turning things over in his mind this way and that, and endlessly investigating without definitive conclusion. It was a temperamental difference and a philosophical one, but the nub of the problem that brought their cordial relationship to an end was their disagreement about the nature of evil.

THE QUESTION OF EVIL

What White could not have known when he first met Jung was that the seventy-year-old man was still in the grip of his creative daemon. It would not let him rest until he died sixteen years later. Even people close to him were continually surprised by his new insights and directions. Victor White was in for some shocking surprises.

Jung conceived the theory of archetypes after his break with Freud in 1913 and elaborated on it in the 1920s and 1930s. This theory formed the intellectual framework for his discussions of such Christian symbols as the Trinity and Christ and Christian rituals like the Mass. Jung's published writings gave White reasonable grounds to assume some reliability. He could expect a solid foundation of empirically based scientific observation and a consistent interpretation of psychological reality derived from it. White could see a clear opening for a dialogue in which theology could perhaps add further detail to analytical psychology and lead it toward its logical conclusion. Revelation caps human science on the march to truth, according to Thomist philosophy. Where human knowledge of the unconscious reaches its limit and comes to a halt, revelation might go ahead and complete the picture.

Jung would have none of this. What theology offered in its images and teachings, he interpreted as an expression of its one-sidedness and dogmatic partiality. Theology for Jung is a conscious elaboration of psychological experience, which in the end departs significantly from its source—the raw experience of the unconscious—and falls into the trap laid by ego defenses. The result is that theology tends toward the one-sidedness of ego-consciousness. It cannot take psychology further; it can only block scientific investigation.

In theology, Jung judged, the ego with its rationalizing tendencies takes over and cuts away those aspects of the full God image that do not agree with its presuppositions and needs. The case of Brother Klaus illustrates this beautifully, and the doctrine of evil as *privatio boni* is a doctrinal example of this same rationalizing tendency. This doctrine turned out to be an intractable barrier that wedged itself between Jung and White and could not be removed. Jung wanted to interpret it psychologically and thereby overcome it; White wanted to accept it and use it as a guide for psychology. It was a land mine that blew up in their faces and destroyed their relationship.

The notion that evil can be defined as "the absence of good" (*privatio boni*) made eminent sense to White and no sense at all to Jung. At first White thought it was only a problem of logic, which could easily be removed once the terms were defined and understood. But much more is at stake here than mere logic. What this definition rests on is the dogmatic assertion that God is completely known, and known to be wholly good. By definition (of the ego, Jung would say), there is no evil in God, and He is in no way responsible for even the slightest trace of evil in the world. Evil comes about, according to this theology, when a being turns away from God. God does not want humans to turn away from Him and reject Him, but humankind is free to do so. The absence of goodness (=God) created by this willful human refusal is what constitutes evil.

White was a supremely qualified philosopher and a razor sharp logician, but he could not convince Jung (no dummy either) that God is purely good. Jung was antagonistic toward this intellectual approach. Categories and clear definitions are things of the conscious mind, not of immediate experience and certainly not of the unconscious. Religious experiences of the kind Jung had in mind do not offer clear pictures of a purely good God. But the notion that God is wholly good and that there is no evil in Him is bedrock Christian teaching, and White, an ordained Roman Catholic priest and a convinced Christian theologian, could not possibly depart from this certainty. What evil there is in the world—and Christian doctrine holds that there is plenty of it, due to human sin—is there because God has been rejected. Humans have the freedom to reject God and to live in the darkness of their own creation. But God's plan is always good, and His will invariably is directed toward the light.

White thought he could bring Jung around to realizing that analytical psychology and its keystone—the archetype of the self—implied the same thing. White would ask: Is it not true that it is the ego that goes off the tracks and cultivates evil out of its lack of insight and inflation and desire for control, while the self is always aligned with truth, health, wholeness, and positive growth? Does not individuation—a person's lifelong journey toward wholeness and consciousness—imply that the self which guides its trajectory is purely good? Given an affirmative answer to these questions, analytical psychology would be in perfect, if unwitting, agreement with Christian teaching.

At this point, Jung, the master and creator of analytical psychology, vigorously shook his head and thundered "Nein." Evil is as real as good, God is as dark as He/She is light, and the doctrine of evil as *privatio boni* is a convenient rationalization of the ego-dominated Christian theological tradition. Theology does not take the reality of the unconscious seriously into account. In a sense, it is impious.

CHRISTIANITY AS INTERPRETED BY ANALYTICAL PSYCHOLOGY

Standing outside the theological circle, Jung interpreted Christian doctrine and practice from the perspective of analytical psychology. Analytical psychology, he held, is based on scientific and clinical observation and on self-critical investigation of the psyche, especially the unconscious. As such, it is permanently open to revision and challenge. It is unlike theological doctrine, which claims immutable veracity and finality. It is not dogmatic. It is a perspective that generates interpretive tools for grasping and exploring the inner world and investigating experiences of the nonrational.

From the standpoint of analytical psychology, religious experience is seen as an eruption of the unconscious and an expression of latent psychic structures and dynamics. Theological doctrines and rituals, on the contrary, are products of the ego's understanding and represent, largely, rationalizations of those experiences. For Jung, the raw data from the unconscious—in the form of dreams, visions, and synchronicities—was a much more reliable guide to truth about the God image than theology ever could be.

In the perspective offered by analytical psychology, an entire religious tradition can be considered a gigantic collective psyche. It displays evidence of primary experience of the unconscious (the "revelation"), the conscious elaboration in its thinking about these experiences (the "theology"), and various ritualistic recreations of these primary experience of the unconscious (the "rites"). The declared heresies represent the repressed thoughts and images of this psyche and make up its shadow and its "personal unconscious." The dominant institutions and their leaders are its ego. The emphasized doctrines, elaborated as absolute dogmas, express its one-sidedness and defensiveness against the threat of the unconscious and against further influence from it (i.e., new revelations). The rites and rituals both reconnect the present worshippers to the original primal experience of the unconscious "*in illo tempore*" (Eliade's expression) and also defend them from the threatening eruption of new contents from the unconscious.

Religions protect people from God, ironically, even while they connect people to aspects of God in a safe and contained way. Religions are therefore therapeutic institutions, harbors of safety and comfort in a psychic world filled with all sorts of fearful and often destructive potential. Were people not protected from God by their religious institutions, they would be subject to primary religious experience with its potential for inducing psychotic-like states of consciousness.

While White thought he was talking about God with his theological language, therefore, Jung considered that he was referring to a second-hand experience of the unconscious plus a whole layer of highly rationalized defensive sediment covering it in the form of traditional theology.

For Jung, as stated earlier, the experience of God was a fearful onslaught of unwanted, unexpected, and often terrifying mental contents. The human experience of God, however, is not limited to mental and emotional states. There is also synchronicity to consider. The archetype of the self (in analytical psychology, the equivalent of the God term) manifests both mentally and physically, also both individually and collectively. So world history, with its complexity of mental and material features and its mixture of good and evil, was for Jung also a revelation of the Divine. Human history can, of course, be seen as the result of humankind's rejection of God's invitation to grace and wholeness, a product of human sin, shortsightedness, and willfulness. This is the church's position, but it was not Jung's. Jung read the past two thousand years of Christian history as a two-phased revelation of the collective psychological structure underlying this historical period. In the first phase (lasting until approximately 1000 CE), there was a strenuous development of the spiritual nature of humankind, in part to separate this period in Western history from the preceding paganism with its emphasis on physicality and sensual pleasure. In the second phase (extending from 1000 CE through the twentieth century), the emphasis reversed, and there was a focused concentration of attention on the natural world, leading to modern science and philosophical materialism. This two-phase movement in Western history is revelatory of a pair of opposites—spirit vs. matter—within the archetypal structure underlying this period of time.

God is that which humans posit when they refer to the ultimate patterning power behind the flux of time and history. God is the ground of being and the creator of order. By studying the evolving order, one may catch a glimpse of the hidden hand guiding its movements. Ever the empiricist, Jung would cite evidence for God's evil (at least from humankind's point of view) as well as for His goodness. If one considers one side of God, His goodness for instance, one must also be prepared to register His other side, His evil. Colloquially Jung would say that God has two hands, a right and a left. He blesses and He curses; He gives and He takes away. Look at the story of Job! Jung applied the lesson of Job to collective history and to the experience of individuals. Looked at that way, he concluded, one may love God, but one *must* fear Him.

In his argument with Victor White over the doctrine of evil as *privatio boni* and God as only good, we can see Jung attempting to rectify an imbalance in the Christian conception of God. Unfettered by any of the doctrinal limitations placed on theologians by Christian teaching, Jung could consider other religious views as standing on a par with Christian revelation. He felt as much respect for the insights of Taoism and Buddhism and for the teachings of North American native wise men as he did for those of the Bible and the Church Fathers. What he gleaned from them was a God image that represents wholeness in its basic structure and promotes it in its dynamic movements. This image embraces all aspects of reality, which from a human viewpoint (the ego) are often divided into polarities or even split into irreconcilable opposites.

The pairs, good/evil and masculine/feminine, are typical instances of this tendency to split. Human beings, in their effort to understand the world and to cope with its challenges, sort and label many aspects of experienced reality by using the distinguishing features of these polarities. Because of the human propensity toward narcissistic self-centeredness, features of the natural world such as earthquakes and floods are called "evil," while other features such as lush landscapes and abundant harvests are called "good." People will thank God for the latter and perhaps curse Him for the former. From a larger, nonhuman perspective these are merely products of natural forces and have nothing to do with human needs or judgment. But people distort reality by splitting and transform aspects of it into the bizarre offspring of fantasy. The psychologist tries to correct these defensive distortions and to restore a more balanced appraisal of reality, based on direct experience and observation rather than on elaborate mental justifications and rationalizations. To Jung, the doctrine of evil as *privatio boni* was such a distortion. It is the psychologist's job to interpret distortions and to help patients remove them from consciousness. Of course, White the theologian did not see it that way.

JUNG'S MISSION

If we ask Jung why he cared about all of this theological business enough to spend so much time and energy on it, we enter into the complex territory of psychological motivation and of unconscious as

18

well as conscious intention. One quite evident point that can be gleaned from his writings is that Jung felt a doctor's obligation to help those patients who suffered from the distortions inflicted on them by religious education and upbringing. Every psychotherapist faces the challenge of removing the pathogenic effects of some religious teachings. The doctrine that God is good and that all evil in the world must be assigned to humans can lead in some people to an intolerable emphasis on their own sinfulness. In some sensitive souls, this teaching works in tandem with tendencies toward obsessive thinking and compulsive behavior. The problem of "scruples" (an extreme, neurotic exaggeration of one's own sinfulness) is well known in Christian religious life. A person's entire life can become heavily shrouded in the guilt generated by normal human desires for pleasure, sexuality being one of the most common of these. So one of Jung's motivations in addressing a theological doctrine like *privatio boni* was to rectify the balance of responsibility. Not only humans, but God too is responsible for evil in the world. "God made me do it," if offered as a defense for an immoral thought like the destruction of the Basel Cathedral, would have to be taken seriously in the inner judgment halls of one's conscience.

Beyond his concern for such patients, however, I believe Jung felt a therapeutic responsibility toward the Christian tradition as a whole, as though *it* were an ailing patient in need of therapy. The ailments are complex. There is the splitting—spirit vs. body, good vs. evil, masculine vs. feminine—and there is the repression of the second of each of these pairs from the dominant center of consciousness, the prevailing God image. This has led to a historical moment of crisis, in which the Christian tradition must transform itself or enter into a long and painful dying process. In our time, Christianity has little to contribute to culture because it is out of touch with the unconscious and the *Zeitgeist*. The only solution is to undertake a transformation process, like that of individuals who enter therapy and rediscover themselves in depth. Out of this engagement with the unconscious comes the impetus for new life, based on a transformed inner world and a new sense of identity. The self-image of Christianity must become more inclusive and more capable of embracing wholeness. This is the fundamental problem of traditional Christianity. The old bottles cannot adequately contain the new wine of the spirit.

In a letter to Victor White, Jung gives the following advice to the priest, who at the time was suffering a perceived injustice at the hands of his superiors: "It depends very much indeed upon the way you envisage your position with reference to the Church. I should advocate an analytical attitude, which is permissible as well as honest, viz. take the Church as your ailing employer and your colleagues as the unconscious inmates of a hospital" (*Letters*, Vol. 2, p. 172). Here Jung is suggesting to White more or less what he himself adopted vis-à-vis the Christian tradition, an attitude of doctor to ailing patient. Jung recognized in the historical picture of Christianity features held in common with his suffering psychiatric patients. There was a history of repression of incompatible tendencies (the heresies, such as Gnosticism and alchemy); the concomitant development of one-sided structures in consciousness (the accepted doctrines and practices); the psychic death through loss of meaning and energy in middle and old age (the contemporary churches in Europe); and a crisis that could not be met because the living connection to the unconscious had been lost. It was this situation that Jung attempted to address in his writings on Christian doctrine, image, and ritual in the last thirty years of his life.

JUNG'S METHOD

Not included in this anthology are Jung's writings on clinical themes and methods, which are needed to understand fully my argument here. In the treatment of patients, Jung advocates becoming psychologically involved with them by allowing oneself to become affected emotionally by their suffering. The doctor deliberately becomes infected with their illnesses in order to feel what they are feeling. This is the basis of empathy, and it sets up a resonance between doctor and patient. When this happens, the doctor is able to diagnose and treat the patient "from within," so to speak. By going inward, he or she is also going outward to the other. And what the doctor discovers by going inward into his or her own unconscious has an application to the patient. The healing comes about bilaterally. The physician heals him/herself, and the patient is cured with the medicine derived from this process. This method of treatment is an entirely different model of healing from the detached, white-coated, surgical medical practices of Western societies. Jung's therapeutic approach to Christianity is of this type. By going into himself, observing his own dreams, following his unconsciously determined impulses and intuition, he came upon themes and images and ideas that may be useful to Christianity. He cured himself of Christianity's illness, and the writings contained in this anthology represent the healing medicine he found in his inner process.

Answer to Job (CW 11) is a prime example of this method at work.

Jung wrote it in a feverish burst of passion while recovering from an illness in the years following World War II. Many of the ideas in this work, of course, had been incubating in him for many years prior to the writing. Nevertheless, the text itself was composed under the direction of his passionate personal engagement with physical suffering, old age depression, and grave doubts about God's goodness in the grim aftermath of the European collapse of culture and values during the evil years of war and holocaust. All of this could be found mirrored in the Christianity of the day. Similarly, his book *Aion*, a study of Christian history in the Age of Pisces, grew out of dreams and a surprising inner urge to write about the Christ symbol. These literary productions represent the response of his consciousness to the ailing religious and cultural environment in which he was living at the time.

By publishing these reflections and putting the weight of his considerable scientific and medical reputation behind them, Jung was attempting to treat the patient, Christian tradition and culture, as well as himself. In doing so, he took the considerable risk of diminishing his own personal standing in the scientific world. In fact, he was severely criticized by theologians and ignored by scientists, who most probably considered these as the ramblings of an old man in his dotage. Only a few people saw much value in these works.

THE VALUE OF JUNG'S WRITINGS FOR CHRISTIANITY

What can we say today about the value of Jung's writings on Christianity? Certainly they are a unique contribution to Christian thought and practice. For those who live within the confines of the Christian theological circle, they are probably still beyond the pale. Jung's views on the further evolution of Christian doctrine will not be shared by many (if any at all) conventional theologians. To conceive of God as Quaternity rather than as Trinity integrates evil and the feminine into the Divine structure and creates a more balanced symbol of wholeness and totality. What Jung does is open a way to transformation of the God image and also to the synthesis of Eastern and Western religious thought at a profound level through a more inclusive symbol of the Godhead. The implications of this transformation include a perception of God as a Male-Female and a Light-Dark unity, a symbol of wholeness.

Practically, Jung advocates inclusion of dreams, visions, and individual religious experience as essential features of an on-going revelatory process of the Divine. Dreams are to be put on a par with the Biblical

21

testimony, the witness of "heretics," and the accepted doctrinal pronouncements of the past. The Divine reality is not to be set apart from the human but rather seen as participant in a common process of evolution and an on-going development of consciousness. The image of God is never to be seen as final and complete, and humans are co-creators of new dimensions of meaning and understanding. Jung's writings propose a process theology of a psychologically attuned type.

Jung was not naive enough to believe that Christianity would be ready for his therapeutic ministrations any time soon. He had his eye on the distant future. His confidence is placed more in the unconscious process of collective evolution and development than in the notion that intelligent people might eventually discover them and find them useful. He felt that his writings, which emerged from his own depths and which he actually served rather than controlled or dictated, would be of value to people in the future. Time is on his side. The transformation of the God image is underway, and Jung saw himself simply as its servant and spokesperson, using the limited means at his command to advance a process that will unfold over the coming millennium.

It is impossible to predict accurately how Christian doctrine and practice will change in the coming centuries. Jung would not have been among those to wish for or to imagine Christianity's further deterioration or demise. Its transformation, however, is inevitable. As non-Europeans more and more constitute the majority in all Christian denominations, their cultural and social diversity is bound to have a powerful effect. And as other major religious traditions become more familiar and are accepted as existing on a par with Christian views and conceptions, there is bound to be mutual integration and deep internal influence. Should intelligent life be discovered elsewhere in the universe, as seems highly likely today, there will be an added urgency to engage in comparison and exchange of views about spiritual realities. In all of these discussions, Jung's conception of a deep archetypal background to conscious human thought, experience, and perception can be, and for some certainly will be, a useful tool for orientation and understanding.

Murray Stein

REFERENCES

Jung, C.G. 1968. *Aion: Researches into the phenomenology of the self.* In *Collected Works*, Vol. 9, Part 2. Princeton: Princeton University Press.

————. 1961. *Memories, dreams, reflections.* New York: Random House.

————. 1969. *Psychology and religion: West and East.* In *Collected Works,* Vol. 11. Princeton: Princeton University Press.

————. 1970. *Mysterium Coniunctionis.* In *Collected Works,* Vol. 14. Princeton: Princeton University Press.

————. 1973. *Letters,* Vol. 1. Princeton: Princeton University Press.

————. 1975. *Letters,* Vol. 2. Princeton: Princeton University Press.

Lammers, Ann. 1994. *In God's shadow: The collaboration of Victor White and C.G. Jung.* New York: Paulist Press.

Stein, Murray. 1985. *Jung's treatment of Christianity.* Wilmette, Illinois: Chiron Publications.

PART I

JUNG'S RELATIONSHIP TO
CHRISTIANITY

1

A FATHER'S UNFINISHED WORK

From *Memories, Dreams, Reflections,* pp. 52–63

With my father it was quite different. I would have liked to lay my religious difficulties before him and ask him for advice, but I did not do so because it seemed to me that I knew in advance what he would be obliged to reply out of respect for his office. How right I was in this assumption was demonstrated to me soon afterward. My father personally gave me my instruction for confirmation. It bored me to death. One day I was leafing through the catechism, hoping to find something besides the sentimental-sounding and usually incomprehensible as well as uninteresting expatiations on Lord Jesus. I came across the paragraph on the Trinity. Here was something that challenged my interest: a oneness which was simultaneously a threeness. This was a problem that fascinated me because of its inner contradiction. I waited longingly for the moment when we would reach this question. But when we got that far, my father said, "We now come to the Trinity, but we'll skip that, for I really understand nothing of it myself." I admired my father's honesty, but on the other hand I was profoundly disappointed and said to myself, "There we have it; they know nothing about it and don't give it a thought. Then how can I talk about my secret?"

I made vain, tentative attempts with certain of my schoolfellows who struck me as reflective. I awakened no response, but, on the contrary, a stupefaction that warned me off.

In spite of the boredom, I made every effort to believe without understanding—an attitude which seemed to correspond with my father's —and prepared myself for Communion, on which I had set my last hopes. This was, I thought, merely a memorial meal, a kind of anniversary celebration for Lord Jesus who had died 1890—30 = 1860 years ago. But still, he had let fall certain hints such as, "Take, eat, this is my body," meaning that we should eat the Communion bread as if it were his body, which after all had originally been flesh. Likewise we were to drink the wine which had originally been blood. It was clear to me that

27

in this fashion we were to incorporate him into ourselves. This seemed to me so preposterous an impossibility that I was sure some great mystery must lie behind it, and that I would participate in this mystery in the course of Communion, on which my father seemed to place so high a value.

As was customary, a member of the church committee stood godfather to me. He was a nice, taciturn old man, a wheelwright in whose workshop I had often stood, watching his skill with lathe and adze. Now he came, solemnly transformed by frock coat and top hat, and took me to church, where my father in his familiar robes stood behind the altar and read prayers from the liturgy. On the white cloth covering the altar lay large trays filled with small pieces of bread. I could see that the bread came from our baker, whose baked goods were generally poor and flat in taste. From a pewter jug, wine was poured into a pewter cup. My father ate a piece of the bread, took a swallow of the wine—I knew the tavern from which it had come—and passed the cup to one of the old men. All were stiff, solemn, and, it seemed to me, uninterested. I looked on in suspense, but could not see or guess whether anything unusual was going on inside the old men. The atmosphere was the same as that of all other performances in church—baptisms, funerals, and so on. I had the impression that something was being performed here in the traditionally correct manner. My father, too, seemed to be chiefly concerned with going through it all according to rule, and it was part of this rule that the appropriate words were read or spoken with emphasis. There was no mention of the fact that it was now 1860 years since Jesus had died, whereas in all other memorial services the date was stressed. I saw no sadness and no joy, and felt that the feast was meager in every respect, considering the extraordinary importance of the person whose memory was being celebrated. It did not compare at all with secular festivals.

Suddenly my turn came. I ate the bread; it tasted flat, as I had expected. The wine, of which I took only the smallest sip, was thin and rather sour, plainly not of the best. Then came the final prayer, and the people went out, neither depressed nor illumined with joy, but with faces that said, "So that's that."

I walked home with my father, intensely conscious that I was wearing a new black felt hat and a new black suit which was already beginning to turn into a frock coat. It was a kind of lengthened jacket that spread out into two little wings over the seat, and between these was a slit with a pocket into which I could tuck a handkerchief—which seemed to me a grown-up, manly gesture. I felt socially elevated and by implication accepted into the society of men. That day, too, Sunday dinner was an unusually good one. I would be able to stroll about in my new suit all day. But otherwise I was empty and did not know what I was feeling.

Only gradually, in the course of the following days, did it dawn on me that nothing had happened. I had reached the pinnacle of religious initiation, had expected something—I knew not what—to happen, and nothing at all had happened. I knew that God could do stupendous things to me, things of fire and unearthly light; but this ceremony contained no trace of God—not for me, at any rate. To be sure, there had been talk about Him, but it had all amounted to no more than words. Among the others I had noticed nothing of the vast despair, the overpowering elation and outpouring of grace which for me constituted the essence of God. I had observed no sign of "communion," of "union, becoming one with . . ." With whom? With Jesus? Yet he was only a man who had died 1860 years ago. Why should a person become one with him? He was called the "Son of God"—a demigod, therefore, like the Greek heroes: how then could an ordinary person become one with him? This was called the "Christian religion," but none of it had anything to do with God as I had experienced Him. On the other hand it was quite clear that Jesus, the man, did have to do with God; he had despaired in Gethsemane and on the cross, after having taught that God was a kind and loving father. He too, then, must have seen the fearfulness of God. That I could understand, but what was the purpose of this wretched memorial service with the flat bread and the sour wine? Slowly I came to understand that this Communion had been a fatal experience for me. It had proved hollow; more than that, it had proved to be a total loss. I knew that I would never again be able to participate in this ceremony. "Why, that is not religion at all," I thought. "It is an absence of God; the church is a place I should not go to. It is not life which is there, but death."

I was seized with the most vehement pity for my father. All at once I understood the tragedy of his profession and his life. He was struggling with a death whose existence he could not admit. An abyss had opened between him and me, and I saw no possibility of ever bridging it, for it was infinite in extent. I could not plunge my dear and generous father, who in so many matters left me to myself and had never tyrannized over me, into that despair and sacrilege which were necessary for an experience of divine grace. Only God could do that. I had no right to; it would be inhuman. God is not human, I thought; that is His greatness, that nothing human impinges on Him. He is kind and terrible—both at once—and is therefore a great peril from which everyone naturally tries to save himself. People cling one-sidedly to His love and goodness, for fear they will fall victim to the tempter and destroyer.

Jesus, too, had noticed that, and had therefore taught: "Lead us not into temptation."

My sense of union with the Church and with the human world, so far as I knew it, was shattered. I had, so it seemed to me, suffered the greatest defeat of my life. The religious outlook which I imagined constituted my sole meaningful relation with the universe had disintegrated; I could no longer participate in the general faith, but found myself involved in something inexpressible, in my secret, which I could share with no one. It was terrible and—this was the worst of it—vulgar and ridiculous also, a diabolical mockery.

I began to ponder: What must one think of God? I had not invented that thought about God and the cathedral, still less the dream that had befallen me at the age of three. A stronger will than mine had imposed both on me. Had nature been responsible? But nature was nothing other than the will of the Creator. Nor did it help to accuse the devil, for he too was a creature of God. God alone was real—an annihilating fire and an indescribable grace.

What about the failure of Communion to affect me? Was that my own failure? I had prepared for it in all earnestness, had hoped for an experience of grace and illumination, and nothing had happened. God had been absent. For God's sake I now found myself cut off from the Church and from my father's and everybody else's faith. Insofar as they all represented the Christian religion, I was an outsider. This knowledge filled me with a sadness which was to overshadow all the years until the time I entered the university.

I began looking in my father's relatively modest library—which in those days seemed impressive to me—for books that would tell me what was known about God. At first I found only the traditional conceptions, but not what I was seeking—a writer who thought independently. At last I hit upon Biedermann's *Christliche Dogmatik*, published in 1869. Here, apparently, was a man who thought for himself, who worked out his own views. I learned from him that religion was "a spiritual act consisting in man's establishing his own relationship to God." I disagreed with that, for I understood religion as something that God did to me; it was an act on His part, to which I must simply yield, for He was the stronger. My "religion" recognized no human relationship to God, for how could anyone relate to something so little known as God? I must know more about God in order to establish a relationship to him. In Biedermann's chapter on "The Nature of God" I found that God showed Himself to be a "personality to be conceived after the analogy of the human ego: the unique, utterly supramundane ego who embraces the entire cosmos."

As far as I knew the Bible, this definition seemed to fit. God has a personality and is the ego of the universe, just as I myself am the ego of my psychic and physical being. But here I encountered a formidable obstacle. Personality, after all, surely signifies character. Now, character is one thing and not another; that is to say, it involves certain specific attributes. But if God is everything, how can He still possess a distinguishable character? On the other hand, if He does have a character, He can only be the ego of a subjective, limited world. Moreover, what kind of character or what kind of personality does He have? Everything depends on that, for unless one knows the answer one cannot establish a relationship to Him.

I felt the strongest resistances to imagining God by analogy with my own ego. That seemed to me boundlessly arrogant, if not downright blasphemous. My ego was, in any case, difficult enough for me to grasp. In the first place, I was aware that it consisted of two contradictory aspects: No. 1 and No. 2. Second, in both its aspects my ego was extremely limited, subject to all possible self-deceptions and errors, moods, emotions, passions, and sins. It suffered far more defeats than triumphs, was childish, vain, self-seeking, defiant, in need of love, covetous, unjust, sensitive, lazy, irresponsible, and so on. To my sorrow it lacked many of the virtues and talents I admired and envied in others. How could this be the analogy according to which we were to imagine the nature of God?

Eagerly I looked up the other characteristics of God, and found them all listed in the way familiar to me from my instruction for confirmation. I found that according to Article 172, "the most immediate expression of the supramundane nature of God is 1) *negative*: His invisibility to men," etc., "and 2) *positive*: His dwelling in Heaven," etc. This was disastrous, for at once there rushed to my mind the blasphemous vision which God directly or indirectly (i.e., via the devil) had imposed on my will.

Article 183 informed me that "God's supramundane nature with regard to the moral world" consists in His "justice," which is not merely "judicial" but is also "an expression of His holy being." I had hoped that this paragraph would say something about God's dark aspects which were giving me so much trouble: His vindictiveness, His dangerous wrathfulness, His incomprehensible conduct toward the creatures His omnipotence had made, whose inadequacies He must know by virtue of that same omnipotence, and whom moreover it pleased Him to lead astray, or at least to test, even though He knew in advance the outcome of His experiments. What, indeed, was God's character? What would we say of a human personality who behaved in this manner? I did not dare to think this question out to its conclusion. And then I read that God, "although sufficient unto Himself and needing nothing outside Himself," had created the world "out of His satisfaction," and "as a natural world has filled it with His goodness and as a moral world desires to fill it with His love."

At first I pondered over the perplexing word "satisfaction." Satisfaction with what or with whom? Obviously with the world, for He had looked upon His work and called it good. But it was just this that I had never understood. Certainly the world is immeasurably beautiful, but it is quite as horrible. In a small village in the country, where there are few people and nothing much happens, "old age, disease, and death" are experienced more intensely, in greater detail, and more nakedly than elsewhere. Although I was not yet sixteen years old I had seen a great deal of the reality of the life of man and beast, and in church and school I had heard enough of the sufferings and corruption of the world. God could at most have felt "satisfaction" with paradise, but then He Himself had taken good care that the glory of paradise should not last too long by planting in it that poisonous serpent, the devil. Had He taken satisfaction in that too? I felt certain that Biedermann did not mean this, but was simply babbling on in that mindless way that characterized religious instruction, not even aware that he was writing nonsense. As I saw it, it was not at all unreasonable to suppose that God, for all that He probably did not feel any such cruel satisfaction in the unmerited sufferings of man and beast, had nevertheless intended to create a world of contradictions in which one creature devoured another and life meant simply being born to die. The "wonderful harmonies" of natural law looked to me more like a chaos tamed by fearful effort, and the "eternal" starry firmament with its predetermined orbits seemed plainly an accumulation of random bodies without order or meaning. For no one could really see the constellations people spoke about. They were mere arbitrary configurations.

I either did not see or gravely doubted that God filled the natural world with His goodness. This, apparently, was another of those points which must not be reasoned about but must be believed. In fact, if God is the highest good, why is the world, His creation, so imperfect, so corrupt, so pitiable? "Obviously it has been infected and thrown into confusion by the devil," I thought. But the devil, too, was a creature of God. I had to read up on the devil. He seemed to be highly important after all. I again opened Biedermann's book on Christian dogmatics and looked for the answer to this burning question. What were the reasons for suffering, imperfection, and evil? I could find nothing.

That finished it for me. This weighty tome on dogmatics was nothing but fancy drivel; worse still, it was a fraud or a specimen of uncommon stupidity whose sole aim was to obscure the truth. I was disillusioned and even indignant, and once more seized with pity for my father, who had fallen victim to this mumbo-jumbo.

But somewhere and at some time there must have been people who sought the truth as I was doing, who thought rationally and did not wish to deceive themselves and others and deny the sorrowful reality of the world. It was about this time that my mother, or rather, her No. 2 personality, suddenly and without preamble said, "You must read Goethe's *Faust* one of these days." We had a handsome edition of Goethe, and I picked out *Faust.* It poured into my soul like a miraculous balm. "Here at last," I thought, "is someone who takes the devil seriously and even concludes a blood pact with him—with the adversary who has the power to frustrate God's plan to make a perfect world." I regretted Faust's behavior, for to my mind he should not have been so one-sided and so easily tricked. He should have been cleverer and also more moral. How childish he was to gamble away his soul so frivolously! Faust was plainly a bit of a windbag. I had the impression that the weight of the drama and its significance lay chiefly on the side of Mephistopheles. It would not have grieved me if Faust's soul had gone to hell. He deserved it. I did not like the idea of the "cheated devil" at the end, for after all Mephistopheles had been anything but a stupid devil, and it was contrary to logic for him to be tricked by silly little angels. Mephistopheles seemed to me cheated in quite a different sense: he had not received his promised rights because Faust, that somewhat characterless fellow, had carried his swindle through right into the Hereafter. There, admittedly, his puerility came to light, but, as I saw it, he did not deserve the initiation into the great mysteries. I would have given him a taste of purgatorial fires. The real problem, it seemed to me, lay with Mephistopheles, whose whole figure made the deepest impression on me, and who, I vaguely sensed, had a relationship to the mystery of the Mothers.[1] At any rate Mephistopheles and the great initiation at the end remained for me a wonderful and mysterious experience on the fringes of my conscious world.

At last I had found confirmation that there were or had been people

---

[1] *Faust*, Part Two, trans. by Philip Wayne (Harmondsworth, England, Penguin Books Ltd, 1959), pp. 76 ff.

who saw evil and its universal power, and—more important—the mysterious role it played in delivering man from darkness and suffering. To that extent Goethe became, in my eyes, a prophet. But I could not forgive him for having dismissed Mephistopheles by a mere trick, by a bit of jiggery-pokery. For me that was too theological, too frivolous and irresponsible, and I was deeply sorry that Goethe too had fallen for those cunning devices by which evil is rendered innocuous.

In reading the drama I had discovered that Faust had been a philosopher of sorts, and although he turned away from philosophy, he had obviously learned from it a certain receptivity to the truth. Hitherto I had heard virtually nothing of philosophy, and now a new hope dawned. Perhaps, I thought, there were philosophers who had grappled with these questions and could shed light on them for me.

Since there were no philosophers in my father's library—they were suspect because they thought—I had to content myself with Krug's *General Dictionary of the Philosophical Sciences*, second edition, 1832. I plunged forthwith into the article on God. To my discontent it began with the etymology of the word "God," which, it said, "incontestably" derived from "good" and signified the *ens summum* or *perfectissimum.* The existence of God could not be proved, it continued, nor the innateness of the idea of God. The latter, however, could exist a priori in man, if not in actuality at any rate potentially. In any case our "intellectual powers" must "already be developed to a certain degree before they are capable of engendering so sublime an idea."

This explanation astounded me beyond measure. What is wrong with these "philosophers"? I wondered. Evidently they know of God only by hearsay. The theologians are different in this respect, at any rate; at least they are sure that God exists, even though they make contradictory statements about Him. This lexicographer Krug expresses himself in so involved a manner that it is easy to see he would like to assert that he is already sufficiently convinced of God's existence. Then why doesn't he say so outright? Why does he pretend—as if he really thought that we "engender" the idea of God, and to do so must first have reached a certain level of development? So far as I knew, even the savages wandering naked in their jungles had such ideas. And they were certainly not "philosophers" who sat down to "engender an idea of God." I never engendered any idea of God, either. Of course God cannot be proved, for how could, say, a clothes moth that eats Australian wool prove to other moths that Australia exists? God's existence does not depend on our proofs. How had I arrived at my certainty about God? I was told all sorts of things about Him, yet I could believe nothing. None of it convinced me. That was not where my idea came from. In fact it was not an idea at all—that is, not something thought out. It was not like imagining something and thinking it out and afterward believing it. For example, all that about Lord Jesus was always suspect to me and I never really believed it, although it was impressed upon me far more than God, who was usually only hinted at in the background. Why have I come to take God for granted? Why do these philosophers pretend that God is an idea, a kind of arbitrary assumption which they can engender or not, when it is perfectly plain that He exists, as plain as a brick that falls on your head?

Suddenly I understood that God was, for me at least, one of the most certain and immediate of experiences, After all, I didn't invent that horrible image about the cathedral. On the contrary, it was forced on me and I was compelled, with the utmost cruelty, to think it, and afterward that inexpressible feeling of grace came to me. I had no control over these things. I came to the conclusion that there must be something the matter with these philosophers, for they had the curious notion that God was a kind of hypothesis that could be discussed. I also found it extremely unsatisfying that the philosophers offered no opinions or explanations about the dark deeds of God. These, it seemed to me, merited special attention and consideration from philosophy, since they constituted a problem which, I gathered, was rather a hard one for the theologians. All the greater was my disappointment to discover that the philosophers had apparently never even heard of it.

I therefore passed on to the next topic that interested me, the article on the devil. If, I read, we conceived of the devil as originally evil, we would become entangled in patent contradictions, that is to say, we would fall into dualism. Therefore we would do better to assume that the devil was originally created a good being but had been corrupted by his pride. However, as the author of the article pointed out—and I was glad to see this point made—this hypothesis presupposed the evil it was attempting to explain—namely, pride. For the rest, he continued, the origin of evil was "unexplained and inexplicable"—which meant to me: Like the theologians, he does not want to think about it. The article on evil and its origin proved equally unilluminating.

The account I have given here summarizes trains of thought and developments of ideas which, broken by long intervals, extended over several years. They went on exclusively in my No. 2 personality, and were strictly private. I used my father's library for these researches, secretly and without asking his permission. In the intervals, personality No. 1 openly read all the novels of Gerstäcker, and German translations of the classic English novels. I also began reading German literature, concentrating on those classics which school, with its needlessly laborious explanations of the obvious, had not spoiled for me. I read vastly and planlessly, drama, poetry, history, and later natural science. Reading was not only interesting but provided a welcome and beneficial distraction from the preoccupations of personality No. 2, which in increasing measure were leading me to depressions. For everywhere in the realm of religious questions I encountered only locked doors, and if ever one door should chance to open I was disappointed by what lay behind it. Other people all seemed to have totally different concerns. I felt completely alone with my certainties. More than ever I wanted someone to talk with, but nowhere did I find a point of contact; on the contrary, I sensed in others an estrangement, a distrust, an apprehension which robbed me of speech. That, too, depressed me. I did not know what to make of it. Why has no one had experiences similar to mine? I wondered. Why is there nothing about it in scholarly books? Am I the only one who has had such experiences? Why should I be the only one? It never occurred to me that I might be crazy, for the light and darkness of God seemed to me facts that could be understood even though they oppressed my feelings.

From *Memories, Dreams, Reflections*, pp. 215–21

My memory of my father is of a sufferer stricken with an Amfortas wound, a "fisher king" whose wound would not heal—that Christian suffering for which the alchemists sought the panacea. I as a "dumb" Parsifal was the witness of this sickness during the years of my boyhood, and, like Parsifal, speech failed me. I had only inklings. In actuality my father had never interested himself in theriomorphic Christ-symbolism. On the other hand he had literally lived right up to his death the suffering prefigured and promised by Christ, without ever becoming aware that this was a consequence of the *imitatio Christi*. He regarded his suffering as a personal affliction for which you might ask a doctor's advice; he did not see it as the suffering of the Christian in general. The words of Galatians 2:20: "I live, yet not I, but Christ liveth in me," never penetrated his mind in their full significance, for any thinking about religious matters sent shudders of horror through him. He wanted to rest content with faith, but faith broke faith with him. Such is frequently the reward of the *sacrificium intellectus*. "Not all men can receive this precept, but only those to whom it is given. . . . There are eunuchs who have made themselves eunuchs for the sake of the kingdom of heaven. He who is able to receive this, let him receive it" (Matthew 19:11f.). Blind acceptance never leads to a solution; at best it leads only to a standstill and is paid for heavily in the next generation.

The theriomorphic attributes of the gods show that the gods extend not only into superhuman regions but also into the subhuman realm. The animals are their shadows, as it were, which nature herself associates with the divine image. The *"pisciculi Christianorum"* show that those who imitate Christ are themselves fish—that is, unconscious souls who require the *cura animarum*. The fish laboratory is a synonym for the ecclesiastical "cure of souls." And just as the wounder wounds himself, so the healer heals himself. Significantly, in the dream the decisive activity is carried out by the dead upon the dead, in the world beyond consciousness, that is, in the unconscious.

At that stage of my life, therefore, I was still not conscious of an essential aspect of my task, nor would I have been able to give a satisfactory interpretation of the dream. I could only sense its meaning. I still had to overcome the greatest inner resistances before I could write *Answer to Job.*

The inner root of this book is to be found in *Aion.* There I had dealt with the psychology of Christianity, and Job is a kind of prefiguration of Christ. The link between them is the idea of suffering. Christ is the suffering servant of God, and so was Job. In the case of Christ the sins of the world are the cause of suffering, and the suffering of the Christian is the general answer. This leads inescapably to the question: Who is responsible for these sins? In the final analysis it is God who created the world and its sins, and who therefore became Christ in order to suffer the fate of humanity.

In *Aion* there are references to the bright and dark side of the divine image. I cited the "wrath of God," the commandment to fear God, and the petition "Lead us not into temptation." The ambivalent God-image plays a crucial part in the Book of Job. Job expects that God will, in a sense, stand by him against God; in this we have a picture of God's tragic contradictoriness. This was the main theme of *Answer to Job.*

There were outside forces, too, which impelled me to write this book. The many questions from the public and from patients had made me feel that I must express myself more clearly about the religious problems of modern man. For years I had hesitated to do so, because I was fully aware of the storm I would be unleashing. But at last I could not help being gripped by the problem, in all its urgency and difficulty, and I found myself compelled to give an answer. I did so in the form in which the problem had presented itself to me, that is, as an experience charged with emotion. I chose this form deliberately, in order to avoid giving the impression that I was bent on proclaiming some eternal truth. My *Answer to Job* was meant to be no more than the utterance of a single individual, who hopes and expects to arouse some thoughtfulness in his public. I was far from wanting to enunciate a metaphysical truth. Yet the theologians tax me with that very thing, because theological thinkers are so used to dealing with eternal truths that they know no other kinds. When the physicist says that the atom is of such and such a composition, and when he sketches a model of it, he too does not intend to express anything like an eternal truth. But theologians do not understand the natural sciences and, particularly, psychological thinking. The material of analytical psychology, its principal facts, consist of *statements*—of statements that occur frequently in consistent form at various places and at various times.

The problem of Job in all its ramifications had likewise been foreshadowed in a dream. It started with my paying a visit to my long-deceased father. He was living in the country—I did not know where. I saw a house in the style of the eighteenth century, very roomy, with several rather large outbuildings. It had originally been, I learned, an inn at a spa, and it seemed that many great personages, famous people and princes, had stopped there. Furthermore, several had died and their sarcophagi were in a crypt belonging to the house. My father guarded these as custodian.

He was, as I soon discovered, not only the custodian but also a distinguished scholar in his own right—which he had never been in his lifetime. I met him in his study, and, oddly enough, Dr. Y.—who was about my age—and his son, both psychiatrists, were also present. I do not know whether I had asked a question or whether my father wanted to explain something of his own accord, but in any case he fetched a big Bible down from a shelf, a heavy folio volume like the Merian Bible in my library. The Bible my father held was bound in shiny fishskin. He opened it at the Old Testament—I guessed that he turned to the Pentateuch—and began interpreting a certain passage. He did this so swiftly and so learnedly that I could not follow him. I noted only that what he said betrayed a vast amount of variegated knowledge, the significance of which I dimly apprehended but could not properly judge or grasp. I saw that Dr. Y. understood nothing at all, and his son began to laugh. They thought that my father was going off the deep end and what he said was simply senile prattle. But it was quite clear to me that it was not due to morbid excitement, and that there was nothing silly about what he was saying. On the contrary, his argument was so intelligent and so learned that we in our stupidity simply could not follow it.

38

It dealt with something extremely important which fascinated him. That was why he was speaking with such intensity; his mind was flooded with profound ideas. I was annoyed and thought it was a pity that he had to talk in the presence of three such idiots as we.

The two psychiatrists represented a limited medical point of view which, of course, also infects me as a physician. They represent my shadow—first and second editions of the shadow, father and son.

Then the scene changed. My father and I were in front of the house, facing a kind of shed where, apparently, wood was stacked. We heard loud thumps, as if large chunks of wood were being thrown down or tossed about. I had the impression that at least two workmen must be busy there, but my father indicated to me that the place was haunted. Some sort of poltergeists were making the racket, evidently.

We then entered the house, and I saw that it had very thick walls. We climbed a narrow staircase to the second floor. There a strange sight presented itself: a large hall which was the exact replica of the *divan-i-kaas* (council hall) of Sultan Akbar at Fatehpur Sikri. It was a high, circular room with a gallery running along the wall, from which four bridges led to a basin-shaped center. The basin rested upon a huge column and formed the sultan's round seat. From this elevated place he spoke to his councilors and philosophers, who sat along the walls in the gallery. The whole was a gigantic mandala. It corresponded precisely to the real *divan-i-kaas*.

In the dream I suddenly saw that from the center a steep flight of stairs ascended to a spot high up on the wall—which no longer corresponded to reality. At the top of the stairs was a small door, and my father said, "Now I will lead you into the highest presence." Then he knelt down and touched his forehead to the floor. I imitated him, likewise kneeling, with great emotion. For some reason I could not bring my forehead quite down to the floor—there was perhaps a millimeter to spare. But at least I had made the gesture with him. Suddenly I knew—perhaps my father had told me—that that upper door led to a solitary chamber where lived Uriah, King David's general, whom David had shamefully betrayed for the sake of his wife Bathsheba, by commanding his soldiers to abandon Uriah in the face of the enemy.

I must make a few explanatory remarks concerning this dream. The initial scene describes how the unconscious task which I had left to my "father," that is, to the unconscious, was working out. He was obviously engrossed in the Bible—Genesis?—and eager to communicate his insights. The fishskin marks the Bible as an unconscious content, for fishes are mute and unconscious. My poor father does not succeed in communicating either, for the audience is in part incapable of understanding, in part maliciously stupid.

After this defeat we cross the street to the "other side," where poltergeists are at work. Poltergeist phenomena usually take place in the vicinity of young people before puberty; that is to say, I am still immature and too unconscious. The Indian ambience illustrates the "other side." When I was in India, the mandala structure of the *divan-i-kaas* had in actual fact powerfully impressed me as the representation of a content related to a center. The center is the seat of Akbar the Great, who rules over a subcontinent, who is a "lord of this world," like David. But even higher than David stands his guiltless victim, his loyal general Uriah, whom he abandoned to the enemy. Uriah is a prefiguration of Christ, the god-man who was abandoned by God. "My God, my God, why hast thou forsaken me?" On top of that, David had "taken unto himself" Uriah's wife. Only later did I understand what this allusion to Uriah signified: not only was I forced to speak publicly, and very much to my detriment, about the ambivalence of the God-image in the Old Testament; but also, my wife would be taken from me by death.

These were the things that awaited me, hidden in the unconscious. I had to submit to this fate, and ought really to have touched my forehead to the floor, so that my submission would be complete. But something prevented me from doing so entirely, and kept me just a millimeter away. Something in me was saying, "All very well, but not entirely." Something in me was defiant and determined not to be a dumb fish: and if there were not something of the sort in free men, no Book of Job would have been written several hundred years before the birth of Christ. Man always has some mental reservation, even in the face of divine decrees. Otherwise, where would be his freedom? And what would be the use of that freedom if it could not threaten Him who threatens it?

Uriah, then, lives in a higher place than Akbar. He is even, as the dream said, the "highest presence," an expression which properly is used only of God, unless we are dealing in Byzantinisms. I cannot help thinking here of the Buddha and his relationship to the gods. For the devout Asiatic, the Tathagata is the All-Highest, the Absolute. For that reason Hinayana Buddhism has been suspected of atheism—very wrongly so. By virtue of the power of the gods man is enabled to gain an insight into his Creator. He has even been given the power to annihilate Creation in its essential aspect, that is, man's consciousness of the world. Today he can extinguish all higher life on earth by radioactivity. The idea of world annihilation is already suggested by the Buddha: by means of enlightenment the Nidana chain—the chain of causality which leads inevitably to old age, sickness, and death—can be broken, so that the illusion of Being comes to an end. Schopenhauer's negation of the Will points prophetically to a problem of the future that has already come threateningly close. The dream discloses a thought and a premonition that have long been present in humanity: the idea of the creature that surpasses its creator by a small but decisive factor.

After this excursion into the world of dreams, I must once more come back to my writings. In *Aion* I embarked upon a cycle of problems that needed to be dealt with separately. I had attempted to explain how the appearance of Christ coincided with the beginning of a new aeon, the age of the Fishes. A synchronicity exists between the life of Christ and the objective astronomical event, the entrance of the spring equinox into the sign of Pisces. Christ is therefore the "Fish" (just as Hammurabi before him was the "Ram"), and comes forth as the ruler of the new aeon. This led to the problem of synchronicity, which I discussed in my paper "Synchronicity: An Acausal Connecting Principle."[1]

The Christ problem in *Aion* finally led me to the question of how the phenomenon of the Anthropos—in psychological terms, the self—is expressed in the experience of the individual. I attempted to give an answer to this in *Von den Wurzeln des Bewusstseins* (1954).[2] There I was concerned with the interplay between conscious and unconscious, with the development of consciousness from the unconscious, and with the impact of the greater personality, the inner man, upon the life of every individual.

This investigation was rounded out by the *Mysterium Coniunctionis*, in which I once again took up the problem of the transference, but primarily followed my original intention of representing the whole range of alchemy as a kind of psychology of alchemy, or as an alchemical basis for depth psychology. In *Mysterium Coniunctionis* my psychology was at last given its place in reality and established upon its historical foundations. Thus my task was finished, my work done, and now it can stand. The moment I touched bottom, I reached the bounds of scientific understanding, the transcendental, the nature of the archetype per se, concerning which no further scientific statements can be made.

[1] In C. G. Jung and W. Pauli, *The Interpretation of Nature and the Psyche* (New York and London, 1954); also in *The Structure and Dynamics of the Psyche* (CW 8).
[2] The essays in this book are mostly contained in volumes 8, 9 (i), and 11 of the Collected Works.

2

"THOUGHTS ON THE INTERPRETATION
OF CHRISTIANITY"

From *The Zofingia Lectures*, CW Suppl. A, pars. 237–91

237   People have every right to feel surprised to see a medical student abandon his craft during his clinical training to speak about theological issues. Several considerations might dissuade me from taking this step. I know that I am not going to earn any laurels, but that instead I am running the risk of being sent back to my own little nook with an indignant "Cobbler, stick to your last!"

238   I know that my acquaintance with theological matters is far too sketchy to permit reliable judgments based on a broad knowledge of the field. I know that theologians will find it easy to accuse me of being overhasty in some of my inferences and judgments. They live amid the ideas and concepts of their science, and they will be as swift to detect the imperfect outfit of the intruder, as a medical man would be to note the inevitable flaws displayed by a usurper in the realm of physical science. If any professional theologians are interested in finding out how insecure I feel, I extend to them a friendly invitation to come over (to the medical school) and try their luck on our ground.

239   However, I am determined to take this step into the unknown because of the error that I hate and fear as much as I do living a worthless life. What I want is to dispel error and to create clarity both for myself and for others. Thus I am also moved by *justice*, by the desire to refrain from doing anyone an injustice, and simply to listen and investigate before I form any judgment.

240   But the final and highest cause for my decision to abandon the solid ground under my feet is truth. That truth that since the beginning of

[1] "Preface for my gracious audience!"

time has lain within the shining eyes of the child, with their unheeding, pensive, faraway look; in life with its wild craving and ardent fire, this wretched life beneath the revolving heaven full of transitory stars; and in the staring eye of the dying with their unheeding, pensive, faraway look.

241   The truth compels me to desert my plow before the noontide, to abandon my labor in the fields of my chosen profession, and to ask that we all raise our eyes from our work and look toward the west where the sun, in accordance with ancient custom, will end the day which we have called by name.

242   As an ignorant amateur I hesitate to enter the sanctum sanctorum of an unfamiliar science, and risk being somewhat roughly shown the door again. And yet as a human being I expect hospitality even from adversaries.

THOUGHTS ON THE INTERPRETATION OF CHRISTIANITY, WITH REFERENCE TO THE THEORY OF ALBRECHT RITSCHL

A single spark of the fire of justice, fallen into the soul of a
learned man, is enough to irradiate, purify, and consume his life
and endeavors, so that he no longer has any peace and is forced
to abandon forever that tepid or cold frame of mind in which
run-of-the-mill savants carry out their daily chores.

—Nietzsche

243   If we cast a glance down the long procession of the centuries, we find scattered, like so many points of light, throughout the history of the development and the vicissitudes of worldly powers, strange figures who appear to belong to a different order: alien, almost supramundane beings who relate to the historical conditions just enough to be understood, but who essentially represent a new species of man. The world does not give birth to them, but rather they create a world, a new heaven and a new earth. Their values are different, their truths are new. They know that they are necessary and that we have been waiting for them, that we have awaited them a long time, and that it is for them alone that causal sequence of the world's historical development has plowed the fields and prepared them to receive the seed, or ripened the grain for harvest. They come into the world as if it be-

44

longed to them and see themselves as the incarnation of a purpose for which an infinite number of deeds has prepared the way. They know that they are the meaning and the end toward which the labor of many centuries has been directed, and that now they have become the material representation of this end. They identify with the idea they bring to the world, and they live out this idea feeling that it will endure forever and that it is beyond violation by the exegesis of men. They *are* their own idea, untrammeled and absolute among the minds of their age, and not susceptible to historical analysis, for they experience the products of history not as conditions of their being but rather as the object of their activity, and as their link with the world. They have not evolved from any historical foundation, but know that in their inmost natures they are free of all contingency, and have come only in order to erect on the foundation of history the edifice of their own ideas.

44   One such man was Jesus of Nazareth. He knew this and he did not hesitate to proclaim it to the world.

45   Human beings have never possessed yardsticks with which to measure great minds. For centuries they have debated whether Christ was a god, a god-man, or a man. The Middle Ages assumed the absolute reliability of all the New Testament accounts concerning the person of Christ. The Middle Ages lacked the yardstick by which to measure Christ. A god is *qualitas occulta*; a god-man even more so; and man is absolutely incommensurable with Christ. Thus Christ was a god-man or God, a quality that cannot be further elucidated.

46   The situation has changed radically during the evolution of modern, post-Renaissance philosophy. Over the years epistemology, which constitutes the fundamental problem of all philosophy, has gradually developed a concept essential for general mental operations, namely the concept of the normal man. To be sure, the normal man is not a quantity acknowledged by public statute, but rather is a product of tacit convention, a thing that exists everywhere and nowhere, to which all epistemological results refer implicitly. Just as a Paris cellar now harbors a standard meter by which all other instruments of measurement are calibrated, so, in an indetectable place inside the heads of scientific-minded men, there exists the standard of the normal man that is used to calibrate all scientific-philosophical results.

47   Modern people no longer acknowledge the New Testament accounts to be absolutely reliable, but only relatively reliable. Armed with this judgment, critical scholarship lays hold of the person of Christ, snips a bit off here and another bit off there, and begins—sometimes covertly

45

and sometimes overtly, blatantly, and with a brutal naïveté—to measure him by the standard of the normal man. After he has been distilled through all the artful and capricious mechanisms of the critics' laboratory, the figure of the historical Jesus emerges at the other end. The man with the scientist's retort in his hand is no longer interested in this body which has now been made to conform to the standard of the normal man and patented for international consumption, and leaves it up to the world to decide whether it wishes to welcome this Christ as God, as a god-man, or as a man.

248   The Germanic variety of the species *Homo sapiens* has a reputation for particular sensibility and depth of feeling. This may be true of the German nation as a whole, but great scholars whose achievements are acknowledged in their lifetimes constitute an exception. It is really astounding how little emotion a truth, a piece of scientific knowledge, actually does arouse in our men of learning. How could Kant, who regarded God as a *Ding an sich*, as a "purely negative limiting concept," still have any religion; and how could he himself, as an unknowable *Ding an sich*, exist in the cheerless desert of this "negative limiting concept"? How can Wundt wax enthusiastic over the ethical purpose of the world, when nothing exists that could achieve or enjoy this purpose? How can Hartmann attribute any kind of impulse for ethical action to the void and unfeeling unconscious? And finally, how can Albrecht Ritschl[2] be a committed Christian, when his God is compelled to go through official channels whenever he wishes to do something good for man?

249   An incredible want of sensibility is required to arrive at conclusions like these, and not to feel pierced to the heart. Probably the savants to whom I have alluded suffer from overwork and have no time to experience personally the heights and depths of emotion which must properly attend their views, or to live them out in fear and trembling. A man who fails to live out his own truth will fail to detect its results. And yet it is only by knowing the results of a truth that we become aware of its internal contradictions. As a rule, one does not need to look far to detect some absurdity, some caprice or logical flaw in their ideas.

250   If we wish to make sense of Ritschl's Christianity, we must always keep in mind this want of sensibility which typically characterizes men acknowledged as notable scholars.[3]

---

[2] Albrecht Ritschl (1822–1889), German Protestant theologian, who denied the mystical element in religion; author of *Die Christliche Lehre von der Rechtfertigung und Versöhnung* (1870–1874) (The Christian doctrine of justification and atonement).

[3] *Originally*: This want of feeling so typical for prominent scholars is the most generous

251 Indisputably Ritschl's is the most significant and original of all modern interpretations of Christ and his teachings. I must confess that I was genuinely amazed to encounter so much of solid philosophical value during my study of Ritschl's writings. If we take the theologians at their word, we might expect to find nothing in Ritschl but what theologians term "the simple preachment of the human personality of Christ." But Ritschl's theories are in no way simple or easily accessible. Instead they constitute an extremely artful epistemology which, in genuine Kantian fashion, is calibrated wholly with reference to the normal man; a keen-witted, compelling line of reasoning; a profound intimacy with the philosophical problem of Illuminism; and all in all a first-rate, logical, and extremely conclusive development of Kantian epistemology based on a solid foundation of Lutheranism. All things which our theologians have always taken pains to conceal. For example, quite recently theorists who hold the historical view of Christianity did not say boo when Vischer,[4] in his study, spoke about illuministic knowledge, but instead applauded as if such knowledge were completely compatible with the historical view. I have been listening attentively to theologians for more than two years now, vainly hoping to gain a clue to their mysterious concept of human personality. Vainly I sought to discover where human personality gets its motivational force. Apparently the depiction of his human personality is intended to present us with a clearly-defined image. The formation of an ethical character should result from the holding up of the image, either through some secret correspondence inaccessible to perception or, more naturally, this image is supposed to serve as a model to awaken in us the impulse to imitate Christ. The Ancients were already employing this second method centuries ago, when Theseus or Solon was held up as a model to an Athenian youth. The image of the Buddha is drummed into the Hindu boy, or a holy fakir is paraded before him. A boy who reads *Robinson Crusoe* becomes so enthusiastic about the protagonist that his actions are determined by those of his hero, in accordance with that same law of nature that decrees that a black man cannot refrain from wearing the top hat and studs of the European. If one simply chose to yield to every impulse to mimicry, one could, just for the fun of it, go around with one's head bowed in deep thought, allowing oneself to be possessed by the personality of Hegel, and end up bewitching the world with theories about absolute, a priori Being In-and-Of-Itself,

---

excuse that can be offered for the aberration of modern theology, which Ritschl initiated in a pseudoliterature amalgamated out of Kantian and Lutheran ideas.
[4] F. T. von Vischer, author of *Auch Einer* (1884).

Through-Itself, and For-Itself. We can find as much motivation in any other personality—and even more in those modern personalities with whom we are more familiar—than in the personality of Christ, who is so widely separated from us both in time and through the interpretations. What then is so special about Christ, that he should be the motivational force?[5] Why not another model—Paul or Buddha or Confucius or Zoroaster? The compelling character of moral values derives from metaphysics alone, for as Hartmann says, ethics divorced from metaphysics has no ground to stand on. If we view Christ as a human being, then it makes absolutely no sense to regard him as, in any way, a compelling model for our actions. Under these circumstances it will be a hopeless undertaking to try to convince the world of the necessity of Christian ethics, But if, as Ritschl does, we presuppose the dogma of Christ's divinity, the problem ceases to be that of why Christian ethics is valid in the first place, and is reduced to the more limited problem of the *mode* of determination of ethical action.

252   I will now move on to describe Ritschl's theory of the compelling character of the personality of Christ for Christian moral action.

253   Everything real, that is, every object of cognition, arouses a sensation. It is the function of memory to store up such sensations. At any time memory can reproduce for us the image of an event that originally was real. The image in memory consists of two distinct objects. The first is the image of the original event, and the second is the image of the feeling aroused in us by the original event. Thus the first part of memory contains only the image of the *actus purus*, the pure event, but the second tells us what kind of feeling—pleasure or aversion—the event awakened in us. From this second part of the image in memory arises the idea and the feeling of value that we ascribe to the event, which being pure is, as such, neutral. Thus the image in memory consists of our idea of the pure event, combined with the sense of value. In accordance with the dictum *Nihil est in intellectu, quod non antea fuerit in sensu,*[6] we are accustomed to trace every feeling we experience to an external stimulus. Thus it can easily happen that we relate a feeling to an external, material event, and equate this feeling with a genuine sen-

---

[5] *Deleted*: A theologian really has neither the right nor the power to prevent anyone from taking it into his head to imitate Napoleon or Kaiser Wilhelm. So, when the theologians could not or did not wish to enlighten me, I went to the model on my own, and now I will tell and reveal to you with dispassion what arguments Ritschl presents to justify his doctrine, and what, for unfathomable reasons, the theologians conceal from themselves.

[6] "Nothing exists in the intellect that did not previously exist in the senses" (Aristotle via the Scholastics).

48

sation. In most cases this relation will actually exist, but in some it may not. Probably we are particularly susceptible to such error in matters of religion. I will clarify this with a concrete example.

254   In the time of Christ there was a legend that at certain moments an angel would stir the waters of the pool at Bethesda. Let us suppose that at one time an angel really did stir the water and that someone witnessed this event. This person passed on to others the image of the event as he remembered it. At this point the image in his memory passes into the heads of his audience, and they link this image with the feeling of value that people customarily ascribe to the appearance of an angel. Now the water bubbles up again, in the same way as the image in their memory, and inevitably they associate with the event the sense of value imparted to them by the man who originally told the tale. But being endowed with lively imaginations, they confuse what is merely a subjective feeling with a sensation produced by a material stimulus. But every sensation derives from an actual event external to ourselves, to which we refer the sensation. For this reason people believe that an angel has actually stirred up the water and produced this sensation—or rather this feeling—in them by his presence. Thus the emotion-based hallucination of an angel stems from an unconscious confusion of a feeling felt in the past, which is now merely remembered, with a truly existent feeling produced by objective causes.

255   This is the way Ritschl analyzes objects of a religious nature, above all the problem of the *unio mystica*, the direct relationship of a human being to God and Christ which is claimed by many so-called "pietists."

256   The Gospel-writers transmit to us the image of what they remember about Christ. As we have said, what is communicated is merely the pure, undifferentiated image, but the image is closely linked with the sense of value that has been instilled in the human race. If a man now performs a Christian act consistent with the Christ he remembers, the feeling of value originally transmitted to and instilled in him by the Evangelists, which he recalls in the moment his Christian motivation is realized in action, deceives him into believing that he is experiencing a genuine sensation, and he falls prey to the notion that this sensation results from some objective cause external to himself, namely the actual and effectual presence of Christ. That is, he believes that Christ himself, in an objective and material form, is standing beside him and has entered into a real, tangible relationship with him. The same process explains the direct relationship that allegedly exists between a human being and God.

257   Thus Ritschl rejects any illuministic or subjective knowledge, and

consequently also rejects the *unio mystica*, that object on which all medieval mysticism was focused and which, down to our civilized and enlightened times, has been pursuing its wicked ways inside the heads and hearts of otherwise irreproachable and right-thinking folk. But Ritschl does not maintain this negative attitude, but rather founds his ethics on the power of subjective feeling. He does this with such skill and bewildering dexterity that without incurring the slightest strain or misapprehension, it is possible for him to continue using the same vocabulary, with reference to the god-man relationship, that has hitherto been current in "pietistic" circles. Naturally this fact poses no small obstacle to a genuine and penetrating understanding of Ritschl's theory; this is why, for a nontheologian, the discourse of a dyed-in-the-wool Ritschlian seems to be a conglomeration of contradictions and ambiguities.[7] Of course no theologian will admit that this is the case. But I must say that the technical terms employed by the modern theologian are so abstruse and misleading that even educated people must engage in an abdication of the intellect in order to understand what is meant, on the symbolic or magical level, by a phrase like "religious-ethical motive." And when, finally, a Ritschlian construction is placed on an idea which continues to be addressed under the same old names, one can only gape in amazement and patiently endure the incredible spectacle. At the end one will probably say to one's neighbor: "I suppose that's how it must be?!"

258   Ritschl's foundation of ethics derives from the same epistemological basis as his refutation of Illuminism.

259   The so-called "pietist" says: "I stand in a direct and intimate relationship to God. His nearness and the power of his presence determine me to direct my actions in accordance with his will, i.e., to act morally." On the aforementioned grounds Ritschl refutes the unmediated nature of such a relationship, explaining the *unio mystica* as resulting from the confusion of a subjective feeling of value with an objectively determined sensation. Ritschl develops his foundation of ethics entirely within the sphere of discursive reason and sensory perceptibility. He states: "We cannot demonstrate that others can act on the human mind except within the sphere of active and conscious sensation."

---

[7] *Deleted*: To forestall confusion I will not, in what follows, give you literal quotations from Ritschl, for his syntax is distinguished by its great complexity and, often, its sheer incomprehensibility, at least for those who are merely hearing the words. A sentence which has to be read two or three times before one can understand it will not be comprehensible to someone who hears it read aloud just once.

260   That is, one person can act on another only if the stimulus exerted is received and processed within the other's sphere of consciousness. In fact it is impossible for any human consciousness to be affected except within the sphere of sensory perceptibility, or rather of "conscious sensation."

261   Thus, according to Ritschl, no effect can be exercised on a man's consciousness except by way of conscious sensation. By this theory the possibility, long ago established by science, of the existence of so-called posthypnotic suggestion, is really an impossibility,[8] and so on. Man draws the entire content of consciousness from the sphere of conscious sensation, of sensory perceptibility. Thus he also acquires all motivation for ethical action by way of conscious sensation, in other words from the communications of other human beings. The communication we receive from others is an image drawn from memory. As we have already explained, this image contains only the idea of the thing communicated and the feeling of value we ascribe to the idea. Depending on the degree of value we ascribe to an idea, it may become the motivation of our actions. The subjective feeling of value confers on this idea, which in itself is neutral and passive, the power of motivation, effectiveness, and thus reality. So we lend being and reality to a mere passive idea. We feel our "mental reality," but this reality is determined by a motivation whose only reality derives from the feeling of value we confer upon it. But the reality of the feeling of value has its ground in the reality of self-esteem. Ritschl formulates this rather complex thought in the following terms: "The dignity attached to our mental reality is the sufficient cognitive reason for the reality of everything that contributes to our reality, as a valuable and effective existence in the world."

262   We see, or rather we fail to see, that what we have here is a sort of tall tale in which someone pulls himself out of the swamp by his own topknot.

263   As a rule feelings of value respecting ethical actions are instilled in us by others. The inculcation of these feelings occurs through communication. The child is taught that Christ helped the poor and infirm. This is the *actus purus*, the image in memory that does not involve any power to motivate. The child confers this power on the act after he has been taught that it is good to help the poor. By this process the feeling of value ascribed to the action is intensified so that finally the idea of helping the poor becomes so effective, by virtue of the intensified feeling of value, that it serves to motivate a similar action. The motivation

---

[8] *Deleted*: the same being true of premonitions, etc.

51

of every Christian action is supplied in this way. The Evangelists transmit to us their memory of the deeds of Christ. The feeling of value instilled in us toward ethical action fastens to the idea—neutral in itself—of the moral life of Christ, and confers on this idea that efficacy that it must possess in order to motivate our will. The deeper we penetrate into the historical personality of Christ, the more notions of moral action we adopt, and the more motivations we acquire for our will.

264   Ritschl sees no other way to acquire motivations with respect to value, than the way of conscious sensation, and thus he is entirely dependent on those images in memory, supplied as by the most ancient sources, concerning the life of Christ. Ritschl's theory of the relationship of man with God and Christ derives from this epistemological necessity.

265   Moreover, since Ritschl, too, has built in his mind a tabernacle dedicated to the fictive "normal man," he knows, for reasons already stated, that no man can be acted upon by another outside the sphere of "conscious sensation," and thus that no man has access to any other sources of motivation than are contained in the Holy Scriptures. In Ritschl's view the New Testament, in the final sense, teaches us the life of Christ. Or quite simply, Christ produces his life in us. At this point the so-called "pietist" will fall into a trap and say: This is in fact the *unio mystica.* Far from it! True, the words sound extremely mystical, and St. Francis of Assisi could say them without blushing. We are tempted to cite a slightly amended verse from Goethe:

> One hears the Gospel, but *one* lacks the faith!
> Faith is the dearest child of miracle![9]

266   Ritschl says quietly: "God punishes me through repentance. Christ consoles and encourages me."

267   But keep in mind that this pious sentiment applied only to the extent that the Christ present to the Ritschlian Christian constitutes the sum of all the images in memory handed down by tradition, that is, of all mental images concerning the person of Christ, in conjunction with the feeling of value that we confer on the totality of the images. For the Rieschlian, God and Christ always exist only in a special sense. On the other hand, the "pietist" holds that Christ consoles him, actually and directly, through the power of the Holy Spirit which Christ once promised to send to his own people. But the enlightened Ritschlian, who has learned the lessons of modern civilization, knows that God or Christ is

---

[9] Goethe, *Faust I*, lines 262–263, from "Night, the Gothic Room."

not really materially present (*in substantia*), but only insofar as man, by virtue of the feeling of value that has been instilled in him, confers on the intrinsically unreal mental idea the power of motivating his actions and the property of real existence.

268   In classical antiquity the demigod Prometheus sang happily while he worked:

Here I sit creating human beings . . .[10]

269   The Ritschlian can claim, among other things:

Here I sit creating gods!

270   It appears that modesty increases with the advance of civilization! Furthermore, this compromise which Ritschl effects between Luther and Kant has an ominous taint of Kantian subjectivism and—hard though it is to imagine it—the World as Will and Idea! Oh, if only Schopenhauer had had the pleasure of seeing his ideas turned to account in this way! Perhaps we might modestly suggest to Mr. von Falkenberg that in the next edition of his history of modern philosophy, he might—in addition to the "untimely" non-philosopher Nietzsche[11]—cite Albrecht Ritschl as a secret admirer of Schopenhauer.

271   Many of my audience who are not in the least averse to employing Ritschl's symbolic language[12] may perhaps be horrified to perceive the abyss of anti-Christian notions, underlying this language, which I have just revealed to them. Indeed, assuming that I may always have defended myself with might and main against Ritschl's ideas, they may imagine that I have exaggerated a bit. But in fact I can quote from Ritschl word-for-word passages demonstrating that his brand of Christianity is actually as I have described it, and will do so now.

272   For example, Ritschl reproaches his adversaries who follow a concrete interpretation of Christ's promise: "And lo, I am with you always, even unto the end of the world,"[13] claiming that there exists a direct relationship, a *unio mystica*, between a man and God or Christ. Ritschl

[10] Goethe, "Prometheus."

[11] Jung is alluding to Nietzsche's *Unzeitgemässe Betrachtungen* (Untimely reflections), and to the fact that Nietzsche presented himself not as a philosopher intent on system-building in the traditional German manner but rather as a psychologist with a brilliant and aphoristic style which Nietzsche regarded as modeled on the French.

[12] *Deleted*: who are still gorging themselves on the feast which Ritschl has set before theology.

[13] Matt. 28:20. *Deleted*: or, "For where two or three are gathered together in my name, there am I in the midst of them" [Matt. 18:20].

says of them: "They posit, as the reality of things, what are nothing more than unauthenticated and unstable images in memory."

273   On the other hand Ritschl knows that the only way to act upon a man's sphere of consciousness is through memory, whose power to motivate action is based on the subjective feeling of value. Thus he says: "However, a precise and detailed memory constitutes the form in which the human mind acquires all effectual and meritorious motivations, obedience to which enables us to live up to our proper purpose in life.

274   "For an exact memory is the medium of personal relationships, that is, it enables one person to exercise a continuous effect on another and to be present in him whenever the latter acts on the basis of the former's teaching or instigation. And in the broadest sense this is true of the bond, in religion, between our lives and God, effected through our precise remembrance of Christ. However, we ought not to describe such relationships, and in particular the last-named relationship, as unmediated, for by doing so we declare them to be imaginary. For nothing is real that does not involve a large measure of mediation. But the personal relationship between God or Christ and ourselves is always mediated through our precise memory of the Word, that is, of the law and promise of God, and God acts on us only by means of one or the other of these revelations. The assertion, as a basic principle, of the unmediated nature of any perception or relationship, does away with the possibiltiy of distinguishing between reality and hallucination."

275   Then Ritschl recapitulates once more in order to forestall any possible misinterpretation. "Thus without the mediation of the Word of God, that is, the Law and the Gospel, and without the exact remembrance of this personal revelation of God in Christ, no personal relationship exists between a Christian and God."

276   I believe that this is clear and requires no further commentary. If the high priest who presided over the trial of Christ were not such an unsympathetic figure, one might indeed be tempted to exclaim as he did: "What further need have we of witnesses? behold, now ye have heard his blasphemy" [Matt. 26:65].

277   It remains for us to take a look at the world-view that emerges from Ritschl's epistemology. In the drama of the universe as perceived by Ritschl, God, Christ, and man play a truly pathetic role. A God who exists only to the degree, and can affect the order of the world only to the extent, that human beings ascribe to his image in their memory the power to motivate their actions. Christ is the same fumbling and helpless God turned into a man, and as a man is a wretched dreamer

who suffers from hallucinations and moreover, as Ritschl aptly remarks, is "not very well-versed in the literature of mysticism"—a trait that he loyally shares with his epigone Paul. For Ritschl literally says: "Those who uphold their claim to a direct personal relationship with Christ or God are clearly not very well-versed in the literature of mysticism."

278 We may make light of Ritschl's God, but we can feel nothing but pity for Ritschl's Christian. Every pagan has his gods to whom he can cry out when he feels sorrowful and afraid, even if this god is nothing but a brightly polished boot, a silver button, or a stick of wood. But Ritschl's Christian knows that his God exists only in church, school, and home and owes his efficacy to the subjectively determined power of motivation supplied by memory. And it is to this powerless God that a Christian is supposed to pray for salvation from bodily and spiritual want? God cannot lift a finger, for he exists only historically, in tradition, and in a strictly limited sense. The French could just as easily, and with just as little success, importune Charlemagne to inflict a great defeat on the wretched Germans and liberate Alsace-Lorraine.

79 At this point I will recall that want of feeling typical of notable scholars. This local demon that hops about in the desert of the heart has played a nasty trick on Ritschl.

80 Albrecht Ritschl is much more accessible when approached from a psychological point of view. He was a professor in Göttingen, a Lutheran institution, and was obliged to teach in accordance with Lutheran doctrine; thus he had to be a Lutheran. Ritschl's guideline was that famous blow by which Luther abruptly did away with all mysticism and the entire prophetic tradition of the ancient church. Ritschl himself states: "I am neither obligated nor entitled to teach in another way. Yet it is a noteworthy fact that a theologian like Weiss should dare to judge me by his pietistic pretensions, when I do not deviate from the teachings prescribed by Reformation doctrine."

81 Lutheranism was his absolute basis. In addition, as was proper for a respectable teacher of divinity, he was compelled to grapple with secular philosophy to a sufficient degree to show that Kantian epistemology was entirely compatible with Lutheran Christianity.

82 But the philosopher of Königsberg allows no one to play around with his ideas with impunity. The normal man in Kant's critique of pure reason has little taste for the element of mystery in religion, and seduced Ritschl to deny that mystery which slumbers in every human breast, so that he was swallowed up by that caste of men whose life and work consists in ignoring questions and stimulating certainty.

83 The prodigious history of mystery in the drama of the universe surges

by, swallowing up the puny circles described by Ritschl. An intimation from infinity breathes over all human exegesis and blows it away. But the mystery will remain in the human heart until the end of time.

284   Clearly we have made little progress in understanding the person of Christ. Quite apart from all the absurd interpretations and imputations made concerning Christ—sociopolitical aperçus, ideas which satisfy the desire to "get a human slant on things," and so on, which are cursed by their own absurdity from the moment of their birth—it must still appear very strange to any educated layman who is earnestly struggling to understand Christ, to see how he is treated by theologians, the guardians and keepers of the highest of earthly goods. In their naïveté theologians believe that the world is so sweet and good that the only thing needed to get everyone on earth to fling himself at the feet of this Model enthusiastically is to preach a sermon about the person of Christ. They think that the mere holding-up of the remembered image is sufficient to determine moral action. Apparently many of our theologians are so convinced of the goodness of the world that they believe everyone will immediately ascribe a feeling of value to this remembered image, and so will confer on it the power to act in their hearts. Obviously they do not know how utterly indifferent the world is to sermonizing and preachers who throw up their hands in dismay. The "purely . . . unstable image in memory" *cannot* stir the world because no feeling of value with regard to the person of Christ has yet been instilled in it. The world has not been taught about Christ and has no interest in him. We still know far too little about how Christ viewed himself, about his claim to divinity; and we still understand too little of Christ's concept of his own metaphysical significance to endow him with feelings of value. For the most part, today's practical theologians have in fact abandoned the notion of winning over the world through education and conviction. They simply ignore the moral physiology espoused by their master Ritschl, the second clause of which relates to the feeling of value, and blithely preach away about the historical Jesus whose mere image has no power to motivate. On the contrary, the repetition of this theme every Sunday is turning it into a bore. To avoid the onerous task of educating the human race to accept new points of view, theologians prefer to just shrug their shoulders, say "Non liquet," and give in to a critical world. Indeed, they are willing to concede three-quarters of the personality of Christ—his faith in miracles, his prophetic powers, and his consciousness of his own divinity. They confine themselves to preaching the historical Jesus, Christ as a human being, a departure from Ritschl, but the reduction of a high point to a lesser one. In the end Christ becomes a "naïve idealist," poor

as a churchmouse, stripped of his power and glory and even his keen discernment. Naturally these experiments and concessions substantially reduce the chances of winning the world, and we are already seeing signs that eventually we will be driven to employ Salvation Army techniques, encumber religious services with all sorts of tricky devices, decorate churches inside and out with pretty frippery, install baptismal fonts and communion tables which rotate to the sound of music and come equipped with periodic changes of scenery, and set up, at appropriate spots, automatic sermon-machines which simultaneously function as altars and which, upon the insertion of a dime, will reel out a sermon no more than ten minutes long on any topic desired—all simply in order to ward off, with this din, the deadly boredom that is quietly but surely taking over religious life.

85   Naturally it is much easier and more comfortable to turn a church or a religious service into something amusing; to gamble with values which our forebears shed blood and tears to instill in us; to squander a wealth of knowledge stored up by our ancestors in the course of eighteen hundred years of tumultuous evolution, than to teach people things that must be learned by hard work, and thus to lead them to new and vaster heights.

86   There is no trick to throwing out the baby with the bathwater. And to say, "We are throwing out everything that has been built up around the figure of Christ for eighteen centuries, all the teachings, all the traditions, and will accept only the historical Jesus"—this is not much of a feat either, for as a rule the people who talk this way really have nothing to throw away in the first place. Yet frequently we hear their attitude described as "critical." Our descendants will hardly thank us if we, who are called to make the human race grow and flourish, leave behind us such fruits as a ravaged church composed of intolerable rules and shallow religious concepts which trail off into a wasteland.

87   So here we are, asking ourselves what we ought to do. Why do the sermons about the historical Jesus make no sense? Why are people more interested in attending scientific lectures than in going to church? Why is their interest focused on Darwin, Haeckel, and Büchner?[14] And why today do they not even bother to discuss religious questions which, in the past, people were willing to kill for? Indeed, in certain circles the discussion of religious issues is considered not only awkward but down-

[14] Ernst Haeckel (1834–1919), German biologist, advocate of the nineteenth-century theory of the metamorphosis of species over the course of time. Ludwig Büchner (1824–1899), German materialistic philosopher.

right unseemly. Our society must be educated, we must instill in it a concern for the supreme questions, and only after all this has been done ought we to begin preaching about the so-called historical Jesus and to appeal to the sense of value that people ascribe to Christ. But this sense of value will not arise until the world has grasped the fact that Christ is not a "normal man," any more than he is an element in a world of abstract concepts totally divorced from reality. We should and must interpret Christ as he himself taught us to interpret him. The image of Christ must be restored to the idea he had of himself, namely as a prophet, a man sent by God. The position he occupies in our mental universe must be consistent with his own claims. Modern man must accept the supramundane nature of Christ, no more and no less. If we do not accept it we are no longer Christians, for we are not entitled to bear this name when we have ceased to share the views it implies. But as long as we call ourselves by Christ's name, we are morally bound to observe his teachings in all respects. We *must* believe even what seems impossible, or we will be abusing the name of Christian. This is a harsh prescription, and will be denounced as an abdication of the intellect. But once someone has taken it into his head to be a Christian, he must defend his faith against his critical reason, even at the risk of a new flowering of scholasticism. If he does not wish to do this, there is a very easy way out: he must simply give up his intention to be a Christian. Then he may call himself by any other name he chooses—a man concerned with the preservation of moral decency, or a moral philosopher bent on improving the world. But if our Christianity is to possess any substance whatever, we must once again accept unconditionally the whole of the metaphysical, conceptual universe of the first Christians. To do this will be to drive a painful thorn into our flesh, but for the sake of our title as Christians, we must. I call on everyone, and especially theologians, to remember the truth that Eduard von Hartmann hurled down at the feet of all Christians, and I implore that they hearken to his voice: "The world of metaphysical ideas must always remain the living fountain of feeling in religious worship, which rouses the will to ethical action. Whenever this fountain dries up, worship becomes petrified and turns into a dead, meaningless ceremony, while religious ethics wither into a dry and abstract moralizing or a sentimental phrase-mongering which holds no attraction for anyone!"

288   The mystery of a metaphysical world, a metaphysical order, of the kind that Christ taught and embodied in his own person, must be placed in center stage of the Christian religion, and must occupy its summit as the Prime Mover. Hartmann says: "*No religion whatever* is possible without the premonitory depth and infinite richness of that mystery which shows a different aspect to every human being."

289   No religion has survived, or ever will, without mystery, to which the devotee is most intimately bound. Even modern historically oriented Christianity has its miracles, its mystery. But alas, alas, this miracle par excellence—the effect on man of the person of Christ and man's consequent conversion—is inevitably a fictive miracle in that its cause is not the real presence of Christ (*in substantia*), but only an idea that we, as subjects of cognition, have endowed with the power to motivate our actions. By a strict definition of the term "miracle," the altered conduct of somebody converted in accordance with Ritschl's view of causation cannot constitute a miracle, for the efficient cause of this conduct is that idea which predominates over the will, an idea whose reality is determined by the reality of the subject who knows it. In ordinary, unstilted scientific language this is called autosuggestion. And nowadays the concept of autosuggestion no longer falls into the category of miracle, for if it did, we would also be forced to marvel daily at the miracle of gravitation. We often hear theologians say: It is in fact the great miracle, which makes clear to us the immediate effect which Christ exercises on our lives, that a person can be totally transformed when he grasps the person of Christ. If they interpret this phenomenon in the same way as Ritschl, this would mean that the miracle in question is no greater than if a hypochondriac who has read about tuberculosis were himself to start coughing and spitting. But if they interpret it, in Christian terms, as referring to the material, substantial presence of Christ, then it is indeed a great miracle. But then why not do away with Ritschl's nomenclature too, along with the concept of the historical Jesus,[15] which has meaning only if it is used by an adherent of Ritschl's ideas? For in this case Christ is a metaphysical figure with whom we are bound in a mystical union which raises us up out of the sensory world. And in this case, we laymen should dispense with the idea of the historical Jesus, for it now has a fixed meaning derived from Ritschl, and lends itself to no further interpretation but only to *misin*terpretation. In this case the theologian ought rather to speak in the language of Heinrich Suso, which does not lend itself to misunderstanding, or in the profound and obscure images of a Jakob Böhme. By doing so he will approach the summit of religious feeling more nearly than through the insipid phrases of progressive theology.

290   I leave it up to every man who desires to be a Christian to decide whether or not a *unio mystica* is possible. And every man who bears this name with honor will come to a positive decision, for Christ viewed

---

[15] *Deleted*: The concept of personhood? Why not do away with the exact remembrance of tradition?

himself as one who possessed both ability and desire to remain with his people "even unto the end of the world." This is a dangerous view and inevitably brings with it that peril feared by Ritschl, namely that it eliminates any possibility of distinguishing between reality and hallucination. In its train follow the entire mystical tradition, the problems of asceticism and of ecstatic knowledge, and those of the divinity of Christ and the infallibility of his teachings. Any consistent realization of the mystical idea must inevitably reintroduce debate concerning the objects of scholastic speculation, and thereby come close to the possibility of social and scientific indifference and call into question the further progress of civilization. These are all ominous, far-reaching, and bewildering possibilities which it would not occur to anyone to be concerned about if it were not for the fact that during the thousand years of the Middle Ages, mankind witnessed their reign for long periods. Anyone who wishes to hold fast to the metaphysical reality of the elements of Christian faith must realize these dangers and difficulties and must never lose sight of the fact that Christianity represents nothing less than the break with an entire world, a dehumanization of man, a "revaluation of all values" (Nietzsche). There is not one single element of civilization that can turn a profit on Christian teachings. Everything takes second place to the one great question, that of the inner spiritualization of the individual and the concomitant disintegration of the existing order of nature. Christ came to bring not peace but a sword, for he unleashes the conflict of the dualistic, divided will.

291   For almost two thousand years, from its birth in the theology of John until its decline in Schopenhauer, that dangerous interpretation of Christian faith which formed the foundation of the medieval worldview has fascinated the most distinguished minds. This is cause enough to doubt that it has been completely extinguished, and cause to expect that we have not yet seen the last lightning bolt flare up out of its dark reaches.

Plurimi pertransibunt, et multiplex erit scientia![16]

[16] "Many shall perish, and manifold shall be knowledge!"

3

THE EXPERIENCE OF "RELIGIOUS REALITIES"

From *Letters*, vol. 2, pp. 257–64

Dear Pastor Bernet,   13 June 1955

At last I have got down to reading and studying your book[1] which you so kindly sent me. Please put the slowness of this procedure down to my old age! It was certainly not lack of interest that kept me reading so long, but rather a curiosity or—more accurately—a need to familiarize myself with and learn to understand the theological mode of thinking, which is so alien to me. I have been able to assimilate this thinking only very fragmentarily, if at all, in spite or perhaps because of the fact that I come from a theological milieu on my mother's side, and my father was himself a clergyman. It was the tragedy of my youth to see my father cracking up before my eyes on the problem of his faith and dying an early death.[2] This was the objective outer event that opened my eyes to the importance of religion. Subjective inner experiences prevented me from drawing negative conclusions about religion from my father's fate, much as I was tempted to do so. I grew up in the heyday of scientific materialism, studied natural science and medicine, and became a psychiatrist. My education offered me nothing but arguments against religion on the one hand, and on the other the charisma of faith was denied me. I was thrown back on experience alone. Always Paul's experience on the road to Damascus hovered before me, and I asked myself how his fate would have fallen out but for his vision. Yet this experience came upon him while he was blindly pursuing his own way. As a young man I drew the conclusion that you must obviously fulfill your destiny in order to get to the point where a *donum gratiae* might happen along. But I was far from certain, and always kept the possibility in mind that on this road I might end up in a black hole. I have remained true to this attitude all my life.

---

[1] *Inhalt und Grenze der religiösen Erfahrung* (1952).
[2] Cf. *Memories*, pp. 91ff./96ff.

61

From this you can easily see the origin of my psychology: only by going my own way, integrating my capacities headlong (like Paul), and thus creating a foundation for myself, could something be vouchsafed to me or built upon it, no matter where it came from, and of which I could be reasonably sure that it was not merely one of my own neglected capacities.

The only way open to me was the experience of religious realities which I had to accept without regard to their truth. In this matter I have no criterion except the fact that they seem meaningful to me and harmonize with man's best utterances. I don't know whether the archetype is "true" or not. I only know that it lives and that I have not made it.

Since the number of possibilities is limited, one soon comes to a frontier, or rather to frontiers which recede behind one another presumably up to the point of death. The experience of these frontiers gradually brings the conviction that what is experienced is an endless approximation. The goal of this approximation seems to be anticipated by archetypal symbols which represent something like the circumambulation of a centre. With increasing approximation to the centre there is a corresponding depotentiation of the ego in favour of the influence of the "empty" centre, which is certainly not identical with the archetype but is the thing the archetype points to. As the Chinese would say, the archetype is only the *name* of Tao, not Tao itself. Just as the Jesuits translated Tao as "God," so we can describe the "emptiness"[3] of the centre as "God." Emptiness in this sense doesn't mean "absence" or "vacancy," but something unknowable which is endowed with the highest intensity. If I call this unknowable the "self," all that has happened is that the effects of the unknowable have been given an aggregate name, but its contents are not affected in any way. An indeterminably large part of my own being is included in it, but because this part is the unconscious I cannot indicate its limits or its extent. The self is therefore a *borderline concept*, not by any means filled out with the known psychic processes. On the one hand it includes the phenomena of synchronicity, on the other its archetype is embedded in the brain structure and is physiologically verifiable: through electrical stimulation of a certain area of the brain-stem of an epileptic it is possible to produce mandala visions (*quadratura circuli*). From synchronistic phenomena we learn that a peculiar feature of the psychoid[4] background is

---

[3] For the Buddhist concept of *sunyata*, emptiness, cf. Evans-Wentz, 8 Dec. 38, n. 3. Also "Psychology and Religion," CW 11, par. 136.

[4] Cf. Dr. H., 30 Aug. 51, n. 5.

transgressivity[5] in space and time. This brings us directly to the frontier of transcendence, beyond which human statements can only be mythological.

The whole course of individuation is dialectical, and the so-called "end" is the confrontation of the ego with the "emptiness" of the centre. Here the limit of possible experience is reached: the ego dissolves as the reference-point of cognition. It cannot coincide with the centre, otherwise we would be insensible; that is to say, the extinction of the ego is at best an endless approximation. But if the ego usurps the centre it loses its object (inflation!).[6]

Even though you add to my "ultimate" an "absolute ultimate," you will hardly maintain that my "ultimate" is not as good an "ultimate" as yours. In any case all possibility of cognition and predication ceases for me at this frontier because of the extinction of the ego. The ego can merely affirm that something vitally important is happening to it. It may conjecture that it has come up against something greater, that it feels powerless against this greater power; that it can cognize nothing further; that in the course of the integration process it has become convinced of its finiteness, just as before it was compelled to take practical account of the existence of an ineluctable archetype. The ego has to acknowledge many gods before it attains the centre where no god helps it any longer against another god.

It now occurs to me—and I hope I am not deceiving myself—that from the point where you introduce the "absolute ultimate" which is meant to replace my descriptive concept of the self by an empty abstraction, the archetype is increasingly detached from its dynamic background and gradually turned into a purely intellectual formula. In this way it is neutralized, and you can then say "one can live with it quite well." But you overlook the fact that the self-constellating archetypes and the resultant situations steadily gain in numinosity, indeed are sometimes imbued with a positively eerie daemonism and bring the danger of psychosis threateningly close. The upsurging archetypal material is the stuff of which mental illnesses are made. In the individuation process the ego is brought face to face with an unknown superior power which is likely to cut the ground from under its feet and blow consciousness to bits. The archetype is not just the formal condition for mythological statements but an overwhelming force comparable to nothing I know. In view of the terrors of this confrontation I would

---

[5] "Synchronicity," CW 8, par. 964.
[6] *Aion*, CW 9, ii, pars. 44f., 79.

never dream of addressing this menacing and fascinating opponent familiarly as "Thou," though paradoxically it also has this aspect. All talk of this opponent is mythology. All statements about and beyond the "ultimate" are anthropomorphisms and, if anyone should think that when he says "God" he has also predicated God, he is endowing his words with *magical power*. Like a primitive, he is incapable of distinguishing the verbal image from reality. In one breath he will endorse the statement *Deus est ineffabilis* without a thought, but in the next he will be speaking of God as though he could express him.

It seems to me—and I beg your pardon in advance if I am doing you an injustice—that something of the sort has happened to you. You write, apparently without any misgivings, that I equate God with the self. You seem not to have noticed that I speak of the *God-image and not of God* because it is quite beyond me to say anything about God at all. It is more than astonishing that you have failed to perceive this fundamental distinction, it is shattering. I don't know what you must take me for if you can impute such stupidities to me after you yourself have correctly presented my epistemological standpoint at the beginning of your book. I have in all conscience never supposed that in discussing the psychic structure of the God-image I have taken God himself in hand. I am not a word-magician or word-fetishist who thinks he can posit or call up a metaphysical reality with his incantations. Don't Protestant critics accuse the Catholic Mass of magic when it asserts that by pronouncing the words *Hoc est corpus meum* Christ is actually present?

In *Job* and elsewhere I am always explicitly speaking of the *God-image*. If my theologian critics choose to overlook this, the fault lies with them and not with me. They obviously think that the little word "God" conjures him up in reality, just as the Mass forces Christ to appear through the words of the Consecration. (Naturally I am aware of the dissident Catholic explanation of this.) I do not share your overvaluation of words, and have never regarded the equation Christ = Logos as anything else than an interesting symbol conditioned by its time.

This credulity and entrapment in words is becoming more and more striking nowadays. Proof of this is the rise of such a comical philosophy as existentialism, which labours to help being become being through the magical power of the word. People still believe that they can posit or replace reality by words, or that something has happened when a thing is given a different name. If I call the "ultimate" the self and you call it the "absolute ultimate," its ultimateness is not changed one whit. The name means far less to me than the view associated with it. You seem to think that I enjoy romping about in a circus of archetypal figures and that I take them for ultimate realities which block my view of the Ineffable. They guide but they also mislead; how much I reserve my criticism for them you can see in *Answer to Job*, where I subject archetypal statements to what you call "blasphemous" criticism. The very fact that you consider this critique of anthropomorphisms worthy of condemnation proves how strongly you are bound to these psychic products by word-magic. If theologians think that whenever they say "God" then God is, they are deifying anthropomorphisms, psychic structures and myths. This is exactly what I don't do, for, I must repeat, I speak exclusively of the *God-image* in *Job*. Who talks of divine knowledge and divine revelation? Certainly not me. "Ultimately" I have really reached the ultimate with my presumptuous anthropomorphisms which feign knowledge and revelation! I see many God-images of various kinds; I find myself compelled to make mythological statements, but I know that none of them expresses or captures the immeasurable Other, even if I were to assert it did.

However interesting or enthralling metaphysical statements may be, I must still criticize them as anthropomorphisms. But here the theologian buttonholes me, asseverating that *his* anthropomorphism is God and damning anyone who criticizes any anthropomorphic weaknesses, defects, and contradictions in it as a blasphemer. It is not God who is insulted by the worm but the theologian, who can't or won't admit that his concept is anthropomorphic. With this he puts an end to the much needed discussion and understanding of religious statements. Just as Bultmann's demythologizing procedure stops at the point where the demagicking of words no longer seems advisable to him, so the theologian treats exactly the same concept as mythological, i.e., anthropomorphic at one moment and as an inviolable taboo at the next.

I have begged four distinguished (academic) theologians to tell me what exactly is the attitude of modern Protestantism to the question of the identity of the God of the Old Testament with the God of the New, between whom the layman thinks he can spot quite a number of differences. The question is so harmless that it is like asking what the difference is between Freud's view of the unconscious and mine. Two didn't answer at all despite repeated requests. The third told me that there was no longer any talk of God in the theological literature of the last twenty years anyway. The fourth said the question was very easy to answer: Yahweh was simply a somewhat archaic God-concept in comparison with that of the New Testament. Whereupon I replied: "Look, my dear Professor, this is just the kind of psychologism the theologians accuse me of. Suddenly the divine revelation in the OT is nothing but an archaic *concept* and the revelation in the NT is simply a modern one. But the next moment this same revelation is God himself and no concept at all."

So you ride the hobby-horse of your choice. In order to do away with such tricks, I stick to my proposal that we take all talk of God as mythological and discuss these mythologems honestly. As soon as we open our mouths we speak in traditional verbal images, and even when we merely think we think in age-old psychic structures. If God were to reveal himself to us we have nothing except our psychic organs to register his revelation and could not express it except in the images of our everyday speech.

Let the Protestant theologian therefore abandon his hieratic word-magic and his alleged knowledge of God through faith and admit to the layman that he is mythologizing and is just as incapable as he is of expressing God himself. Let him not vilify and condemn and twist the arguments of others who are struggling just as earnestly to understand the mysteries of religion, even if he finds these arguments personally disagreeable or wrong in themselves. (I cannot exempt you, for one, from the obligation to give due regard to the epistemological premises of *Answer to Job* if you want to criticize it.)

So long as we are conscious of ourselves, we are supported by the psyche and its structures and at the same time imprisoned in them with no possibility of getting outside ourselves. We would not feel and be aware of ourselves at all were we not always confronted with the unknown power. Without this we would not be conscious of our separateness, just as there is no consciousness without an object.

We are not delivered from the "sin" of mythologizing by saying that we are "saved" or "redeemed" through the revelation of God in Christ, for this is simply another mythologem which does, however, contain a psychological truth. Consequently we can understand the "feeling of redemption" which is bound up with this mythologem; but the statement "revelation in Christ" merely affirms that a myth of this kind exists which evidently belongs to the symbolism of the self.

What impresses me most profoundly in discussions with theologians of both camps is that metaphysical statements are made apparently without the slightest awareness that they are talking in mythic images which pass directly as the "word of God." For this reason it is so often thoughtlessly assumed that I do the same thing, whereas quite to the contrary I am trained by my daily professional work to distinguish scrupulously between idea and reality. The recognition of projections is indeed one of the most important tasks of psychotherapy.

I have read your erudite book with great interest and profit and find it all the more regrettable that in spite of your admirably objective presentation of my standpoint at the beginning you nevertheless go off the rails at the end. You think *I* have deviated from my epistemological position in *Job*. Had you read the introduction you could never have pronounced this false judgment.

I can understand very well that you are shocked by the book; I was too, and by the original Job into the bargain. I feel that you have in general too poor an opinion of me when you charge me with the arrogance of wanting to write an *exegesis* of Job. I don't know a word of Hebrew. As a layman, I have only tried to read the translated text with psychological common sense, on the assumption, certainly, that I am dealing with anthropomorphisms and not with magical words that conjure up God himself. If in the Jewish commentaries the high priest takes the liberty of admonishing Adonai to remember his good rather than his bad qualities,[7] it is no longer so shocking if I avail myself of a similar criticism, especially as I am not even addressing Adonai, as the high priest did, but merely the anthropomorphic God-image, and expressly refrain from all metaphysical utterances, which the high priest did not. You will scarcely suppose that, despite my assurance to the contrary, the mere pronouncing of God's name conjures up God himself. At all events Adonai took the high priest's criticism and a number of other equally drastic observations without a murmur, thereby showing himself to be more tolerant than certain theologians. The reason why mythic statements invariably lead to word-magic is that the archetype possesses a numinous autonomy and has a psychic life of its own. I have dealt with this particular difficulty at some length in *Job*. Perhaps I may remark in conclusion that the theory of archetypes is more difficult, and I am not quite so stupid as you apparently think.

I cannot omit to thank you, all the same, for the great trouble you have taken in going into my proposition so thoroughly. It is obvious that this cannot be done without difficulties and misunderstandings, especially in view of the fact that our age is still for the most part trapped in its belief in words. Ancient Greece was on an even lower level, as the term *phrenes* with its psychic connotation shows.[8] The Pueblo Indians of New Mexico still think in the "heart" and not in the

[7] *Aion*, par. 110.

[8] The midriff or diaphragm; among the pre-Socratics, the seat of consciousness. In Homer, however, *phrenes* meant the lungs.

head.[9] Tantra Yoga gives the classic localizations of thought: *anahata*, thinking (or localization of consciousness) in the chest region (*phrenes*); *visuddha* (localized in the larynx), verbal thinking; and *ajna*,[10] vision, symbolized by an eye in the forehead, which is attained only when verbal image and object are no longer identical, i.e., when their *participation mystique*[11] is abolished.

I have this advance of human consciousness particularly at heart. It is a difficult task to which I have devoted all my life's work. This is the reason why I venture to plague you with such a long letter.[12]

Yours sincerely, C. G. JUNG

[9] Memories, p. 248/233.

[10] *Anahata, visuddha,* and *ajna* are three of the seven *chakras* in Kundalini Yoga. Cf. Kotschnig, 23 July 34, n. 2, and "The Realities of Practical Psychotherapy," CW 16 (2nd edn.), Appendix, par. 560.

[11] A term coined by Lévy-Bruhl for the "prelogical" mentality of primitives, but later abandoned by him. Jung made frequent use of it to denote the state of projection in which internal and external events are inextricably mixed up, resulting in an irrational and unconscious identity of inside and outside.

[12] A decade later, B. published extracts from Jung's letter with comments in an essay on Jung in *Tendenzen der Theologie im 20. Jahrhundert. Eine Geschichte in Porträts*, ed. H. J. Schulz (1966). He concluded: ". . . this outsider of theology has, with the relentless determination with which be demands experience of man, with his uncomfortable criticism of ecclesiastical talk of God, with his bold vision in particular of the Protestant Church, urged upon contemporary theological thought questions which in the interest of theology are absolutely necessary and which in their rigour show the way."

4

"WHY I AM NOT A CATHOLIC"

From *The Symbolic Life*, CW 18, pars. 1466–72

466   *Firstly*: Because I am a practical Christian to whom love and justice to his brother mean more than dogmatic speculations about whose ultimate truth or untruth no human being can ever have certain knowledge. The relation to my brother and the unity of the true "catholic" Christendom is to me infinitely more important than "justification by *fide sola*." As a Christian I have to share the burden of my brother's wrongness, and that is most heavy when I do not know whether in the end he is not more right than I. I hold it to be immoral, in any case entirely unchristian, to put my brother in the wrong (i.e., to call him fool, ass, spiteful, obdurate, etc.) simply because I suppose myself to be in possession of the absolute truth. Every totalitarian claim gradually isolates itself because it excludes so many people as "defectors, lost, fallen, apostate, heretic," and so forth. The totalitarian maneuvers himself into a corner, no matter how large his original following. I hold all confessionalism to be completely unchristian.

467   *Secondly*: Because I am a doctor. If I possessed the absolute truth I could do nothing further than to press into my patient's hand a book of devotion or confessional guidance, just what is no longer of any help to him. When, on the other hand, I discover in his untruth a truth, in his confusion an order, in his lostness something that has been found, then I have helped him. This requires an incomparably greater self-abnegation and self-surrender for my brother's sake than if I assessed, correctly from the standpoint of one confession, the motivations of another.

468   You underestimate the immense number of those of goodwill, but to whom confessionalism blocks the doors. A Christian has to concern himself, especially if he is a physician of souls, with the spirituality of

[(Translated by H. N.) Written as part of a letter to H. Irminger of Zurich, 22 Sept. 1944, but not sent; instead, Jung retained it in his literary papers. For the letter to Irminger, see *Jung: Letters*, ed. G. Adler, vol. 1.]

69

the reputedly unspiritual (spirit = confessionalism!) and he can do this only if he speaks their language and certainly not if, in the deterrent way of confessionalism, he sounds the kerygmatic trumpet, hoarse with age. Whoever talks in today's world of an absolute and single truth is speaking in an obsolete dialect and not in any way in the language of mankind. Christianity possesses a εὐαγγέλιον, good tidings from God, but no textbook of a dogma with claim to totality. Therefore it is hard to understand why God should never have sent more than one message. Christian modesty in any case strictly forbids assuming that God did not send εὐαγγέλια in other languages, not just in Greek, to other nations. If we think otherwise our thinking is in the deepest sense unchristian. The Christian—my idea of Christian—knows no curse formulas; indeed he does not even sanction the curse put on the innocent fig-tree by the rabbi Jesus, nor does he lend his ear to the missionary Paul of Tarsus when he forbids cursing to the Christian and then he himself curses the next moment.

1469   *Thirdly*: Because I am a man of science.

1470   The Catholic doctrine, as you present it to me so splendidly, is familiar to me to that extent. I am convinced of its "truth" in so far as it formulates determinable psychological facts, and thus far I accept this truth without further ado. But where I lack such empirical psychological foundations it does not help me in the least to believe in anything beyond them, for that would not compensate for my missing knowledge; nor could I ever surrender to the self-delusion of knowing something where I merely believe. I am now nearly seventy years old, but the charisma of belief has never arisen in me. Perhaps I am too overweening, too conceited; perhaps you are right in thinking that the cosmos circles around the God Jung. But in any case I have never succeeded in thinking that what I believe, feel, think, and understand is the only and final truth and that I enjoy the unspeakable privilege of God-likeness by being the possessor of the sole truth. You see that, although I can estimate the charisma of faith and its blessedness, the acceptance of "faith" is impossible for me because it says nothing to me.

1471   You will naturally remonstrate that, after all, I talk about "God." I do this with the same right as humanity has from the beginning equated the numinous effects of certain psychological facts with an unknown primal cause called God. This cause is beyond my understanding, and therefore I can say nothing further about it except that I am convinced of the existence of such a cause, and indeed with the same logic by which one may conclude from the disturbance of a planet's course the existence of a yet unknown heavenly body. To be sure, I do not believe in the absolute validity of the law of causality, which is why I guard against "positing" God as cause, for by this I would have given him a precise definition.

472   Such restraint is surely an offense to confessors of the Faith. But according to the fundamental Christian commandment I must not only bear with and understand my schismatic Protestant brother, but also my brothers in Arabia and India. They, too, have received strange but no less notable tidings which it is my obligation to understand. As a European, I am burdened most heavily by my unexpectedly dark brother, who confronts me with his antichristian Neo-Paganism. This extends far beyond the borders of Germany as the most pernicious schism that has ever beset Christianity. And though I deny it a thousand times, *it is also in me.* One cannot come to terms with this conflict by imputing wrong to someone else and the undoubted right to onself. This conflict I can solve first of all only within myself and not in another.

PART II

JUNG'S PSYCHOLOGICAL APPROACH TO CHRISTIAN DOCTRINE, RITUAL, AND SYMBOL

1

"CHRIST, A SYMBOL OF THE SELF"

From *Aion*, CW 9ii, pars. 68–126

68   The dechristianization of our world, the Luciferian development of science and technology, and the frightful material and moral destruction left behind by the second World War have been compared more than once with the *eschatological* events foretold in the New Testament. These, as we know, are concerned with the coming of the Antichrist: "This is Antichrist, who denieth the Father and the Son."[1] "Every Spirit that dissolveth Jesus . . . is Antichrist . . . of whom you have heard that he cometh."[2] The Apocalypse is full of expectations of terrible things that will take place at the end of time, before the marriage of the Lamb. This shows plainly that the *anima christiana* has a sure knowledge not only of the existence of an adversary but also of his future usurpation of power.

69   Why—my reader will ask—do I discourse here upon Christ and his adversary, the Antichrist? Our discourse necessarily brings us to Christ, because he is the still living myth of our culture. He is our culture hero, who, regardless of his historical existence, embodies the myth of the divine Primordial Man, the mystic Adam. It is he who occupies the centre of the Christian mandala, who is the Lord of the Tetramorph, i.e., the four symbols of the evangelists, which are like the four columns of his throne. He is in us and we in him. His kingdom is the pearl of great price, the treasure buried in the field, the grain of mus-

---

[1] I John 2:22 (DV).
[2] I John 4:3 (DV). The traditional view of the Church is based on II Thessalonians 2:3ff., which speaks of the apostasy, of the ἄνθρωπος τῆς ἀνομίας (man of lawlessness) and the υἱὸς τῆς ἀπωλείας (son of perdition) who herald the coming of the Lord. This "lawless one" will set himself up in the place of God, but will finally be slain by the Lord Jesus "with the breath of his mouth." He will work wonders κατ᾽ ἐνέργειαν τοῦ σατανᾶ (according to the working of Satan). Above all, he will reveal himself by his *lying and deceitfulness.* Daniel 11:36ff. is regarded as a prototype.

tard seed which will become a great tree, and the heavenly city.[3] As Christ is in us, so also is his heavenly kingdom.[4]

70   These few, familiar references should be sufficient to make the psychological position of the Christ symbol quite clear. *Christ exemplifies the archetype of the self.*[5] He represents a totality of a divine or heavenly kind, a glorified man, a son of God *sine macula peccati*, unspotted by sin. As *Adam secundus* he corresponds to the first Adam before the Fall, when the latter was still a pure image of God, of which Tertullian (d. 222) says: "And this therefore is to be considered as the image of God in man, that the human spirit has the same motions and senses as God has, though not in the same way as God has them."[6] Origen (185–254) is very much more explicit: The *imago Dei* imprinted on the soul, not on the body,[7] is an image of an image, "for my soul is not directly the image of God, but is made after the likeness of the former image."[8] Christ, on the other hand, is the true image of God,[9] after whose like-

---

[3] For "city" cf. *Psychology and Alchemy*, pp. 104ff.

[4] Ἡ βασιλεία τοῦ θεοῦ ἐντὸς ὑμῶν ἔστιν (The kingdom of God is within you [or "among you"]). "The kingdom of God cometh not with observation: neither shall they say, Lo here! or, lo there!" for it is within and everywhere. (Luke 17:20f.) "It is not of this [external] world." (John 18:36.) The likeness of the kingdom of God to man is explicitly stated in the parable of the sower (Matthew 13:24. Cf. also Matthew 13:45, 18:23, 22:2). The papyrus fragments from Oxyrhynchus say: . . . ἡ βασ[ιλεία τῶν οὐρανῶν] ἐντὸς ὑμῶν [ἐ]στι [καὶ ὅστις ἂν ἑαυτὸν] γνῶ ταύτην εὑρή[σει] ἑαυτοὺς γνώσεσθε κτλ. (The kingdom of heaven is within you, and whosoever knoweth himself shall find it. Know yourselves.) Cf. James, *The Apocryphal New Testament*, p. 26, and Grenfell and Hunt, *New Sayings of Jesus*, p. 15.

[5] Cf. my observations on Christ as archetype in "A Psychological Approach to the Dogma of the Trinity," pars. 226ff.

[6] "Et haec ergo imago censenda est Dei in homine, quod eosdem motus et sensus habeat humanus animus, quos et Deus, licet non tales quales Deus" (*Adv. Marcion.*, II, xvi; in Migne, *P.L.*, vol. 2, col. 304).

[7] *Contra Celsum*, VIII, 49 (Migne, *P.G.*, vol. 11, col. 1590): "In anima, non in corpore impressus sit imaginis conditoris character" (The character of the image of the Creator is imprinted on the soul, not on the body). (Cf. trans. by H. Chadwick, p. 488.)

[8] *In Lucam homilia*, VIII (Migne, *P.G.*, vol. 13, col. 1820): "Si considerem Dominum Salvatorem imaginem esse invisibilis Dei, et videam animam meam factam ad imaginem conditoris, ut imago esset imaginis: neque enim anima mea specialiter imago est Dei, sed ad similitudinem imaginis prioris effecta est" (If I consider that the Lord and Saviour is the image of the invisible God, I see that my soul is made after the image of the Creator, so as to be an image of an image; for my soul is not directly the image of God, but is made after the likeness of the former image).

[9] *De principiis*, I, ii, 8 (Migne, *P.G.*, vol. 11, col. 156): "Salvator figura est substantiae vel subsistentiae Dei" (The Saviour is the figure of the substance or subsistence of God). *In Genesim homilia*, I, 13 (Migne, *P.G.*, vol. 12. col. 156): "Quae est ergo alia imago Dei ad cuius imaginis similitudinem factus est homo, nisi Salvator noster, qui est primogenitus

ness our inner man is made, invisible, incorporeal, incorrupt, and immortal.[10] The God-image in us reveals itself through "prudentia, iustitia, moderatio, virtus, sapientia et disciplina."[11]

71   St. Augustine (354–430) distinguishes between the God-image which is Christ and the image which is implanted in man as a means or possibility of becoming like God.[12] The God-image is not in the corporeal man, but in the *anima rationalis*, the possession of which distinguishes man from animals. "The God-image is within, not in the body. . . . Where the understanding is, where the mind is, where the power of investigating truth is, there God has his image."[13] Therefore we should remind ourselves, says Augustine, that we are fashioned after the image of God nowhere save in the understanding: ". . . but where man knows himself to be made after the image of God, there he knows there is something more in him than is given to the beasts."[14] From this it is clear that the God-image is, so to speak, identical with the *anima rationalis*. The latter is the higher spiritual man, the *homo coelestis* of St Paul.[15] Like Adam before the Fall, Christ is an embodiment of the God-image,[16] whose totality is specially emphasized by St. Augustine. "The Word," he

---

omnis creaturae?" (What else therefore is the image of God after the likeness of which image man was made, but our Saviour, who is the first born of every creature?) *Selecta in Genesim*, IX, 6 (Migne, *P.G.*, vol. 12, col. 107): "Imago autem Del invisibilis salvator" (But the image of the invisible God is the saviour).

[10] *In Gen. hom.*, I, 13 (Migne, *P.G.*, vol. 12, col. 155): "Is autem qui ad imaginem Dei factus est et ad similitudinem, interior homo noster est, invisibilis et incorporalis, et incorruptus atque immortalis" (But that which is made after the image and similitude of God is our inner man, invisible, incorporeal, incorrupt, and immortal).

[11] *De princip.*, IV, 37 (Migne, *P.G.*, vol. 11, col. 412).

[12] *Retractationes*, I, xxvi (Migne, *P.L.*, vol. 32, col. 626): "(Unigenitus) . . . tantummodo imago est, non ad imaginem" (The Only-Begotten . . . alone is the image, not after the image).

[13] *Enarrationes in Psalmos*, XLVIII, Sermo II (Migne, *P.L.*, vol. 36, col. 564): "Imago Dei intus est, non est in corpore . . . ubi est intellectus, ubi est mens, ubi ratio investigandae veritatis etc. ibi habet Deus imaginem suam." Also ibid., Psalm XLII, 6 (Migne, *P.L.*, vol. 36, col. 480): "Ergo intelligimus habere nos aliquid ubi imago Dei est, mentem scilicet atque rationem" (Therefore we understand that we have something in which the image of God is, namely mind and reason). Sermo XC, 10 (Migne, *P.L.*, vol. 38, col. 566): "Veritas quaeritur in Dei imagine" (Truth is sought in the image of God), but against this the *Liber de vera religione* says: "in interiore homine habitat veritas" (truth dwells in the inner man). From this it is clear that the *imago Dei* coincides with the *interior homo*.

[14] *Enarr. in Ps.*, LIV, 3 (Migne, *P.L.*, vol. 36, col. 629): ". . . ubi autem homo ad imaginem Dei factum se novit, ibi aliquid in se agnoscit amplius esse quam datum est pecoribus."

[15] I Cor. 15:47.

[16] *In Joannis Evangelium*, Tract. LXXVIII, 3 (Migne, *P.L.*, vol. 35, col. 1836): "Christus est Deus, anima rationalis et caro" (Christ is God, a rational soul and a body).

says, "took on complete manhood, as it were in its fulness: the soul and body of a man. And if you would have me put it more exactly—since even a beast of the field has a 'soul' and a body—when I say a human soul and human flesh, I mean he took upon him a complete human soul."[17]

72 The God-image in man was not destroyed by the Fall but was only damaged and corrupted ("deformed"), and can be restored through God's grace. The scope of the integration is suggested by the *descensus ad inferos*, the descent of Christ's soul to hell, its work of redemption embracing even the dead. The psychological equivalent of this is the integration of the collective unconscious which forms an essential part of the individuation process. St. Augustine says: "Therefore our end must be our perfection, but our perfection is Christ,"[18] since he is the perfect God-image. For this reason he is also called "King." His bride (*sponsa*) is the human soul, which "in an inwardly hidden spiritual mystery is joined to the Word, that two may be in one flesh," to correspond with the mystic marriage of Christ and the Church.[19] Concurrently with the continuance of this *hieros gamos* in the dogma and rites of the Church, the symbolism developed in the course of the Middle Ages into the alchemical conjunction of opposites, or "chymical wedding," thus giving rise on the one hand to the concept of the *lapis philosophorum*, signifying totality, and on the other hand to the concept of chemical combination.

73 The God-image in man that was damaged by the first sin can be "reformed"[20] with the help of God, in accordance with Romans 12:2:

---

[17] Sermo CCXXXVII, 4 (Migne, *P.L.*, vol. 38, col. 1124): "(Verbum) suscepit totum quasi plenum hominem, animam et corpus hominis. Et si aliquid scrupulosius vis audire; quia animam et carnem habet et pecus, cum dico animam humanam et carnem humanam, totam animam humanam accepit."

[18] *Enarr. in Ps.*, LIV, 1 (Migne, *P.L.*, vol. 36, col. 628).

[19] *Contra Faustum*, XXII, 38 (Migne, *P.L.*, vol. 42, col. 424): "Est enim et sancta Ecclesia Domino Jesu Christo in occulto uxor. Occulte quippe atque intus in abscondito secreto spirituali anima humana inhaeret Verbo Dei, ut sint duo in carne una." Cf. St. Augustine's *Reply to Faustus the Manichaean* (trans. by Richard Stothert, p. 433): "The holy Church, too, is in secret the spouse of the Lord Jesus Christ. For it is secretly, and in the hidden depths of the spirit, that the soul of man is joined to the word of God, so that they are two in one flesh." St. Augustine is referring here to Eph. 5:31f.: "For this cause shall a man leave his father and mother, and shall be joined unto his wife, and they two shall be one flesh. This is a great mystery: but I speak concerning Christ and the Church."

[20] Augustine, *De Trinitate*, XIV, 22 (Migne, *P.L.*, vol. 42, col. 1053): "Reformamini in novitate mentis vostrae, ut incipiat illa imago ab illo reformari, a quo formata est" (Be reformed in the newness of your mind; the beginning of the image's reforming must come from him who first formed it) (trans. by John Burnaby, p. 120).

"And be not conformed to this world, but be transformed by the renewal of your mind, that you may prove what is . . . the will of God"
(RSV). The totality images which the unconscious produces in the
course of an individuation process are similar "reformations" of an *a
priori* archetype (the mandala).[21] As I have already emphasized, the
spontaneous symbols of the self, or of wholeness, cannot in practice be
distinguished from a God-image. Despite the word μεταμορφοῦσθε
('be transformed') in the Greek text of the above quotation, the "renewal" (ἀνακαίνωσις, *reformatio*) of the mind is not meant as an actual
alteration of consciousness, but rather as the restoration of an original
condition, an apocatastasis. This is in exact agreement with the empirical findings of psychology, that there is an ever-present archetype of
wholeness[22] which may easily disappear from the purview of consciousness or may never be perceived at all until a consciousness illuminated
by conversion recognizes it in the figure of Christ. As a result of this
"anamnesis" the original state of oneness with the God-image is restored. It brings about an integration, a bridging of the split in the
personality caused by the instincts striving apart in different and mutually contradictory directions. The only time the split does not occur is
when a person is still as legitimately unconscious of his instinctual life
as an animal. But it proves harmful and impossible to endure when an
artificial unconsciousness—a repression—no longer reflects the life of
the instincts.

74   There can be no doubt that the original Christian conception of the
imago Dei embodied in Christ meant an all-embracing totality that even
includes the animal side of man. Nevertheless the Christ-symbol lacks
wholeness in the modern psychological sense, since it does not include
the dark side of things but specifically excludes it in the form of a
Luciferian opponent. Although the exclusion of the power of evil was
something the Christian consciousness was well aware of, all it lost in
effect was an insubstantial shadow, for, through the doctrine of the
privatio boni first propounded by Origen, evil was characterized as a
mere diminution of good and thus deprived of substance. According to
the teachings of the Church, evil is simply "the accidental lack of perfection." This assumption resulted in the proposition "omne bonum a
Deo, omne malum ab homine." Another logical consequence was the
subsequent elimination of the devil in certain Protestant sects.

75   Thanks to the doctrine of the *privatio boni*, wholeness seemed guar-
anteed in the figure of Christ. One must, however, take evil rather

---

[21] Cf. "Concerning Mandala Symbolism," in Part I of vol. 9.
[22] *Psychology and Alchemy*, pars. 323ff.

more substantially when one meets it on the plane of empirical psychology. There it is simply the opposite of good. In the ancient world the Gnostics, whose arguments were very much influenced by psychic experience, tackled the problem of evil on a broader basis than the Church Fathers. For instance, one of the things they taught was that Christ "cast off his shadow from himself."[23] If we give this view the weight it deserves, we can easily recognize the cut-off counterpart in the figure of Antichrist. The Antichrist develops in legend as a perverse imitator of Christ's life. He is a true ἀντίμιμὸν πνεῦμα, an imitating spirit of evil who follows in Christ's footsteps like a shadow following the body. This complementing of the bright but one-sided figure of the Redeemer—we even find traces of it in the New Testament—must be of especial significance. And indeed considerable attention was paid to it quite early.

76   If we see the traditional figure of Christ as a parallel to the psychic manifestation of the self, then the Antichrist would correspond to the shadow of the self, namely the dark half of the human totality, which ought not to be judged too optimistically. So far as we can judge from experience, light and shadow are so evenly distributed in man's nature that his psychic totality appears, to say the least of it, in a somewhat murky light. The psychological concept of the self, in part derived from our knowledge of the whole man, but for the rest depicting itself spontaneously in the products of the unconscious as an archetypal quaternity bound together by inner antinomies, cannot omit the shadow that belongs to the light figure, for without it this figure lacks body and humanity. In the empirical self, light and shadow form a paradoxical unity. In the Christian concept, on the other hand, the archetype is hopelessly split into two irreconcilable halves, leading ultimately to a metaphysical dualism—the final separation of the kingdom of heaven from the fiery world of the damned.

---

[23] Irenaeus (*Adversus haereses*, II, 5, 1) records the Gnostic teaching that when Christ, as the demiurgic Logos, created his mother's being, he "cast her out of the Pleroma—that is, he cut her off from knowledge." For creation took place outside the pleroma, in the shadow and the void. According to Valentinus (*Adv. haer.*, I, 11, 1), Christ did not spring from the Aeons of the pleroma, but from the mother who was outside it. She bore him, he says, "not without a kind of shadow." But he, "being masculine" cast off the shadow from himself and returned to the Pleroma (καὶ τοῦτον [Χριστὸν] μὲν ἅτε ἄρρενα ὑπάρχοντα ἀποκόψαντα ἀφ᾽ ἑαυτοῦ τὴν σκιάν, ἀναδραμεῖν εἰς τὸ Πλήρωμα κτλ.), while his mother, "being left behind in the shadow, and deprived of spiritual substance," there gave birth to the real "Demiurge and Pantokrator of the lower world." But the shadow which lies over the world is, as we know from the Gospels, the *princeps huius mundi*, the devil. Cf. *The Writings of Irenaeus*, I, pp. 45f.

77   For anyone who has a positive attitude towards Christianity the problem of the Antichrist is a hard nut to crack. It is nothing less than the
counterstroke of the devil, provoked by God's Incarnation; for the devil
attains his true stature as the adversary of Christ, and hence of God,
only after the rise of Christianity, while as late as the Book of Job he
was still one of God's sons and on familiar terms with Yahweh.[24] Psychologically the case is clear, since the dogmatic figure of Christ is so sublime and spotless that everything else turns dark beside it. It is, in fact,
so one-sidedly perfect that it demands a psychic complement to restore
the balance. This inevitable opposition led very early to the doctrine of
the two sons of God, of whom the elder was called Satanaël.[25] The
coming of the Antichrist is not just a prophetic prediction—it is an
inexorable psychological law whose existence, though unknown to the
author of the Johannine Epistles, brought him a sure knowledge of the
impending enantiodromia. Consequently he wrote as if he were conscious of the inner necessity for this transformation, though we may be
sure that the idea seemed to him like a divine revelation. In reality
every intensified differentiation of the Christ-image brings about a corresponding accentuation of its unconscious complement, thereby increasing the tension between above and below.

78   In making these statements we are keeping entirely within the
sphere of Christian psychology and symbolism. A factor that no one
has reckoned with, however, is the fatality inherent in the Christian
disposition itself, which leads inevitably to a reversal of its spirit—not
through the obscure workings of chance but in accordance with psychological law. The ideal of spirituality striving for the heights was
doomed to clash with the materialistic earth-bound passion to conquer
matter and master the world. This change became visible at the time of
the "Renaissance." The word means "rebirth," and it referred to the
renewal of the antique spirit. We know today that this spirit was chiefly
a mask; it was not the spirit of antiquity that was reborn, but the spirit
of medieval Christianity that underwent strange pagan transformations,
exchanging the heavenly goal for an earthly one, and the vertical of
the Gothic style for a horizontal perspective (voyages of discovery, exploration of the world and of nature). The subsequent developments
that led to the Enlightenment and the French Revolution have produced a worldwide situation today which can only be called "antichristian" in a sense that confirms the early Christian anticipation of the

[24] Cf. R. Schärf, "Die Gestalt des Satans im Alten Testament."
[25] "The Spirit Mercurius," par. 271.

"end of time." It is as if, with the coming of Christ, opposites that were latent till then had become manifest, or as if a pendulum had swung violently to one side and were now carrying out the complementary movement in the opposite direction. No tree, it is said, can grow to heaven unless its roots reach down to hell. The double meaning of this movement lies in the nature of the pendulum. Christ is without spot, but right at the beginning of his career there occurs the encounter with Satan, the Adversary, who represents the counterpole of that tremendous tension in the world psyche which Christ's advent signified. He is the "mysterium iniquitatis" that accompanies the "sol iustitiae" as inseparably as the shadow belongs to the light, in exactly the same way, so the Ebionites[26] and Euchites[27] thought, that one brother cleaves to the other. Both strive for a kingdom: one for the kingdom of heaven, the other for the "principatus huius mundi." We hear of a reign of a "thousand years" and of a "coming of the Antichrist," just as if a partition of worlds and epochs had taken place between two royal brothers. The meeting with Satan was therefore more than mere chance; it was a link in the chain.

79   Just as we have to remember the gods of antiquity in order to appreciate the psychological value of the anima/animus archetype, so Christ is our nearest analogy of the self and its meaning. It is naturally not a question of a collective value artificially manufactured or arbitrarily awarded, but of one that is effective and present *per se*, and that makes its effectiveness felt whether the subject is conscious of it or not. Yet, although the attributes of Christ (consubstantiality with the Father, co-eternity, filiation, parthenogenesis, crucifixion, Lamb sacrificed between opposites, One divided into Many, etc.) undoubtedly mark him out as an embodiment of the self, looked at from the psychological angle he corresponds to only one half of the archetype. The other half appears in the Antichrist. The latter is just as much a manifestation of the self, except that he consists of its dark aspect. Both are Christian symbols, and they have the same meaning as the image of the Saviour crucified between two thieves. This great symbol tells us that the progressive development and differentiation of consciousness leads to an ever more menacing awareness of the conflict and involves nothing less than a crucifixion of the ego, its agonizing suspension between irrecon-

---

[26] Jewish Christians who formed a Gnostic-syncretistic party.

[27] A Gnostic sect mentioned in Epiphanius, *Panarium adversus octoginta haereses*, LXXX, 1–3, and in Michael Psellus, *De daemonibus* (in Marsilius Ficinus, *Auctores Platonici* [*Iamblichus de mysteriis Aegyptiorum*], Venice, 1497).

cilable opposites.[28] Naturally there can be no question of a total extinction of the ego, for then the focus of consciousness would be destroyed, and the result would be complete unconsciousness. The relative abolition of the ego affects only those supreme and ultimate
decisions which confront us in situations where there are insoluble
conflicts of duty. This means, in other words, that in such cases the ego
is a suffering bystander who decides nothing but must submit to a decision and surrender unconditionally. The "genius" of man, the higher
and more spacious part of him whose extent no one knows, has the
final word. It is therefore well to examine carefully the psychological
aspects of the individuation process in the light of Christian tradition,
which can describe it for us with an exactness and impressiveness far
surpassing our feeble attempts, even though the Christian image of the
self—Christ—lacks the shadow that properly belongs to it.

80   The reason for this, as already indicated, is the doctrine of the Summum Bonum. Irenaeus says very rightly, in refuting the Gnostics, that

---

[28] "Oportuit autem ut alter illorum extremorum isque optimus appellaretur Dei filius
propter suam excellentiam; alter vero ipsi *ex diametro oppositus*, mali daemonis, Satanae
diabolique filius diceretur" (But it is fitting that one of these two extremes, and that the
best, should be called the Son of God because of his excellence, and the other, *diametrically opposed* to him, the son of the evil demon, of Satan and the devil) (Origen,
Contra Celsum, VI, 45; in Migne, *P.G.*, vol. 11, col. 1367; cf. trans. by Chadwick, p. 362).
The opposites even condition one another: "Ubi quid malum est . . . ibi necessario
bonum esse malo contrarium. . . . Alterum ex altero sequitur: proinde aut utrumque
tollendum est negandumque bona et mala esse; aut admisso altero maximeque malo,
bonum quoque admissum oportet." (Where there is evil . . . there must needs be good
contrary to the evil. . . . The one follows from the other; hence we must either do away
with both, and deny that good and evil exist, or if we admit the one, and particularly evil,
we must also admit the good.) (*Contra Celsum*, II, 51; in Migne, *P.G.*, vol. 11, col. 878; cf.
trans. by Chadwick, p. 106.) In contrast to this clear, logical statement Origen cannot
help asserting elsewhere that the "Powers, Thrones, and Principalities" down to the evil
spirits and impure demons "do not have it—the contrary virtue—substantially" ("non
substantialiter id habeant scl. virtus adversaria"), and that they were not created evil but
chose the condition of wickedness ("malitiae gradus") of their own free will. (*De principiis*, I, VIII, 4; in Migne, *P.G.*, vol. 11, col. 179.) Origen is already committed, at least by
implication, to the definition of God as the Summum Bonum, and hence betrays the
inclination to deprive evil of substance. He comes very close to the Augustinian conception of the *privatio boni* when he says: "Certum namque est malum esse bono carere" (For
it is certain that to be evil means to be deprived of good). But this sentence is immediately preceded by the following: "Recedere autem a bono, non aliud est quam effici in
malo" (To turn aside from good is nothing other than to be perfected in evil) (*De principiis*, II, IX, 2; in Migne, *P.G.*, vol. 11, cols. 226–27). This shows clearly that an increase in
the one means a diminution of the other, so that good and evil represent equivalent
halves of an opposition.

exception must be taken to the "light of their Father," because it "could not illuminate and fill even those things which were within it,"[29] namely the shadow and the void. It seemed to him scandalous and reprehensible to suppose that within the pleroma of light there could be a "dark and formless void." For the Christian neither God nor Christ could be a paradox; they had to have a single meaning, and this holds true to the present day. No one knew, and apparently (with a few commendable exceptions) no one knows even now, that the hybris of the speculative intellect had already emboldened the ancients to propound a philosophical definition of God that more or less obliged him to be the Summum Bonum. A Protestant theologian has even had the temerity to assert that "God *can* only be good." Yahweh could certainly have taught him a thing or two in this respect, if he himself is unable to see his intellectual trespass against God's freedom and omnipotence. This forcible usurpation of the Summum Bonum naturally has its reasons, the origins of which lie far back in the past (though I cannot enter into this here). Nevertheless, it is the effective source of the concept of the *privatio boni*, which nullifies the reality of evil and can be found as early as Basil the Great (330–79) and Dionysius the Areopagite (2nd half of the 4th century), and is fully developed in Augustine.

81   The earliest authority of all for the later axiom "Omne bonum a Deo, omne malum ab homine" is Tatian (2nd century), who says: "Nothing evil was created by God; we ourselves have produced all wickedness."[30] This view is also adopted by Theophilus of Antioch (2nd century) in his treatise *Ad Autolycum*.[31]

82   Basil says:

You must not look upon God as the author of the existence of evil, nor consider that evil has any subsistence in itself [ἰδίαν ὑπόστασιν τοῦ κακοῦ εἶναι]. For evil does not subsist as a living being does, nor can we set before our eyes any substantial essence [οὐσίαν ἐνυπόστατον] thereof. For evil is the privation [στέρησις] of good. . . . And thus evil does not inhere in its own substance [ἐν ἰδίᾳ ὑπάρξει], but arises from the mutilation [πηρώμασιν] of the soul.[32] Neither is it uncreated, as the wicked say who set up evil for the equal of good . . . nor is it created. For if all things are of God, how can evil arise from good?[33]

---

[29] *Adv. haer.*, II, 4, 3.
[30] *Oratio ad Graecos* (Migne, *P.G.*, vol. 6, col. 829).
[31] Migne, *P.G.*, vol. 6, col. 1080.
[32] Basil thought that the darkness of the world came from the shadow cast by the body of heaven. *Hexaemeron*, II, 5 (Migne, *P.G.*, vol. 29, col. 40).
[33] *Homilia: Quod Deus non est auctor malorum* (Migne, *P.G.*, vol. 31, col. 341).

CHRIST, A SYMBOL OF SELF

83   Another passage sheds light on the logic of this statement. In the
second homily of the *Hexaemeron*, Basil says:

It is equally impious to say that evil has its origin from God, because the contrary cannot proceed from the contrary. Life does not engender death, darkness is not the origin of light, sickness is not the maker of health. . . . Now if
evil is neither uncreated nor created by God, whence comes its nature? That
evil exists no one living in the world will deny. What shall we say, then? That
evil is not a living and animated entity, but a condition [διάθεσις] of the soul
opposed to virtue, proceeding from light-minded [ῥαθύμοις] persons on account of their falling away from good. . . . Each of us should acknowledge that
he is the first author of the wickedness in him.[34]

84   The perfectly natural fact that when you say "high" you immediately
postulate "low" is here twisted into a causal relationship and reduced to
absurdity, since it is sufficiently obvious that darkness produces no light
and light produces no darkness. The idea of good and evil, however, is
the premise for any moral judgment. They are a logically equivalent
pair of opposites and, as such, the *sine qua non* of all acts of cognition.
From the empirical standpoint we cannot say more than this. And from
this standpoint we would have to assert that good and evil, being coex-
istent halves of a moral judgment, do not derive from one another but
are always there together. Evil, like good, belongs to the category of
human values, and we are the authors of moral value judgments, but
only to a limited degree are we authors of the facts submitted to our
moral judgment. These facts are called by one person good and by
another evil. Only in capital cases is there anything like a *consensus
generalis*. If we hold with Basil that man is the author of evil, we are
saying in the same breath that he is also the author of good. But man is
first and foremost the author merely of judgments; in relation to the
facts judged, his responsibility is not so easy to determine. In order to
do this, we would have to give a clear definition of the extent of his
free will. The psychiatrist knows what a desperately difficult task this is.
85   For these reasons the psychologist shrinks from metaphysical assertions but must criticize the admittedly human foundations of the *privatio boni*. When therefore Basil asserts on the one hand that evil has
no substance of its own but arises from a "mutilation of the soul," and
if on the other hand he is convinced that evil really exists, then the
relative reality of evil is grounded on a real "mutilation" of the soul

[34] *De spiritu sancto* (Migne, *P.G.*, vol. 29, col. 37). Cf. *Nine Homilies of the Hexaemeron*, trans.
by Blomfield Jackson, pp. 61f.

which must have an equally real cause. If the soul was originally created good, then it has really been corrupted and by something that is real, even if this is nothing more than carelessness, indifference, and frivolity, which are the meaning of the word ῥαθυμία. When something—I must stress this with all possible emphasis—is traced back to a psychic condition or fact, it is very definitely not reduced to nothing and thereby nullified, but is shifted on to the plane of *psychic reality*, which is very much easier to establish empirically than, say, the reality of the devil in dogma, who according to the authentic sources was not invented by man at all but existed long before he did. If the devil fell away from God of his own free will, this proves firstly that evil was in the world before man, and therefore that man cannot be the sole author of it, and secondly that the devil already had a "mutilated" soul for which we must hold a real cause responsible. The basic flaw in Basil's argument is the *petitio principii* that lands him in insoluble contradictions: it is laid down from the start that the independent existence of evil must be denied even in face of the eternity of the devil as asserted by dogma. The historical reason for this was the threat presented by Manichaean dualism. This is especially clear in the treatise of Titus of Bostra (d. *c.* 370), entitled *Adversus Manichaeos*,[35] where he states in refutation of the Manichaeans that, so far as substance is concerned, there is no such thing as evil.

86   John Chrysostom (*c.* 344–407) uses, instead of στέρησις (*privatio*), the expression ἐκτροπὴ τοῦ καλοῦ (deviation, or turning away, from good). He says: "Evil is nothing other than a turning away from good, and therefore evil is secondary in relation to good."[36]

87   Dionysius the Areopagite gives a detailed explanation of evil in the fourth chapter of *De divinis nominibus*. Evil, he says, cannot come from good, because if it came from good it would not be evil. But since everything that exists comes from good, everything is in some way good, but "evil does not exist at all" (τὸ δὲ κακὸν οὔτε ὄν ἐστιν).

88   Evil in its nature is neither a thing nor does it bring anything forth.

Evil does not exist at all and is neither good nor productive of good [οὐκ ἔστι καθόλου τὸ κακὸν οὔτε ἀγαθὸν οὔτε ἀγαθοποιόν].

All things which are, by the very fact that they are, are good and come from good; but in so far as they are deprived of good, they are neither good nor do they exist.

That which has no existence is not altogether evil, for the absolutely non-

---

[35] Migne, *P.G.*, vol. 18, cols. 1132f.
[36] *Responsiones ad orthodoxas* (Migne, *P.G.*, vol. 6, cols. 1313–14).

existent will be nothing, unless it be thought of as subsisting in the good super-essentially [κατὰ τὸ ὑπερούσιον]. Good, then, as absolutely existing and as absolutely non-existing, will stand in the foremost and highest place [πολλῷ πρότερον ὑπεριδρύμενον], while evil is neither in that which exists nor in that which does not exist [τὸ δὲ κακὸν οὔτε ἐν τοῖς οὖσιν, οὔτε ἐν τοῖς μὴ οὖσιν].[37]

89   These quotations show with what emphasis the reality of evil was de-nied by the Church Fathers. As already mentioned, this hangs together with the Church's attitude to Manichaean dualism, as can plainly be seen in St. Augustine. In his polemic against the Manichaeans and Mar-cionites he makes the following declaration:

For this reason all things are good, since some things are better than others and the goodness of the less good adds to the glory of the better. . . . Those things we call evil, then, are defects in good things, and quite incapable of existing in their own right outside good things. . . . But those very defects tes-tify to the natural goodness of things. For what is evil by reason of a defect must obviously be good of its own nature. For a defect is something contrary to nature, something which damages the nature of a thing—and it can do so only by diminishing that thing's goodness. *Evil therefore is nothing but the privation of good.* And thus it can have no existence anywhere except in some good thing. . . . So there can be things which are good without any evil in them, such as God himself, and the higher celestial beings; but there can be no evil things without good. For if evils cause no damage to anything, they are not evils; if they do damage something, they diminish its goodness; and if they damage it still more, it is because it still has some goodness which they dimin-ish; and if they swallow it up altogether, nothing of its nature is left to be damaged. And so there will be no evil by which it can be damaged, since there is then no nature left whose goodness any damage can diminish.[38]

<hr/>

[37] Migne, *P.G.*, vol. 3, cols. 716–18. Cf. the *Works of Dionysius the Areopagite*, trans. by John Parker, I, pp. 53ff.

[38] "Nunc vero ideo suni omnia bona, quia sunt aliis alia meliora, et bonitas inferiorum addit laudibus meliorum. . . . Ea vero quae dicuntur mala, aut vitia sunt rerum bonarum, quae omnino extra res bonas per se ipsa alicubi esse non possunt. . . . Sed ipsa quoque vitia testimonium perhibent bonitati naturarum. Quod enim malum est per vitium, pro-fecto bonum est per naturam. Vitium quippe contra naturam est, quia naturae nocet; nec noceret, nisi bonum eius minueret. *Non est ergo malum nisi privatio boni.* Ac per hoc nusquam est nisi in re aliqua bona. . . . Ac per hoc bona sine malis esse possunt, sicut ipse Deus, et quaeque superiora coelestia; mala vero sine bonis esse non possunt. Si enim nihil nocent, mala non sunt; si autem nocent, bonum minuunt; et si amplius nocent, habent adhuc bonum quod minuant; et si totum consumunt, nihil naturae remanebit qui noceatur; ac per hoc nec malum erit a quo noceatur, quando, natura defuerit, cuius bonum nocendo minuatur." (*Contra adversarium legis et prophetarum*, I, 4f.; in Migne, *P.L.*,

90   The *Liber Sententiarum ex Augustino* says (CLXXVI): "Evil is not a substance,[39] for as it has not God for its author, it does not exist; and so the
defect of corruption is nothing else than the desire or act of a mis-
directed will."[40] Augustine agrees with this when he says: "The steel is
not evil; but the man who uses the steel for a criminal purpose, he is
evil."[41]

91   These quotations clearly exemplify the standpoint of Dionysius and
Augustine: evil has no substance or existence in itself, since it is merely
a diminution of good, which alone has substance. Evil is a *vitium*, a bad
use of things as a result of erroneous decisions of the will (blindness
due to evil desire, etc.). Thomas Aquinas, the great theoretician of the
Church, says with reference to the above quotation from Dionysius:

> One opposite is known through the other, as darkness is known through
> light. Hence also what evil is must be known from the nature of good. Now we
> have said above that good is everything appetible; and thus, since every nature
> desires its own being and its own perfection, it must necessarily be said that the
> being and perfection of every created thing is essentially good. Hence it cannot
> be that evil signifies a being, or any form or nature. Therefore it must be that
> by the name of evil is signified the absence of good.[42]
>
> Evil is not a being, whereas good is a being.[43]
>
> That every agent works for an end clearly follows from the fact that every
> agent tends to something definite. Now that to which an agent tends definitely

---

vol. 42, cols. 606–7.) Although the *Dialogus Quaestionum LXV* is not an authentic writing
of Augustine's, it reflects his standpoint very clearly. Quaest. XVI: "Cum Deus omnia
bona creaverit, nihilque sit quod non ab illo conditum sit, unde malum? Resp. Malum
natura non est; sed *privatio boni* hoc nomen accepit. Denique bonum potest esse sine
malo, sed malum non potest esse sine bono, nec potest esse malum ubi non fuerit
bonum. . . . Ideoque quando dicimus bonum, naturam laudamus; quando dicimus
malum, non naturam sed vitium, quod est bonae naturae contrarium reprehendimus."
(Question XVI: Since God created all things good and there is nothing which was not
created by him, whence arises evil? Answer: Evil is not a natural thing, it is rather the
name given to the privation of good. Thus there can be good without evil, but there
cannot be evil without good, nor can there be evil where there is no good. . . . Therefore, when we call a thing good, we praise its inherent nature; when we call a thing evil,
we blame not its nature, but some defect in it contrary to its nature, which is good.)
[39] "Iniquity has no substance" (CCXXVIII). "There is a nature in which there is no evil—
in which, indeed, there can be no evil. But it is impossible for a nature to exist in which
there is no good" (CLX).
[40] *Augustini Opera omnia*, Maurist edn., X, Part 2, cols. 2561–2618.
[41] *Sermones supposititii*, Sermo I, 3, Maurist edn., V, col. 2287.
[42] *Summa theologica*, I, q. 48, ad 1 (trans. by the Fathers of the English Dominican Province, II, p. 264).
[43] Ibid., I, q. 48, ad 3 (trans., p. 268).

must needs be befitting to that agent, since the latter would not tend to it save on account of some fittingness thereto. But that which is befitting to a thing is good for it. Therefore every agent works for a good.[44]

92   St. Thomas himself recalls the saying of Aristotle that "the thing is the whiter, the less it is mixed with black,"[45] without mentioning, however, that the reverse proposition: "the thing is the blacker, the less it is mixed with white," not only has the same validity as the first but is also its logical equivalent. He might also have mentioned that not only darkness is known through light, but that, conversely, light is known through darkness.

93   As only that which works is real, so, according to St. Thomas, only good is real in the sense of "existing." His argument, however, introduces a good that is tantamount to "convenient, sufficient, appropriate, suitable." One ought therefore to translate "omne agens agit propter bonum" as: "Every agent works for the sake of what suits it." That's what the devil does too, as we all know. He too has an "appetite" and strives after perfection—not in good but in evil. Even so, one could hardly conclude from this that his striving is "essentially good."

94   Obviously evil can be represented as a diminution of good, but with this kind of logic one could just as well say: The temperature of the Arctic winter, which freezes our noses and ears, is relatively speaking only a little below the heat prevailing at the equator. For the Arctic temperature seldom falls much lower than 230° C. above absolute zero. All things on earth are "warm" in the sense that nowhere is absolute zero even approximately reached. Similarly, all things are more or less "good," and just as cold is nothing but a diminution of warmth, so evil is nothing but a diminution of good. The *privatio boni* argument remains a euphemistic *petitio principii* no matter whether evil is regarded as a lesser good or as an effect of the finiteness and limitedness of created things. The false conclusion necessarily follows from the premise "Deus = Summum Bonum," since it is unthinkable that the perfect good could ever have created evil. It merely created the good and the less good (which last is simply called "worse" by laymen).[46] Just

---

[44] ". . . Quod autem conveniens est alicui est illi bonum. Ergo omne agens agit propter bonum" (*Summa contra Gentiles*, III, ch. 3, trans. by the English Dominican Fathers, vol. III, p. 7).

[45] *Summa theologica*, I, q. 48, ad 2 (trans., II, p. 266, citing Aristotle's *Topics*, iii, 4).

[46] In the Decrees of the 4th Lateran Council we read: "For the devil and the other demons as created by God were naturally good, but became evil of their own motion." Denzinger and Bannwart. *Enchiridion symbolorum*, p. 189.

as we freeze miserably despite a temperature of 230° above absolute zero, so there are people and things that, although created by God, are good only to the minimal and bad to the maximal degree.

95   It is probably from this tendency to deny any reality to evil that we get the axiom "Omne bonum a Deo, omne malum ab homine." This is a contradiction of the truth that he who created the heat is also responsible for the cold ("the goodness of the less good"). We can certainly hand it to Augustine that all natures are good, yet just not good enough to prevent their badness from being equally obvious.

*

96   One could hardly call the things that have happened, and still happen, in the concentration camps of the dictator states an "accidental lack of perfection"—it would sound like mockery.

97   Psychology does not know what good and evil are in themselves; it knows them only as judgments about relationships. "Good" is what seems suitable, acceptable, or valuable from a certain point of view; evil is its opposite. If the things we call good are "really" good, then there must be evil things that are "real" too. It is evident that psychology is concerned with a more or less subjective judgment, i.e., with a psychic antithesis that cannot be avoided in naming value relationships: "good" denotes something that is not bad, and "bad" something that is not good. There are things which from a certain point of view are extremely evil, that is to say dangerous. There are also things in human nature which are very dangerous and which therefore seem proportionately evil to anyone standing in their line of fire. It is pointless to gloss over these evil things, because that only lulls one into a sense of false security. Human nature is capable of an infinite amount of evil, and the evil deeds are as real as the good ones so far as human experience goes and so far as the psyche judges and differentiates between them. Only unconsciousness makes no difference between good and evil. Inside the psychological realm one honestly does not know which of them predominates in the world. We hope, merely, that good does— i.e., what seems suitable to us. No one could possibly say what the general good might be. No amount of insight into the relativity and fallibility of our moral judgment can deliver us from these defects, and those who deem themselves beyond good and evil are usually the worst tormentors of mankind, because they are twisted with the pain and fear of their own sickness.

98   Today as never before it is important that human beings should not overlook the danger of the evil lurking within them. It is unfortunately only too real, which is why psychology must insist on the reality of evil

and must reject any definition that regards it as insignificant or actually non-existent. Psychology is an empirical science and deals with realities. As a psychologist, therefore, I have neither the inclination nor the competence to mix myself up with metaphysics. Only, I have to get polemical when metaphysics encroaches on experience and interprets it in a way that is not justified empirically. My criticism of the *privatio boni* holds only so far as psychological experience goes. From the scientific point of view the *privatio boni*, as must be apparent to everyone, is founded on a *petitio principii*, where what invariably comes out at the end is what you put in at the beginning. Arguments of this kind have no power of conviction. But the fact that such arguments are not only used but are undoubtedly believed is something that cannot be disposed of so easily. It proves that there is a tendency, existing right from the start, to give priority to "good, " and to do so with all the means in our power, whether suitable or unsuitable. So if Christian metaphysics clings to the *privatio boni*, it is giving expression to the tendency always to increase the good and diminish the bad. The *privatio boni* may therefore be a metaphysical truth. I presume to no judgment on this matter. I must only insist that in our field of experience white and black, light and dark, good and bad, are equivalent opposites which always predicate one another.

99   This elementary fact was correctly appreciated in the so-called Clementine Homilies,[47] a collection of Gnostic-Christian writings dating from about A.D. 150. The unknown author understands good and evil as the right and left hand of God, and views the whole of creation in terms of syzygies, or pairs of opposites. In much the same way the follower of Bardesanes, Marinus, sees good as "light" and pertaining to the right hand ($\delta\varepsilon\xi\iota\acute{o}v$), and evil as "dark" and pertaining to the left hand ($\dot{\alpha}\varrho\iota\sigma\tau\varepsilon\varrho\acute{o}v$).[48] The left also corresponds to the feminine. Thus in Irenaeus (*Adv. haer.*, I, 30, 3), Sophia Prounikos is called Sinistra. Clement finds this altogether compatible with the idea of God's unity. Provided that one has an anthropomorphic God-image—and every God-image is anthropomorphic in a more or less subtle way—the logic and naturalness of Clement's view can hardly be contested. At all events this

---

[47] Harnack (*Lehrbuch der Dogmengeschichte*, p. 332) ascribes the Clementine Homilies to the beginning of the 4th cent. and is of the opinion that they contain "no source that could be attributed with any certainty to the 2nd century." He thinks that Islam is far superior to this theology. Yahweh and Allah are unreflected God-images, whereas in the Clementine Homilies there is a psychological and reflective spirit at work. It is not immediately evident why this should bring about a disintegration of the God-concept, as Harnack thinks. Fear of psychology should not be carried too far.

[48] *Der Dialog des Adamantius*, III, 4 (ed. by van de Sande Bakhuyzen, p. 119).

view, which may be some two hundred years older than the quotations given above, proves that the reality of evil does not necessarily lead to Manichaean dualism and so does not endanger the unity of the God-image. As a matter of fact, it guarantees that unity on a plane beyond the crucial difference between the Yahwistic and the Christian points of view. Yahweh is notoriously unjust, and injustice is not good. The God of Christianity, on the other hand, is *only* good. There is no denying that Clement's theology helps us to get over this contradiction in a way that fits the psychological facts.

100   It is therefore worth following up Clement's line of thought a little more closely. "God," he says, "appointed two kingdoms [βασιλείας] and two ages [αἰῶνας], determining that the present world should be given over to evil [πονηρῷ], because it is small and passes quickly away. But he promised to preserve the future world for good, because it is great and eternal." Clement goes on to say that this division into two corresponds to the structure of man: the body comes from the female, who is characterized by emotionality; the spirit comes from the male, who stands for rationality. He calls body and spirit the "two tri-ads."[49]

Man is a compound of two mixtures [φυραμάτων, lit. 'pastes'], the female and the male. Wherefore also two ways have been laid before him—those of obe-dience and of disobedience to law; and two kingdoms have been established—the one called the kingdom of heaven, and the other the kingdom of those who are now rulers upon earth. . . . Of these two, the one does violence to the other. Moreover these two rulers are the swift hands of God.

That is a reference to Deuteronomy 32:39: "I will kill and I will make to live" (DV). He kills with the left hand and saves with the right.

These two principles have not their substance outside of God, for there is no other primal source [ἀρχή]. Nor have they been sent forth from God as ani-mals, for they were of the same mind [ὁμόδοξοι] with him. . . . But from God were sent forth the four first elements—hot and cold, moist and dry. In conse-quence of this, he is the Father of every substance [οὐσίας], but not of the knowledge which arises from the mixing of the elements.[50] For when these were combined from without, choice [προαίρεσις] was begotten in them as a child.[51]

[49] The female or somatic triad consist of ἐπιθυμία (desire), ὀργή (anger), and λύπη (grief); the male, of λογισμός (reflection), γνῶσις (knowledge), and φόβος (fear). Cf. the triad of functions in "The Phenomenology of the Spirit in Fairy-tales," Part I of vol. 9, pars. 425ff.
[50] P. de Lagarde (*Clementina*, p. 190) has here . . . πάσης οὐσίας . . . οὔσης γνώμης. The reading οὐ τῆς seems to me to make more sense.
[51] Ch. III: τῆς μετὰ τὴν κρᾶσιν.

92

That is to say, through the mixing of the four elements inequalities arose which caused uncertainty and so necessitated decisions or acts of choice. The four elements form the fourfold substance of the body (τετραγενὴς τοῦ σώματος οὐσία) and also of evil (τοῦ πονηροῦ). This substance was "carefully discriminated and sent forth from God, but when it was combined from without, according to the will of him who sent it forth, there arose, as a result of the combination, the preference which rejoices in evils [ἡ κακοῖς χαίρουσα προαίρεσις]."[52]

01 The last sentence is to be understood as follows: The fourfold substance is eternal (οὖσα ἀεί) and God's child. But the tendency to evil was added from outside to the mixture willed by God (κατὰ τὴν τοῦ θεοῦ βούλησιν ἔξω τῇ κράσει συμβέβηκεν). Thus evil is not created by God or by any one else, nor was it projected out of him, nor did it arise of itself. Peter, who is engaged in these reflections, is evidently not quite sure how the matter stands.

02 It seems as if, without God's intending it (and possibly without his knowing it) the mixture of the four elements took a wrong turning, though this is rather hard to square with Clement's idea of the opposite hands of God "doing violence to one another." Obviously Peter, the leader of the dialogue, finds it rather difficult to attribute the cause of evil to the Creator in so many words.

03 The author of the Homilies espouses a Petrine Christianity distinctly "High Church" or ritualistic in flavour. This, taken together with his doctrine of the dual aspect of God, brings him into close relationship with the early Jewish-Christian Church, where, according to the testimony of Epiphanius, we find the Ebionite notion that God had two sons, an elder one, Satan, and a younger one, Christ.[53] Michaias, one of the speakers in the dialogue, suggests as much when he remarks that if good and evil were begotten in the same way they must be brothers.[54]

04 In the (Jewish-Christian?) apocalypse, the "Ascension of Isaiah," we find, in the middle section, Isaiah's vision of the seven heavens through which he was rapt.[55] First he saw Sammaël and his hosts, against whom a "great battle" was raging in the firmament. The angel then wafted

---

[52] *The Clementine Homilies and the Apostolical Constitutions*, trans. by Thomas Smith et al., pp. 312ff. (slightly modified).
[53] *Panarium*, ed. by Oehler, I, p. 267.
[54] *Clement. Hom.* XX, ch. VII. Since there is no trace in peudo-Clement of the defensive attitude towards Manichaean dualism which is so characteristic of the later writers, it is possible that the Homilies date back to the beginning of the 3rd cent., if not earlier.
[55] Hennecke, *Neutestamentliche Apokryphen*, pp. 309ff.

him beyond this into the first heaven and led him before a throne. On the right of the throne stood angels who were more beautiful than the angels on the left. Those on the right "all sang praises with *one* voice," but the ones on the left sang *after* them, and their singing was not like the singing of the first. In the second heaven all the angels were more beautiful than in the first heaven, and there was no difference between them, either here or in any of the higher heavens. Evidently Sammaël still has a noticeable influence on the first heaven, since the angels on the left are not so beautiful there. Also, the lower heavens are not so splendid as the upper ones, though each surpasses the other in splendour. The devil, like the Gnostic archons, dwells in the firmament, and he and his angels presumably correspond to astrological gods and influences. The gradation of splendour, going all the way up to the topmost heaven, shows that his sphere interpenetrates with the divine sphere of the Trinity, whose light in turn filters down as far as the lowest heaven. This paints a picture of complementary opposites balancing one another like right and left hands. Significantly enough, this vision, like the Clementine Homilies, belongs to the pre-Manichaean period (second century), when there was as yet no need for Christianity to fight against its Manichaean competitors. It might easily be a description of a genuine yang-yin relationship, a picture that comes closer to the actual truth than the *privatio boni*. Moreover, it does not damage monotheism in any way, since it unites the opposites just as yang and yin are united in Tao (which the Jesuits quite logically translated as "God"). It is as if Manichaean dualism first made the Fathers conscious of the fact that until then, without clearly realizing it, they had always believed firmly in the substantiality of evil. This sudden realization might well have led them to the dangerously anthropomorphic assumption that what man cannot unite, God cannot unite either. The early Christians, thanks to their greater unconsciousness, were able to avoid this mistake.

105   Perhaps we may risk the conjecture that the problem of the Yahwistic God-image, which had been constellated in men's minds ever since the Book of Job, continued to be discussed in Gnostic circles and in syncretistic Judaism generally, all the more eagerly as the Christian answer to this question—namely the unanimous decision in favour of God's goodness[56]—did not satisfy the conservative Jews. In this respect, therefore, it is significant that the doctrine of the two antithetical sons of God originated with the Jewish Christians living in Palestine. Inside

---

[56] Cf. Matt. 19:17 and Mark 10:18.

Christianity itself the doctrine spread to the Bogomils and Cathars; in Judaism it influenced religious speculation and found lasting expression in the two sides of the cabalistic Tree of the Sephiroth, which were named *hesed* (love) and din (justice). A rabbinical scholar, Zwi Werblowsky, has been kind enough to put together for me a number of passages from Hebrew literature which have bearing on this problem.

06   R. Joseph taught: "What is the meaning of the verse, 'And none of you shall go out at the door of his house until the morning?' (Exodus 12:22.)[57] Once permission has been granted to the destroyer, he does not distinguish between the righteous and the wicked. Indeed, he even begins with the righteous."[58] Commenting on Exodus 33:5 ("If for a single moment I should go up among you, I would consume you"), the midrash says: "Yahweh means he could wax wroth with you for a moment—for that is the length of his wrath, as is said in Isaiah 26:20, 'Hide yourselves for a little moment until the wrath is past'—and destroy you." Yahweh gives warning here of his unbridled irascibility. If in this moment of divine wrath a curse is uttered, it will indubitably be effective. That is why Balaam, "who knows the thoughts of the Most High,"[59] when called upon by Balak to curse Israel, was so dangerous an enemy, because he knew the moment of Yahweh's wrath.[60]

07   God's love and mercy are named his right hand, but his justice and his administration of it are named his left hand. Thus we read in I Kings 22:19: "I saw the Lord sitting on his throne, and all the host of heaven standing beside him on his right hand and on his left." The midrash comments: "Is there right and left on high? This means that the intercessors stand on the right and the accusers on the left."[61] The comment on Exodus 15:6 ("Thy right hand, O Lord, glorious in power, thy right hand, O Lord, shatters the enemy") runs: "When the children of Israel perform God's will, they make the left hand his right hand. When they do not do his will, they make even the right hand his left hand."[62] "God's left hand dashes to pieces; his right hand is glorious to save."[63]

08   The dangerous aspect of Yahweh's justice comes out in the following

---

[57] A reference to the slaying of the first-born in Egypt.

[58] *Nezikin* I, Baba Kamma 60 (in *The Babylonian Talmud*, trans. and ed. by Isidore Epstein, p. 348 [hereafter abbr. *BT*]; slightly modified).

[59] Numbers 24:16.

[60] *Zera'im* I, Berakoth 7a (*BT*, p. 31).

[61] *Midrash Tanchuma Shemoth* XVII.

[62] Cf. *Pentateuch with Targum Onkelos . . . and Rashi's Commentary*, trans. by M. Rosenbaum and A. M. Silbermann, II, p. 76.

[63] Midrash on Song of Sol. 2:6.

passage: "Even so said the Holy One, blessed be He: If I create the world on the basis of mercy alone, its sins will be great; but on the basis of justice alone the world cannot exist. Hence I will create it on the basis of justice and mercy, and may it then stand!"[64] The midrash on Genesis 18:23 (Abraham's plea for Sodom) says (Abraham speaking): "If thou desirest the world to endure, there can be no absolute justice, while if thou desirest absolute justice, the world cannot endure. Yet thou wouldst hold the cord by both ends, desiring both the world and absolute justice. Unless thou forgoest a little, the world cannot endure."[65]

109   Yahweh prefers the repentant sinners even to the righteous, and protects them from his justice by covering them with his hand or by hiding them under his throne.[66]

110   With reference to Habakkuk 2:3 ("For still the vision awaits its time. . . . If it seem slow, wait for it"), R. Jonathan says: "Should you say, *We* wait [for his coming] but *He* does not, it stands written (Isaiah 30:18), 'Therefore will the Lord wait, that he may be gracious unto you.' . . . But since we wait and he waits too, what delays his coming? Divine justice delays it."[67] It is in this sense that we have to understand the prayer of R. Jochanan: "May it be thy will, O Lord our God, to look upon our shame and behold our evil plight. Clothe thyself in thy mercies, cover thyself in thy strength, wrap thyself in thy loving-kindness, and gird thyself with thy graciousness, and may thy goodness and gentleness come before thee."[68] God is properly exhorted to remember his good qualities. There is even a tradition that God prays to himself: "May it be My will that My mercy may suppress My anger, and that My compassion may prevail over My other attributes."[69] This tradition is borne out by the following story:

R. Ishmael the son of Elisha said: I once entered the innermost sanctuary to offer incense, and there I saw Akathriel[70] Jah Jahweh Zebaoth[71] seated upon a high and exalted throne. He said to me, Ishmael, my son, bless me! And I

[64] *Bereshith Rabba* XII, 15 (*Midrash Rabbah translated into English*, ed. by H. Freedman and M. Simon, I, p. 99; slightly modified).
[65] Ibid. XXXIX, 6 (p. 315).
[66] *Mo'ed* IV, Pesahim 119 (*BT*, p. 613); *Nezikin* VI, Sanhedrin II, 103 (*BT*, pp. 698ff.).
[67] *Nezikin* VI, Sanhedrin II, 97 (*BT*, p. 659, modified).
[68] *Zera'im* I. Berakoth 16b (*BT*, p. 98; slightly modified).
[69] Ibid. 7a (p. 30).
[70] "Akathriel" is a made-up word composed of *ktr* = *kether* (throne) and *el*, the name of God.
[71] A string of numinous God names, usually translated as "the Lord of Hosts."

96

answered him: May it be Thy will that Thy mercy may suppress Thy anger, and that Thy compassion may prevail over Thy other attributes, so that Thou mayest deal with Thy children according to the attribute of mercy and stop short of the limit of strict justice! And He nodded to me with His head.[72]

11   It is not difficult to see from these quotations what was the effect of Job's contradictory God-image. It became a subject for religious speculation inside Judaism and, through the medium of the Cabala, it evidently had an influence on Jakob Böhme. In his writings we find a similar ambivalence, namely the love and the "wrath-fire" of God, in which Lucifer burns for ever.[73]

12   Since psychology is not metaphysics, no metaphysical dualism can be derived from, or imputed to, its statements concerning the equivalence of opposites.[74] It knows that equivalent opposites are necessary conditions inherent in the act of cognition, and that without them no discrimination would be possible. It is not exactly probable that anything so intrinsically bound up with the act of cognition should be at the same time a property of the object. It is far easier to suppose that it is primarily our consciousness which names and evaluates the differences between things, and perhaps even creates distinctions where no differences are discernible.

13   I have gone into the doctrine of the *privatio boni* at such length because it is in a sense responsible for a too optimistic conception of the evil in human nature and for a too pessimistic view of the human soul. To offset this, early Christianity, with unerring logic, balanced Christ against an Antichrist. For how can you speak of "high" if there is no "low," or "right" if there is no "left," of "good" if there is no "bad," and the one is as real as the other? Only with Christ did a devil enter the world as the real counterpart of God, and in early Jewish-Christian circles Satan, as already mentioned, was regarded as Christ's elder brother.

14   But there is still another reason why I must lay such critical stress on

---

[72] *Zera'im* I, Berakoth 7 (*BT*, p. 30; slightly modified).

[73] *Aurora*, trans. by John Sparrow, p. 423.

[74] My learned friend Victor White, O.P., in his *Dominican Studies* (II, p. 399), thinks he can detect a Manichaean streak in me. I don't go in for metaphysics, but ecclesiastical philosophy undoubtedly does, and for this reason I must ask what are we to make of hell, damnation, and the devil, if these things are eternal? Theoretically they consist of nothing, and how does that square with the dogma of eternal damnation? But if they consist of something, that something can hardly be good. So where is the danger of dualism? In addition to this my critic should know how very much I stress the unity of the self, this central archetype which is a *complexio oppositorum* par excellence, and that my leanings are therefore towards the very reverse of dualism.

the *privatio boni*. As early as Basil we meet with the tendency to attribute evil to the disposition ($\delta\iota\acute{\alpha}\theta\epsilon\sigma\iota\varsigma$) of the soul, and at the same time to give it a "non-existent" character. Since, according to this author, evil originates in human frivolity and therefore owes its existence to mere negligence, it exists, so to speak, only as a by-product of psychological oversight, and this is such a *quantité négligeable* that evil vanishes altogether in smoke. Frivolity as a cause of evil is certainly a factor to be taken seriously, but it is a factor that can be got rid of by a change of attitude. We *can* act differently, if we want to. Psychological causation is something so elusive and seemingly unreal that everything which is reduced to it inevitably takes on the character of futility or of a purely accidental mistake and is thereby minimized to the utmost. It is an open question how much of our modern undervaluation of the psyche stems from this prejudice. This prejudice is all the more serious in that it causes the psyche to be suspected of being the birthplace of all evil. The Church Fathers can hardly have considered what a fatal power they were ascribing to the soul. One must be positively blind not to see the colossal role that evil plays in the world. Indeed, it took the intervention of God himself to deliver humanity from the curse of evil, for without his intervention man would have been lost. If this paramount power of evil is imputed to the soul, the result can only be a negative inflation—i.e., a daemonic claim to power on the part of the unconscious which makes it all the more formidable. This unavoidable consequence is anticipated in the figure of the Antichrist and is reflected in the course of contemporary events, whose nature is in accord with the Christian aeon of the Fishes, now running to its end.

115   In the world of Christian ideas Christ undoubtedly represents the self.[75] As the apotheosis of individuality, the self has the attributes of uniqueness and of occurring once only in time. But since the psychological self is a transcendent concept, expressing the totality of conscious and unconscious contents, it can only be described in anti-

---

[75] It has been objected that Christ cannot have been a valid symbol of the self, or was only an illusory substitute for it. I can agree with this view only if it refers strictly to the present time, when psychological criticism has become possible, but not if it pretends to judge the pre-psychological age. Christ did not merely *symbolize* wholeness, but, as a psychic phenomenon, he *was* wholeness. This is proved by the symbolism as well as by the phenomenology of the past, for which—be it noted—evil was a *privatio boni*. The idea of totality is, at any given time, as total as one is oneself. Who can guarantee that our conception of totality is not equally in need of completion? The mere concept of totality does not by any means posit it.

nomial terms;[76] that is, the above attributes must be supplemented by their opposites if the transcendental situation is to be characterized correctly. We can do this most simply in the form of a quaternion of opposites:

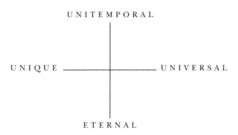

UNITEMPORAL

UNIQUE ——————— UNIVERSAL

ETERNAL

16   This formula expresses not only the psychological self but also the dogmatic figure of Christ. As an historical personage Christ is unitemporal and unique; as God, universal and eternal. Likewise the self: as the essence of individuality it is unitemporal and unique; as an archetypal symbol it is a God-image and therefore universal and eternal.[77] Now if theology describes Christ as simply "good" and "spiritual," something "evil" and "material"—or "chthonic"—is bound to arise on the other side, to represent the Antichrist. The resultant quaternion of opposites is united on the psychological plane by the fact that the self is not deemed exclusively "good" and "spiritual"; consequently its shadow turns out to be much less black. A further result is that the opposites of "good" and "spiritual" need no longer be separated from the whole:

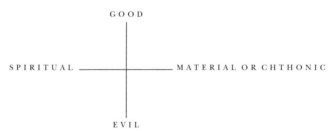

GOOD

SPIRITUAL ——————— MATERIAL OR CHTHONIC

EVIL

17   This *quaternio* characterizes the psychological self. Being a totality, it must by definition include the light and dark aspects, in the same way that the self embraces both masculine and feminine and is therefore

---

[76] Just as the transcendent nature of light can only be expressed through the image of waves and particles.

[77] Cf. *Psychology and Alchemy*, pars. 323ff., and "The Relations between the Ego and the Unconscious," pars. 398ff.

symbolized by the marriage *quaternio*.[78] This last is by no means a new discovery, since according to Hippolytus it was known to the Naassenes.[79] Hence individuation is a "mysterium coniunctionis," the self being experienced as a nuptial union of opposite halves[80] and depicted as a composite whole in mandalas that are drawn spontaneously by patients.

118   It was known, and stated, very early that the man Jesus, the son of Mary, was the *principium individuationis*. Thus Basilides[81] is reported by Hippolytus as saying: "Now Jesus became the first sacrifice in the discrimination of the natures [φυλοκρίνησις], and the Passion came to pass for no other reason than the discrimination of composite things. For in this manner, he says, the sonship that had been left behind in a formless state [ἀμορφία] . . . needed separating into its components [φυλοκρινηθῆναι], in the same way that Jesus was separated."[82] According to the rather complicated teachings of Basilides, the "non-existent" God begot a threefold sonship (υἱότης). The first "son," whose nature was the finest and most subtle, remained up above with the Father. The second son, having a grosser (παχυμερέστερα) nature, descended a bit lower, but received "some such wing as that with which Plato . . . equips the soul in his *Phaedrus*."[83] The third son, as his nature needed purifying (ἀποκαθάρσις), fell deepest into "formlessness." This third "sonship" is obviously the grossest and heaviest because of its impurity. In these three emanations or manifestations of the non-existent God it is not hard to see the trichotomy of spirit, soul, and body (πνευματικόν, ψυχικόν, σαρκικόν). Spirit is the finest and highest; soul, as the *ligamentum spiritus et corporis*, is grosser than spirit, but has "the wings of an eagle,"[84] so that it may lift its heaviness up to the higher regions. Both are of a "subtle" nature and dwell, like the ether and the eagle, in or near the region of light, whereas the body, being heavy, dark, and impure, is deprived of the light but nevertheless contains the divine seed of the third sonship, though still *unconscious and formless*. This seed is as it were awakened by Jesus, purified and made capable of ascension (ἀναδρομή),[85] by virtue of the fact that the opposites were separated in

---

[78] Cf. "The Psychology of the Transference," pars. 425ff.
[79] *Elenchos*, V, 8, 2 (trans. by F. Legge, I, p. 131). Cf. infra, pars. 358ff.
[80] *Psychology and Alchemy*, par. 334, and "The Psychology of the Transference," pars. 457ff.
[81] Basilides lived in the 2nd cent.
[82] *Elenchos*, VII, 27, 12 (cf. Legge trans., II, p. 79).
[83] Ibid., VII, 22, 10 (cf. II, pp. 69–70).
[84] Ibid., VII, 22, 15 (II, p. 70). The eagle has the same significance in alchemy.
[85] This word also occurs in the well-known passage about the *krater* in Zosimos. (Berthelot, *Alch. grecs*, III, li, 8: ἀνάδραμε ἐπὶ τὸ γένος τὸ σόν.

Jesus through the Passion (i.e., through his division into four).[86] Jesus is thus the prototype for the awakening of the third sonship slumbering in the darkness of humanity. He is the "spiritual inner man."[87] He is also a complete trichotomy in himself, for Jesus the Son of Mary represents the incarnate man, but his immediate predecessor is the second Christ, the son of the highest archon of the hebdomad, and his first prefiguration is Christ the son of the highest archon of the ogdoad, the demiurge Yahweh.[88] This trichotomy of Anthropos figures corresponds exactly to the three sonships of the non-existing God and to the division of human nature into three parts. We have therefore three trichotomies:

I	II	III
First sonship	*Christ of the Ogdoad*	*Spirit*
Second sonship	*Christ of the Hebdomad*	*Soul*
Third sonship	*Jesus the Son of Mary*	*Body*

19   It is in the sphere of the dark, heavy body that we must look for the ἀμορφία, the "formlessness" wherein the third sonship lies hidden. As suggested above, this formlessness seems to be practically the equivalent of "unconsciousness." G. Quispel has drawn attention to the con-

---

[86] I must say a word here about the *horos* doctrine of the Valentinians in Irenaeus (*Adv. haer.*, I, 2, 2ff.) *Horos* (boundary) is a "power" or numen identical with Christ, or at least proceeding from him. It has the following synonyms: ὁροθέτης (boundary-fixer), μεταγωγεύς (he who leads across), καρπιστής (emancipator), λυτρώτης (redeemer), σταυρός (cross). In this capacity he is the regulator and mainstay of the universe, like Jesus. When Sophia was "formless and shapeless as an embryo, Christ took pity on her, stretched her out through his Cross and gave her form through his power," so that at least she acquired substance (*Adv. haer.*, I, 4). He also left behind for her an "intimation of immortality." The identity of the Cross with Horos, or with Christ, is clear from the text, an image that we find also in Paulinus of Nola:

> ". . . regnare deum super omnia Christum,
> qui cruce dispensa per quattuor extima ligni
> quattuor adtingit dimensum partibus orbem,
> ut trahat ad uitam populos ex omnibus aris."

(Christ reigns over all things as God, who, on the outstretched cross, reaches out through the four extremities of the wood to the four parts of the wide world, that he may draw unto life the peoples from all lands.) (*Carmina*, ed. by Wilhelm Hartel, Carm. XIX, 639ff., p. 140.) For the Cross as God's "lightning" cf. "A Study in the Process of Individuation," pars. 535f.

[87] *Elenchos*, VII, 27, 5 (Legge trans., II, p. 78).

[88] Ibid., VII, 26, 5 (II, p. 75).

cepts of *ἀγνωσία* in Epiphanius[89] and *ἀνόητον* in Hippolytus,[90] which are best translated by "unconscious." Ἀμορφία, *ἀγνωσία*, and *ἀνόητον* all refer to the initial state of things, to the potentiality of unconscious contents, aptly formulated by Basilides as *οὐκ ὂν σπέρμα τοῦ κόσμου πολύμορφον ὁμοῦ καὶ πολυούσιον* (the non-existent, many-formed, and all-empowering seed of the world).[91]

120   This picture of the third sonship has certain analogies with the medieval *filius philosophorum* and the *filius macrocosmi*, who also symbolize the world-soul slumbering in matter.[92] Even with Basilides the body acquires a special and unexpected significance, since in it and its materiality is lodged a third of the revealed Godhead. This means nothing less than that matter is predicated as having considerable numinosity in itself, and I see this as an anticipation of the "mystic" significance which matter subsequently assumed in alchemy and— later on—in natural science. From a psychological point of view it is particularly important that Jesus corresponds to the third sonship and is the prototype of the "awakener" because the opposites were separated in him through the Passion and so became conscious, whereas in the third sonship itself they remain unconscious so long as the latter is formless and undifferentiated. This amounts to saying that in unconscious humanity there is a latent seed that corresponds to the prototype Jesus. Just as the man Jesus became conscious only through the light that emanated from the higher Christ and separated the natures in him, so the seed in unconscious humanity is awakened by the light emanating from Jesus, and is thereby impelled to a similar discrimination of opposites. This view is entirely in accord with the psychological fact that the archetypal image of the self has been

[89] *Panarium*, XXXI, 5 (Oehler edn., I, p. 314).
[90] *Elenchos*, VII, 22, 16 (Legge trans., II, p. 71 Cf. infra, pars. 298ff.
[91] Ibid., 20, 5 (cf. II, p. 66). Quispel, "Note sur 'Basilide'."
[92] With reference to the psychological nature of Gnostic sayings, see Quispel's "Philo und die altchristliche Häresie," p. 432, where he quotes Irenaeus (*Adv. haer.*, II, 4, 2): "Id quod extra et quod intus dicere eos secundum agnitionem et ignorantiam, sed non secundum localem sententiam" (In speaking of what is outward and what is inward, they refer, not to place, but to what is known and what is not known). (Cf. Legge, I, p. 127.) The sentence that follows immediately after this—"But in the Pleroma, or in that which is contained by the Father, everything that the demiurge or the angels have created is contained by the unspeakable greatness, as the centre in a circle"—is therefore to be taken as a description of unconscious contents. Quispel's view of projection calls for the critical remark that projection does not do away with the *reality* of a psychic content. Nor can a fact be called "unreal" merely because it cannot be described as other than "psychic." Psyche is reality par excellence.

shown to occur in dreams even when no such conceptions exist in the conscious mind of the dreamer.[93]

*

121   I would not like to end this chapter without a few final remarks that are forced on me by the importance of the material we have been discussing. The standpoint of a psychology whose subject is the phenomenology of the psyche is evidently something that is not easy to grasp and is very often misunderstood. If, therefore, at the risk of repeating myself, I come back to fundamentals, I do so only in order to forestall certain wrong impressions which might be occasioned by what I have said, and to spare my reader unnecessary difficulties.

122   The parallel I have drawn here between Christ and the self is not to be taken as anything more than a psychological one, just as the parallel with the fish is mythological. There is no question of any intrusion into the sphere of metaphysics, i.e., of faith. The images of God and Christ which man's religious fantasy projects cannot avoid being anthropomorphic and are admitted to be so; hence they are capable of psychological elucidation like any other symbols. Just as the ancients believed that they had said something important about Christ with their fish symbol, so it seemed to the alchemists that their parallel with the stone served to illuminate and deepen the meaning of the Christ-image. In the course of time, the fish symbolism disappeared completely, and so likewise did the *lapis philosophorum.* Concerning this latter symbol, however, there are plenty of statements to be found which show it in a special light—views and ideas which attach such importance to the stone that one begins to wonder whether, in the end, it was Christ who was taken as a symbol of the stone rather than the other way round. This marks a development which—with the help of certain ideas in the epistles of John and Paul—includes Christ in the realm of immediate inner experience and makes him appear as the figure of the total man. It also links up directly with the psychological evidence for the existence of an archetypal content possessing all those qualities which are characteristic of the Christ-image in its archaic and medieval forms. Modern psychology is therefore confronted with a question very like the one that faced the alchemists: Is the self a symbol of Christ, or is Christ a symbol of the self?

123   In the present study I have affirmed the latter alternative. I have

[93] Cf. *Psychology and Alchemy*, pars. 52ff., 122ff., and "A Study in the Process of Individuation," pars. 542, 550, 581f.

tried to show how the traditional Christ-image concentrates upon itself the characteristics of an archetype—the archetype of the self. My aim and method do not purport to be anything more in principle than, shall we say, the efforts of an art historian to trace the various influences which have contributed towards the formation of a particular Christ-image. Thus we find the concept of the archetype in the history of art as well as in philology and textual criticism. The psychological archetype differs from its parallels in other fields only in one respect: it refers to a living and ubiquitous psychic fact, and this naturally shows the whole situation in a rather different light. One is then tempted to attach greater importance to the immediate and living presence of the archetype than to the idea of the historical Christ. As I have said, there is among certain of the alchemists, too, a tendency to give the *lapis* priority over Christ. Since I am far from cherishing any missionary intentions, I must expressly emphasize that I am not concerned here with confessions of faith but with proven scientific facts. If one inclines to regard the archetype of the self as the real agent and hence takes Christ as a symbol of the self, one must bear in mind that there is a considerable difference between *perfection* and *completeness*. The Christ-image is as good as perfect (at least it is meant to be so), while the archetype (so far as known) denotes completeness but is far from being perfect. It is a paradox, a statement about something indescribable and transcendental. Accordingly the realization of the self, which would logically follow from a recognition of its supremacy, leads to a fundamental conflict, to a real suspension between opposites (reminiscent of the crucified Christ hanging between two thieves), and to an approximate state of wholeness that lacks perfection. To strive after teleiosis in the sense of perfection is not only legitimate but is inborn in man as a peculiarity which provides civilization with one of its strongest roots. This striving is so powerful, even, that it can turn into a passion that draws everything into its service. Natural as it is to seek perfection in one way or another, the archetype fulfils itself in completeness, and this is a τελείωσις of quite another kind. Where the archetype predominates, completeness is *forced* upon us against all our conscious strivings, in accordance with the archaic nature of the archetype. The individual may strive after perfection ("Be you therefore perfect—τέλειοι—as also your heavenly Father is perfect."[94]) but must suffer from the opposite of his intentions for the sake of his completeness. "I find then a law, that, when I would do good, evil is present with me."[95]

[94] Matt. 5:48 (DV).
[95] Rom. 7:21 (AV).

124   The Christ-image fully corresponds to this situation: Christ is the perfect man who is crucified. One could hardly think of a truer picture of the goal of ethical endeavour. At any rate the transcendental idea of the self that serves psychology as a working hypothesis can never match that image because, although it is a symbol, it lacks the character of a revelatory historical event. Like the related ideas of *atman* and *tao* in the East, the idea of the self is at least in part a product of cognition, grounded neither on faith nor on metaphysical speculation but on the experience that under certain conditions the unconscious spontaneously brings forth an archetypal symbol of wholeness. From this we must conclude that some such archetype occurs universally and is endowed with a certain numinosity. And there is in fact any amount of historical evidence as well as modern case material to prove this.[96] These naïve and completely uninfluenced pictorial representations of the symbol show that it is given central and supreme importance precisely because it stands for the conjunction of opposites. Naturally the conjunction can only be understood as a paradox, since a union of opposites can be thought of only as their annihilation. Paradox is a characteristic of all transcendental situations because it alone gives adequate expression to their indescribable nature.

125   Whenever the archetype of the self predominates, the inevitable psychological consequence is a state of conflict vividly exemplified by the Christian symbol of crucifixion—that acute state of unredeemedness which comes to an end only with the words "consummatum est." Recognition of the archetype, therefore, does not in any way circumvent the Christian mystery; rather, it forcibly creates the psychological preconditions without which "redemption" would appear meaningless. "Redemption" does not mean that a burden is taken from one's shoulders which one was never meant to bear. Only the "complete" person knows how unbearable man is to himself. So far as I can see, no relevant objection could be raised from the Christian point of view against anyone accepting the task of individuation imposed on us by nature, and the recognition of our wholeness or completeness, as a binding personal commitment. If he does this consciously and intentionally, he avoids all the unhappy consequences of repressed individuation. In other words, if he voluntarily takes the burden of completeness on himself, he need not find it "happening" to him against his will in a negative form. This is as much as to say that anyone who is destined to descend into a deep pit had better set about it with all

---

[96] Cf. the last two papers in Part I of vol. 9.

the necessary precautions rather than risk falling into the hole backwards.

126   The irreconcilable nature of the opposites in Christian psychology is due to their moral accentuation. This accentuation seems natural to us, although, looked at historically, it is a legacy from the Old Testament with its emphasis on righteousness in the eyes of the law. Such an influence is notably lacking in the East, in the philosophical religions of India and China. Without stopping to discuss the question of whether this exacerbation of the opposites, much as it increases suffering, may not after all correspond to a higher degree of truth, I should like merely to express the hope that the present world situation may be looked upon in the light of the psychological rule alluded to above. Today humanity, as never before, is split into two apparently irreconcilable halves. The psychological rule says that when an inner situation is not made conscious, it happens outside, as fate. That is to say, when the individual remains undivided and does not become conscious of his inner opposite, the world must perforce act out the conflict and be torn into opposing halves.

2

"CHRIST AS ARCHETYPE"

From *Psychology and Religion: West and East,*
CW 11, pars. 226–42

226   The Trinity and its inner life process appear as a closed circle, a self-contained divine drama in which man plays, at most, a passive part. It seizes on him and, for a period of several centuries, forced him to occupy his mind passionately with all sorts of queer problems which today seem incredibly abstruse, if not downright absurd. It is, in the first place, difficult to see what the Trinity could possibly mean for us, either practically, morally, or symbolically. Even theologians often feel that speculation on this subject is a more or less otiose juggling with ideas, and there are not a few who could get along quite comfortably without the divinity of Christ, and for whom the role of the Holy Ghost, both inside and outside the Trinity, is an embarrassment of the first order. Writing of the Athanasian Creed, D. F. Strauss remarks: "The truth is that anyone who has sworn to the Symbolum Quicumque has abjured the laws of human thought." Naturally, the only person who can talk like that is one who is no longer impressed by the revelation of holiness and has fallen back on his own mental activity. This, so far as the revealed archetype is concerned, is an inevitably retrograde step: the liberalistic humanization of Christ goes back to the rival doctrine of homoiousia and to Arianism, while modern anti-trinitarianism has a conception of God that is more Old Testament or Islamic in character than Christian.

227   Obviously, anyone who approaches this problem with rationalistic and intellectualistic assumptions, like D. F. Strauss, is bound to find the patristic discussions and arguments completely nonsensical. But that anyone, and especially a theologian, should fall back on such manifestly incommensurable criteria as reason, logic, and the like, shows that, despite all the mental exertions of the Councils and of scholastic theology, they failed to bequeath to posterity an intellectual understanding of the dogma that would lend the slightest support to belief

in it. There remained only submission to faith and renunciation of one's own desire to understand. Faith, as we know from experience, often comes off second best and has to give in to criticism which may not be at all qualified to deal with the object of faith. Criticism of this kind always puts on an air of great enlightenment—that is to say, it spreads round itself that thick darkness which the Word once tried to penetrate with its light: "And the light shineth in the darkness, and the darkness comprehended it not."

228   Naturally, it never occurs to these critics that their way of approach is incommensurable with their object. They think they have to do with rational facts, whereas it entirely escapes them that it is and always has been primarily a question of irrational psychic phenomena. That this is so can be seen plainly enough from the unhistorical character of the gospels, whose only concern was to represent the miraculous figure of Christ as graphically and impressively as possible. Further evidence of this is supplied by the earliest literary witness, Paul, who was closer to the events in question than the apostles. It is frankly disappointing to see how Paul hardly ever allows the real Jesus of Nazareth to get a word in. Even at this early date (and not only in John) he is completely overlaid, or rather smothered, by metaphysical conceptions: he is the ruler over all daemonic forces, the cosmic saviour, the mediating God-man. The whole pre-Christian and Gnostic theology of the Near East (some of whose roots go still further back) wraps itself about him and turns him before our eyes into a dogmatic figure who has no more need of historicity. At a very early stage, therefore, the real Christ vanished behind the emotions and projections that swarmed about him from far and near; immediately and almost without trace he was absorbed into the surrounding religious systems and moulded into their archetypal exponent. He became the collective figure whom the unconscious of his contemporaries expected to appear, and for this reason it is pointless to ask who he "really" was. Were he human and nothing else, and in this sense historically true, he would probably be no more enlightening a figure than, say, Pythagoras, or Socrates, or Apollonius of Tyana. He opened men's eyes to revelation precisely because he was, from everlasting, God, and therefore unhistorical; and he functioned as such only by virtue of the consensus of unconscious expectation. If nobody had remarked that there was something special about the wonder-working Rabbi from Galilee, the darkness would never have noticed that a light was shining. Whether he lit the light with his own strength, or whether he was the victim of the universal longing for light and broke down under it, are questions which, for

lack of reliable information, only faith can decide. At any rate the documentary reports relating to the general projection and assimilation of the Christ-figure are unequivocal. There is plenty of evidence for the co-operation of the collective unconscious in view of the abundance of parallels from the history of religion. In these circumstances we must ask ourselves what it was in man that was stirred by the Christian message, and what the answer he gave.

229   If we are to answer this psychological question, we must first of all examine the Christ-symbolism contained in the New Testament, together with the patristic allegories and medieval iconography, and compare this material with the archetypal content of the unconscious psyche in order to find out what archetypes have been constellated. The most important of the symbolical statements about Christ are those which reveal the attributes of the hero's life: improbable origin, divine father, hazardous birth, rescue in the nick of time, precocious development, conquest of the mother and of death, miraculous deeds, a tragic, early end, symbolically significant manner of death, postmortem effects (reappearances, signs and marvels, etc.). As the Logos, Son of the Father, *Rex gloriae, Judex mundi*, Redeemer, and Saviour, Christ is himself God, an all-embracing, totality, which, like the definition of Godhead, is expressed iconographically by the circle or mandala.[1] Here I would mention only the traditional representation of the *Rex gloriae* in a mandala, accompanied by a quaternity composed of the four symbols of the evangelists (including the four seasons, four winds, four rivers, and so on). Another symbolism of the same kind is the choir of saints, angels, and elders grouped round Christ (or God) in the centre. Here Christ symbolizes the integration of the kings and prophets of the Old Testament. As a shepherd he is the leader and centre of the flock. He is the vine, and those that hang on him are the branches. His body is bread to be eaten, and his blood wine to be drunk; he is also the mystical body formed by the congregation. In his human manifestation he is the hero and God-man, born without sin, more complete and more perfect than the natural

---

[1] "Deus est circulus cuius centrum est ubique, circumferentia vero nusquam" (God is a circle whose centre is everywhere and the circumference nowhere). This definition occurs in the later literature. In the form "Deus est sphaera infinita" (God is an infinite sphere) it is supposed to have come from the *Liber Hermetis, Liber Termegisti*, Cod. Paris. 6319 (14th cent.); Cod. Vat 3060 (1315). Cf. Baumgartner, *Die Philosophie des Alanus de Insulis*, p. 118. In this connection, mention should be made of the tendency of Gnostic thought to move in a circle, e.g.: "In the beginning was the Word, and the Word was with God, and God was the Word." Cf. Leisegang, *Denkformen*, pp. 6off.

man, who is to him what a child is to an adult, or an animal (sheep) to a human being.

230   These mythological statements, coming from within the Christian sphere as well as from outside it, adumbrate an archetype that expresses itself in essentially the same symbolism and also occurs in individual dreams or in fantasy-like projections upon living people (transference phenomena, hero-worship, etc.). The content of all such symbolic products is the idea of an overpowering, all-embracing, complete or perfect being, represented either by a man of heroic proportions, or by an animal with magical attributes, or by a magical vessel or some other "treasure hard to attain," such as a jewel, ring, crown, or, geometrically, by a mandala. This archetypal idea is a reflection of the individual's wholeness, i.e., of the self, which is present in him as an unconscious image. The conscious mind can form absolutely no conception of this totality, because it includes not only the conscious but also the unconscious psyche, which is, as such, inconceivable and irrepresentable.

231   It was this archetype of the self in the soul of every man that responded to the Christian message, with the result that the concrete Rabbi Jesus was rapidly assimilated by the constellated archetype. In this way Christ realized the idea of the self.[2] But as one can never distinguish empirically between a symbol of the self and a God-image, the two ideas, however much we try to differentiate them, always appear blended together, so that the self appears synonymous with the inner Christ of the Johannine and Pauline writings, and Christ with God ("of one substance with the Father"), just as the atman appears as the individualized self and at the same time as the animating principle of the cosmos, and Tao as a condition of mind and at the same time as the correct behaviour of cosmic events. Psychologically speaking, the domain of "gods" begins where consciousness leaves off, for at that point man is already at the mercy of the natural order, whether he thrive or perish. To the symbols of wholeness that come to him from there he attaches names which vary according to time and place.

232   The self is defined psychologically as the psychic totality of the individual, Anything that a man postulates as being a greater totality than himself can become a symbol of the self. For this reason the symbol of the self is not always as total as the definition would require. Even the Christ-figure is not a totality, for it lacks the nocturnal side of the psyche's nature, the darkness of the spirit, and is also without sin. Without the integration of evil there is no totality, nor can evil be "added to

---

[2] Koepgen (p. 307) puts it very aptly: "Jesus relates everything to his ego, but this ego is not the subjective ego, it is a cosmic ego."

the mixture by force." One could compare Christ as a symbol to the mean of the first mixture: he would then be the middle term of a triad, in which the One and Indivisible is represented by the Father, and the Divisible by the Holy Ghost, who, as we know, can divide himself into tongues of fire. But this triad, according to the *Timaeus*, is not yet a reality. Consequently a second mixture is needed.

233   The goal of psychological, as of biological, development is self-realization, or individuation. But since man knows himself only as an ego, and the self, as a totality, is indescribable and indistinguishable from a God-image, self-realization—to put it in religious or metaphysical terms—amounts to God's incarnation. That is already expressed in the fact that Christ is the son of God. And because individuation is an heroic and often tragic task, the most difficult of all, it involves suffering, a passion of the ego: the ordinary, empirical man we once were is burdened with the fate of losing himself in a greater dimension and being robbed of his fancied freedom of will. He suffers, so to speak, from the violence done to him by the self.[3] The analogous passion of Christ signifies God's suffering on account of the injustice of the world and the darkness of man. The human and the divine suffering set up a relationship of complementarity with compensating effects. Through the Christ-symbol, man can get to know the real meaning of his suffering: he is on the way towards realizing his wholeness. As a result of the integration of conscious and unconscious, his ego enters the "divine" realm, where it participates in "God's suffering." The cause of the suffering is in both cases the same, namely "incarnation," which on the human level appears as "individuation." The divine hero born of man is already threatened with murder; he has nowhere to lay his head, and his death is a gruesome tragedy. The self is no mere concept or logical postulate; it is a psychic reality, only part of it conscious, while for the rest it embraces the life of the unconscious and is therefore inconceivable except in the form of symbols. The drama of the archetypal life of Christ describes in symbolic images the events in the conscious life—as well as in the life that transcends consciousness—of a man who has been transformed by his higher destiny.

III. THE HOLY GHOST

234   The psychological relationship between man and the trinitarian life process is illustrated first by the human nature of Christ, and second by

---

[3] Cf. Jacob's struggle with the angel at the ford.

the descent of the Holy Ghost and his indwelling in man, as predicted and promised by the Christian message. The life of Christ is on the one hand only a short, historical interlude for proclaiming the message, but on the other hand it is an exemplary demonstration of the psychic experiences connected with God's manifestation of himself (or the realization of the self). The important thing for man is not the δεικ-νύμενον and the δρώμενον (what is "shown" and "done"), but what happens afterwards: the seizure of the individual by the Holy Ghost.

235   Here, however, we run into a great difficulty. For if we follow up the theory of the Holy Ghost and carry it a step further (which the Church has not done, for obvious reasons), we come inevitably to the conclusion that if the Father appears in the Son and breathes together with the Son, and the Son leaves the Holy Ghost behind for man, then the Holy Ghost breathes in man, too, and thus is the breath common to man, the Son, and the Father. Man is therefore included in God's worship, and the words of Christ—"Ye are gods" (John 10:34)—appear in a significant light. The doctrine that the Paraclete was expressly left behind for man raises an enormous problem. The triadic formula of Plato would surely be the last word in the matter of logic, but psychologically it is not so at all, because the psychological factor keeps on intruding in the most disturbing way. Why, in the name of all that's wonderful, wasn't it "Father, Mother, and Son?" That would be much more "reasonable" and "natural" than "Father, Son, and Holy Ghost." To this we must answer: it is not just a question of a natural situation, but of a product of human reflection[4] added on to the natural sequence of father and son. Through reflection, "life" and its "soul" are abstracted from Nature and endowed with a separate existence. Father and son are united in the same soul, or, according to the ancient Egyptian view, in the same procreative force, Ka-mutef. Ka-mutef is exactly the same hypostatization of an attribute as the breath or "spiration" of the Godhead.[5]

---

[4] "Reflection" should be understood not simply as an act of thought, but rather as an attitude. [Cf. *Psychological Types*, Def. 8.—EDITORS.] It is a privilege born of human freedom in contradistinction to the compulsion of natural law. As the word itself testifies ("reflection" means literally "bending back"), reflection is a spiritual act that runs counter to the natural process; an act whereby we stop, call something to mind, form a picture, and take up a relation to and come to terms with what we have seen. It should, therefore, be understood as an act of *becoming conscious*.

[5] "Active spiration" is a manifestation of life, an immanent act of Father and Son; "passive spiration," on the other hand, is a quality of the Holy Ghost. According to St. Thomas, spiration does not proceed from the intellect but from the will of the Father

236   This psychological fact spoils the abstract perfection of the triadic formula and makes it a logically incomprehensible construction, since, in some mysterious and unexpected way, an important mental process peculiar to man has been imported into it. If the Holy Ghost is, at one and the same time, the breath of life and a loving spirit and the Third Person in whom the whole trinitarian process culminates, then he is essentially a product of reflection, an hypostatized noumenon tacked on to the natural family-picture of father and son. It is significant that early Christian Gnosticism tried to get round this difficulty by interpreting the Holy Ghost as the Mother.[6] But that would merely have kept him within the archaic family-picture, within the tritheism and polytheism of the patriarchal world. It is, after all, perfectly natural that the father should have a family and that the son should embody the father. This train of thought is quite consistent with the father-world. On the other hand, the mother-interpretation would reduce the specific meaning of the Holy Ghost to a primitive image and destroy the most essential of the qualities attributed to him: not only is he the life common to Father and Son, he is also the Paraclete whom the Son left behind him, to procreate in man and bring forth works of divine parentage. It is of paramount importance that the idea of the Holy Ghost is not a natural image, but a recognition of the living quality of Father and Son, abstractly conceived as the "third" term between the One and the Other. Out of the tension of duality life always produces a "third" that seems somehow incommensurable or paradoxical. Hence, as the "third," the Holy Ghost is bound to be incommensurable and paradoxical too. Unlike Father and Son, he has no name and no character. He is a *function*, but that function is the Third Person of the Godhead.

237   He is psychologically heterogeneous in that he cannot be logically derived from the father-son relationship and can only be understood as an idea introduced by a process of human reflection. The Holy Ghost is an exceedingly "abstract" conception, since a "breath" shared by two figures characterized as distinct and not mutually interchangeable can hardly be conceived at all. Hence one feels it to be an artificial construction of the mind, even though, as the Egyptian Ka-mutef concept shows, it seems somehow to belong to the very essence of the Trinity.

---

and Son. In relation to the Son the Holy Ghost is not a spiration, but a procreative act of the Father.

[6] Cf. the Acts of Thomas (trans. by James, p. 388): "Come, O communion of the male; come, she that knoweth the mysteries of him that is chosen. . . . Come, holy dove that beareth the twin young; come, hidden mother."

113

Despite the fact that we cannot help seeing in the positing of such a concept a product of human reflection, this reflection need not necessarily have been a conscious act. It could equally well owe its existence to a "revelation," i.e., to an unconscious reflection,[7] and hence to an autonomous functioning of the unconscious, or rather of the self, whose symbols, as we have already said, cannot be distinguished from God-images. A religious interpretation will therefore insist that this hypostasis was a divine revelation. While it cannot raise any objections to such a notion, psychology must hold fast to the conceptual nature of the hypostasis, for in the last analysis the Trinity, too, is an anthropomorphic configuration, gradually taking shape through strenuous mental and spiritual effort, even though already preformed by the timeless archetype.

238   This separating, recognizing, and assigning of qualities is a mental activity which, although unconscious at first, gradually filters through to consciousness as the work proceeds. What started off by merely happening to consciousness later becomes integrated in it as its own activity. So long as a mental or indeed any psychic process at all is unconscious, it is subject to the law governing archetypal dispositions, which are organized and arranged round the self. And since the self cannot be distinguished from an archetypal God-image, it would be equally true to say of any such arrangement that it conforms to natural law and that it is an act of God's will. (Every metaphysical statement is, *ipso facto*, unprovable.) Inasmuch, then, as acts of cognition and judgment are essential qualities of consciousness, any accumulation of unconscious acts of this sort[8] will have the effect of strengthening and widening consciousness, as one can see for oneself in any thorough analysis of the unconscious. Consequently, man's achievement of consciousness appears as the result of prefigurative archetypal processes or—to put it metaphysically—as part of the divine life-process. In other words, God becomes manifest in the human act of reflection.

239   The nature of this conception (i.e., the hypostatizing of a quality) meets the need evinced by primitive thought to form a more or less abstract idea by endowing each individual quality with a concrete existence of its own. Just as the Holy Ghost is a legacy left to man, so, conversely, the concept of the Holy Ghost is something begotten by man and bears the stamp of its human progenitor. And just as Christ took on man's bodily nature, so through the Holy Ghost man as a spiritual force

[7] For this seeming *contradictio in adjecto* see "On the Nature of the Psyche," p. 172.
[8] The existence of such process is evidenced by the content of dreams.

114

is surreptitiously included in the mystery of the Trinity, thereby raising it far above the naturalistic level of the triad and thus beyond the Platonic triunity. The Trinity, therefore, discloses itself as a symbol that comprehends the essence of the divine *and* the human. It is, as Koepgen[9] says, "a revelation not only of God but at the same time of man."

240   The Gnostic interpretation of the Holy Ghost as the Mother contains a core of truth in that Mary was the instrument of God's birth and so became involved in the trinitarian drama as a human being. The Mother of God can, therefore, be regarded as a symbol of mankind's essential participation in the Trinity. The psychological justification for this assumption lies in the fact that thinking, which originally had its source in the self-revelations of the unconscious, was felt to be the manifestation of a power external to consciousness. The primitive does not think; the thoughts come to him. We ourselves still feel certain particularly enlightening ideas as "in-fluences," "in-spirations," etc. Where judgments and flashes of insight are transmitted by unconscious activity, they are often attributed to an archetypal feminine figure, the anima or mother-beloved. It then seems as if the inspiration came from the mother or from the beloved, the "femme inspiratrice." In view of this, the Holy Ghost would have a tendency to exchange his neuter designation ($\tau\grave{o}\ \pi\nu\varepsilon\tilde{v}\mu\alpha$) for a feminine one. (It may be noted that the Hebrew word for spirit—*ruach*—is predominantly feminine.) Holy Ghost and Logos merge in the Gnostic idea of Sophia, and again in the Sapientia of the medieval natural philosophers, who said of her: "In gremio matris sedet sapientia patris" (the wisdom of the father lies in the lap of the mother). These psychological relationships do something to explain why the Holy Ghost was interpreted as the mother, but they add nothing to our understanding of the Holy Ghost as such, because it is impossible to see how the mother could come third when her natural place would be second.

241   Since the Holy Ghost is an hypostasis of "life," posited by an act of reflection, he appears, on account of his peculiar nature, as a separate and incommensurable "third," whose very peculiarities testify that it is neither a compromise nor a mere triadic appendage, but rather the logically unexpected resolution of tension between Father and Son. The fact that it is precisely a process of human reflection that irrationally creates the uniting "third" is itself connected with the nature of the drama of redemption, whereby God descends into the human realm and man mounts up to the realm of divinity.

[9] *Die Gnosis des Christentums,* p. 194.

242   Thinking in the magic circle of the Trinity, or trinitarian thinking, is in truth motivated by the "Holy Spirit" in so far as it is never a question of mere cogitation but of giving expression to imponderable psychic events. The driving forces that work themselves out in this thinking are not conscious motives; they spring from an historical occurrence rooted, in its turn, in those obscure psychic conditions for which one could hardly find a better or more succinct formula than the "change from father to son," from unity to duality, from non-reflection to criticism. To the extent that personal motives are lacking in trinitarian thinking, and the forces motivating it derive from impersonal and collective psychic conditions, it expresses a need of the unconscious psyche far surpassing all personal needs. This need, aided by human thought, produced the symbol of the Trinity, which was destined to serve as a saving formula of wholeness in an epoch of change and psychic transformation. Manifestations of a psychic activity not caused or consciously willed by man himself have always been felt to be daemonic, divine, or "holy," in the sense that they treat and make whole. His ideas of God behave as do all images arising out of the unconscious: they compensate or complete the general mood or attitude of the moment, and it is only through the integration of these unconscious images that a man becomes a psychic whole. The "merely conscious" man who is all ego is a mere fragment, in so far as he seems to exist apart from the unconscious. But the more the unconscious is split off, the more formidable the shape in which it appears to the conscious mind—if not in divine form, then in the more unfavourable form of obsessions and outbursts of affect.[10] Gods are personifications of unconscious contents, for they reveal themselves to us through the unconscious activ-

[10] In the *Rituale Romanum* ("On the Exorcism of Persons Possessed by the Devil": 1952 edn., pp. 839ff.), states of possession are expressly distinguished from diseases. We are told that the exorcist must learn to know the signs by which the possessed person may be distinguished from "those suffering from melancholy or any morbid condition." The criteria of possession are: ". . . speaking fluently in unknown tongues or understanding those who speak them; revealing things that take place at a distance or in secret; giving evidence of greater strength than is natural in view of one's age or condition; and other things of the same kind." The Church's idea of possession, therefore, is limited to extremely rare cases, whereas I would use it in a much wider sense as designating a frequently occurring psychic phenomenon: any autonomous complex not subject to the conscious will exerts a possessive effect on consciousness proportional to its strength and limits the latter's freedom. On the question of the Church's distinction between disease and possession, see Tonquédec, *Les Maladies nerveuses ou mentales et les manifestations diaboliques.*

ity of the psyche.[11] Trinitarian thinking had something of the same quality, and its passionate profundity rouses in us latecomers a näive astonishment. We no longer know, or have not yet discovered, what depths in the soul were stirred by that great turning-point in human history. The Holy Ghost seems to have faded away without having found the answer to the question he set humanity.

---

[11] I am always coming up against the misunderstanding that a psychological treatment or explanation reduces God to "nothing but" psychology. It is not a question of God at all, but of man's ideas of God, as I have repeatedly emphasized. There are people who do have such ideas and who form such conceptions, and these things are the proper study of psychology.

3

"FATHER, SON, AND SPIRIT"

From *Psychology and Religion: West and East,*
CW 11, pars. 194–206

194   I have dwelt at some length on the views of the Babylonians and
Egyptians, and on Platonist philosophy, in order to give the reader
some conception of the trinitarian and unitarian ideas that were in
existence many centuries before the birth of Christianity. Whether
these ideas were handed down to posterity as a result of migration and
tradition or whether they arose spontaneously in each case is a question of little importance. The important thing is that they occurred
because, once having sprung forth from the unconscious of the human
race (and not just in Asia Minor!), they could re-arise anywhere at any
time. It is, for instance, more than doubtful whether the Church Fathers who devised the *homoousios* formula were even remotely acquainted with the ancient Egyptian theology of kingship. Nevertheless,
they neither paused in their labours nor rested until they had finally
reconstructed the ancient Egyptian archetype. Much the same sort of
thing happened when, in A.D. 431, at the Council of Ephesus, whose
streets had once rung with hymns of praise to many-breasted Diana,
the Virgin Mary was declared the θεοτόκος, 'birth-giver of the god.'[1] As
we know from Epiphanius,[2] there was even a sect, the Collyridians, who
worshipped Mary after the manner of an antique goddess. Her cult
had its chief centres in Arabia, Thrace, and Upper Scythia, the most
enthusiastic devotees being women. Their provocations moved Epiphanius to the rebuke that "the whole female sex is slippery and prone to
error, with a mind that is very petty and narrow."[3] It is clear from this
chastening sermon that there were priestesses who on certain feast days

---

[1] Here one might recall the legend that, after the death of Christ, Mary betook herself
with John to Ephesus, where she is said to have lived until her death.

[2] *Panarium (Contra octoginta haereses)* LXXIX. See Migne, *P.G.*, vol. 41, cols. 739ff.

[3] "Quod genus lubricum et in errorem proclive, ac pusilli admodum et angusti animi esse
solet."

decorated a wagon or four-cornered seat and covered it with linen, on which they placed offerings of bakemeats "in the name of Mary" (εἰς ὄνομα τῆς Μαρίας), afterwards partaking of the sacrificial meal. This plainly amounted to a Eucharistic feast in honour of Mary, at which wheaten bread was eaten. The orthodox standpoint of the time is aptly expressed in the words of Epiphanius: "Let Mary be held in honour, and let the Father and the Son and the Holy Ghost be adored, but let no one adore Mary."

195   Thus the archetype reasserted itself, since, as I have tried to show, archetypal ideas are part of the indestructible foundations of the human mind. However long they are forgotten and buried, always they return, sometimes in the strangest guise, with a personal twist to them or intellectually distorted, as in the case of the Arian heresy, but continually reproducing themselves in new forms representing the timeless truths that are innate in man's nature.[4]

196   Even though Plato's influence on the thinkers of the next few centuries can hardly be overestimated, his philosophically formulated triad cannot be held responsible for the origins of the Christian dogma of the Trinity. For we are concerned here not with any philosophical, that is conscious, assumptions but with unconscious, archetypal forms. The Platonic formula for the triad contradicts the Christian Trinity in one essential point: the triad is built on opposition, whereas the Trinity contains no opposition of any kind, but is, on the contrary, a complete harmony in itself. The three Persons are characterized in such a manner that they cannot possibly be derived from Platonic premises, while the terms Father, Son, and Holy Ghost do not proceed in any sense from the number three. At most, the Platonic formula supplies the intellectual scaffolding for contents that come from quite other sources. The Trinity may be conceived platonically as to its form, but for its content we have to rely on psychic factors, on irrational data that cannot be logically determined beforehand. In other words, we have to distinguish between the *logical idea* of the Trinity and its *psychological reality*. The latter brings us back to the very much more ancient Egyptian ideas and hence to the archetype, which provides the authentic and eternal justification for the existence of any trinitarian idea at all.

197   The psychological datum consists of Father, Son, and Holy Ghost. If we posit "Father," then "Son" logically follows; but "Holy Ghost" does

_____

[4] The special emphasis I lay on archetypal predispositions does not mean that mythologems are of exclusively psychic origin. I am not overlooking the social conditions that are just as necessary for their production.

not follow logically from either "Father" or "Son." So we must be dealing here with a special factor that rests on a different presupposition. According to the old doctrine, the Holy Ghost is "vera persona, quae a filio et patre missa est" (a real person who is sent by the Son and the Father). The "processio a patre filioque" (procession from the Father and the Son) is a "spiration" and not a "begetting." This somewhat peculiar idea corresponds to the separation, which still existed in the Middle Ages, of "corpus" and "spiramen," the latter being understood as something more than mere "breath." What it really denoted was the *anima*, which, as its name shows, is a breath-being (*anemos* = wind). Although an activity of the body, it was thought of as an independent substance (or hypostasis) existing alongside the body. The underlying idea is that the body "lives," and that "life" is something superadded and autonomous, conceived as a soul unattached to the body. Applying this idea to the Trinity formula, we would have to say: Father, Son, and Life—the life proceeding from both or lived by both. The Holy Ghost as "life" is a concept that cannot be derived logically from the identity of Father and Son, but is, rather, a psychological idea, a datum based on an irrational, primordial image. This primordial image is the archetype, and we find it expressed most clearly in the Egyptian theology of kingship. There, as we have seen, the archetype takes the form of God the father, Ka-mutef (the begetter), and the son. The *ka* is the life-spirit, the animating principle of men and gods, and therefore can be legitimately interpreted as the soul or spiritual double. He is the "life" of the dead man, and thus corresponds on the one hand to the living man's soul, and on the other to his "spirit" or "genius." We have seen that Ka-mutef is a hypostatization of procreative power.[5] In the same way, the Holy Ghost is hypostatized procreative power and life-force.[6] Hence, in the Christian Trinity, we are confronted with a distinctly archaic idea, whose extraordinary value lies precisely in the fact that it is a supreme, hypostatic representation of an abstract thought (two-dimensional triad). The form is still concretistic, in that the archetype is represented by the relationship "Father" and "Son." Were it nothing but that, it would only be a dyad. The third element, however, the

[5] The *ka* of the king even has an individual name. Thus "the living *ka* of the Lord of the Two Lands," Thutmosis III, was called the "victorious bull which shines in Thebes." Erman, *Life in Ancient Egypt*, p. 307.
[6] The "doubling" of the spirit occurs also in the Old Testament, though more as a "potency" emanating from God than as an hypostasis. Nevertheless, Isaiah 48:16 looks very like a hypostasis in the Septuagint text: Κύριος Κύριος ἀπεστειλέν με καὶ τὸ πνεῦμα αὐτοῦ (The Lord the Lord sent me and his spirit).

CHRISTIAN DOCTRINE, RITUAL, AND SYMBOL

connecting link between "Father" and "Son," is spirit and not a human figure. The masculine father-son relationship is thus lifted out of the natural order (which includes mothers and daughters) and translated to a sphere from which the feminine element is excluded: in ancient Egypt as in Christianity the Theotokos stands outside the Trinity. One has only to think of Jesus's brusque rejection of his mother at the marriage in Cana: "Woman, what have I to do with thee?" (John 2:4), and also earlier, when she sought the twelve-year-old child in the temple: "How is it that ye sought me? wist ye not that I must be about my Father's business?" (Luke 2:49). We shall probably not be wrong in assuming that this special sphere to which the father-son relationship is removed is the sphere of primitive mysteries and masculine initiations. Among certain tribes, women are forbidden to look at the mysteries on pain of death. Through the initiations the young men are systematically alienated from their mothers and are reborn as spirits. The celibacy of the priesthood is a continuation of this archetypal idea.[7]

198   The intellectual operation that lies concealed in the higher father-son relationship consists in the extrapolation of an invisible figure, a "spirit" that is the very essence of masculine life. The life of the body or of a man is posited as something different from the man himself. This led to the idea of a *ka* or immortal soul, able to detach itself from the body and not dependent on it for its existence. In this respect, primitives have extraordinarily well developed ideas about a plurality of souls. Some are immortal, others are only loosely attached to the body and can wander off and get lost in the night, or they lose their way and get caught in a dream. There are even souls that belong to a person without being lodged in his body, like the bush-soul, which dwells outside in the forest, in the body of an animal. The juxtaposition of a person and his "life" has its psychological basis in the fact that a mind which is not very well differentiated cannot think abstractly and is incapable of putting things into categories. It can only take the qualities it perceives and place them side by side: man and his life, or his sickness (visualized as a sort of demon), or his health or prestige (mana, etc.). This is obviously the case with the Egyptian *ka*. Father-son-life (or procreative power), together with rigorous exclusion of the Theotokos, constitute the patriarchal formula that was "in the air" long before the advent of Christianity.

199   The Father is, by definition, the prime cause, the creator, the *auctor rerum*, who, on a level of culture where reflection is still unknown, can

[7] For an instructive account of the Greek background see Harrison, *Themis*, ch. 1.

only be One. The Other follows from the One by splitting off from it. This split need not occur so long as there is no criticism of the *auctor rerum*—so long, that is to say, as a culture refrains from all reflection about the One and does not start criticizing the Creator's handiwork. A feeling of oneness, far removed from critical judgment and moral conflict, leaves the Father's authority unimpaired.

200   I had occasion to observe this original oneness of the father-world when I was with a tribe of Negroes on Mount Elgon. These people professed to believe that the Creator had made everything good and beautiful. "But what about the bad animals that kill your cattle?" I asked. They replied: "The lion is good and beautiful." "And your horrible diseases?" "You lie in the sun, and it is beautiful." I was impressed by their optimism. But at six o'clock in the evening this philosophy came to a sudden stop, as I was soon to discover. After sunset, another world took over—the dark world of the Ayik, who is everything evil, dangerous, and terrifying. The optimistic philosophy ends and a philosophy of fear, ghosts, and magical spells for averting the Evil One begins. Then, at sunrise, the optimism starts off again without any trace of inner contradiction.

201   Here man, world, and God form a whole, a unity unclouded by criticism. It is the world of the Father, and of man in his childhood state. Despite the fact that twelve hours out of every twenty-four are spent in the world of darkness, and in agonizing belief in this darkness, the doubt never arises as to whether God might not also be the Other. The famous question about the origin of evil does not yet exist in a patriarchal age. Only with the coming of Christianity did it present itself as the principal problem of morality. The world of the Father typifies an age which is characterized by a pristine oneness with the whole of Nature, no matter whether this oneness be beautiful or ugly or awe-inspiring. But once the question is asked: "Whence comes the evil, why is the world so bad and imperfect, why are there diseases and other horrors, why must man suffer?"—then reflection has already begun to judge the Father by his manifest works, and straightway one is conscious of a doubt, which is itself the symptom of a split in the original unity. One comes to the conclusion that creation is imperfect—nay more, that the Creator has not done his job properly, that the goodness and almightiness of the Father cannot be the sole principle of the cosmos. Hence the One has to be supplemented by the Other, with the result that the world of the Father is fundamentally altered and is superseded by the world of the Son.

202   This was the time when the Greeks started criticizing the world, the

time of "gnosis" in its widest sense, which ultimately gave birth to Christianity. The archetype of the redeemer-god and Original Man is age-old—we simply do not know how old. The Son, the revealed god, who voluntarily or involuntarily offers himself for sacrifice as a man, in order to create the world or redeem it from evil, can be traced back to the Purusha of Indian philosophy, and is also found in the Persian conception of the Original Man, Gayomart. Gayomart, son of the god of light, falls victim to the darkness, from which he must be set free in order to redeem the world. He is the prototype of the Gnostic redeemer-figures and of the teachings concerning Christ, redeemer of mankind.

203   It is not hard to see that a critique which raised the question of the origin of evil and of suffering had in mind another world—a world filled with longing for redemption and for that state of perfection in which man was still one with the Father. Longingly he looked back to the world of the Father, but it was lost forever, because an irreversible increase in man's consciousness had taken place in the meantime and made it independent. With this mutation he broke away from the world of the Father and entered upon the world of the Son, with its divine drama of redemption and the ritualistic retelling of those things which the God-man had accomplished during his earthly sojourn.[8] The life of the God-man revealed things that could not possibly have been known at the time when the Father ruled as the One. For the Father, as the original unity, was not a defined or definable object; nor could he, strictly speaking, either be called the "Father" or be one. He only became a "Father" by incarnating in the Son, and by so doing became defined and definable. By becoming a father and a man he revealed to man the secret of his divinity.

204   One of these revelations is the Holy Ghost. As a being who existed before the world was, he is eternal, but he appears empirically in this world only when Christ had left the earthly stage. He will be for the disciples what Christ was for them. He will invest them with the power to do works greater, perhaps, than those of the Son (John 14:12). The Holy Ghost is a figure who deputizes for Christ and who corresponds to what Christ received from the Father. From the Father comes the Son, and common to both is the living activity of the Holy Ghost, who, according to Christian doctrine, is breathed forth ("spirated") by both. As he is the third term common to Father and Son, he puts an end to

[8] Cf. the detailed exposition of the death and rebirth of the divine κοῦρος in Harrison, *Themis.*

124

the duality, to the "doubt" in the Son. He is, in fact, the third element that rounds out the Three and restores the One. The point is that the unfolding of the One reaches its climax in the Holy Ghost after polarizing itself as Father and Son. Its descent into a human body is sufficient in itself to make it become another, to set it in opposition to itself. Thenceforward there are two: the "One" and the "Other," which results in a certain tension.[9] This tension works itself out in the suffering and fate of the Son[10] and, finally, in Christ's admission of abandonment by God (Matthew 27:46).

205   Although the Holy Ghost is the progenitor of the Son (Matthew 1:18), he is also, as the Paraclete, a legacy from him. He continues the work of redemption in mankind at large, by descending upon those who merit divine election. Consequently, the Paraclete is, at least by implication, the crowning figure in the work of redemption on the one hand and in God's revelation of himself on the other. It could, in fact, be said that the Holy Ghost represents the final, complete stage in the evolution of God and the divine drama. For the Trinity is undoubtedly a higher form of God-concept than mere unity, since it corresponds to a level of reflection on which man has become more conscious.

206   The trinitarian conception of a life-process within the Deity, which I have outlined here, was, as we have seen, already in existence in pre-Christian times, its essential features being a continuation and differentiation of the primitive rites of renewal and the cult-legends associated with them. Just as the gods of these mysteries become extinct, so, too, do the mysteries themselves, only to take on new forms in the course of history. A large-scale extinction of the old gods was once more in progress at the beginning of our era, and the birth of a new god, with new mysteries and new emotions, was an occurrence that healed the wound in men's souls. It goes without saying that any conscious borrowing from the existing mystery traditions would have hampered the god's renewal and rebirth. It had to be an entirely unprejudiced revelation which, quite unrelated to anything else, and if possible without preconceptions of any kind, would usher into the world a new $\delta\varrho\acute{\omega}\mu\varepsilon\nu o\nu$ and a new cult-legend. Only at a comparatively late date did people notice the striking parallels with the legend of Dionysus, which they then de-

---

[9] The relation of Father to Son is not arithmetical, since both the One and the Other are still united in the original Unity and are, so to speak, eternally on the point of becoming two. Hence the Son is eternally being begotten by the Father, and Christ's sacrificial death is an eternally present act.

[10] The $\pi\acute{\alpha}\theta\eta$ of Dionysus would be the Greek parallels.

clared to be the work of the devil. This attitude on the part of the early Christians can easily be understood, for Christianity did indeed develop in this unconscious fashion, and furthermore its seeming lack of antecedents proved to be the indispensable condition for its existence as an effective force. Nobody can doubt the manifold superiority of the Christian revelation over its pagan precursors, for which reason it is distinctly superfluous today to insist on the unheralded and unhistorical character of the gospels, seeing that they swarm with historical and psychological assumptions of very ancient origin.

4

THE HOLY GHOST

From *Alchemical Studies*
CW 13, pars. 194–99

THE NATURAL TRANSFORMATION MYSTERY

194   Aniadus (or Aniadum), interpreted by Bodenstein and Dorn as the "efficacity of things," is defined by Ruland as "the regenerated spiritual man in us, the heavenly body implanted in its Christians by the Holy Ghost through the most Holy Sacraments." This interpretation does full justice to the role which Aniadus plays in the writings of Paracelsus. Though it is clearly related to the sacraments and to the Communion in particular, it is equally clear that there was no question of arousing or implanting the inner man in the Christian sense, but of a "scientific" union of the natural with the spiritual man with the aid of arcane techniques of a medical nature. Paracelsus carefully avoids the ecclesiastical terminology and uses instead an esoteric language which is extremely difficult to decipher, for the obvious purpose of segregating the "natural" transformation mystery from the religious one and effectively concealing it from prying eyes. Otherwise the welter of esoteric terms in this treatise would have no explanation. Nor can one escape the impression that this mystery was in some sense opposed to the religious mystery: as the "nettle" and the *flammula* show, the ambiguities of Eros were also included in it.[1] It had far more to do with pagan antiquity, as is evidenced by the *Hypnerotomachia Poliphili*, than with the Christian mystery. Nor is there any reason to suppose that Paracelsus was sniffing out nasty secrets; a more cogent motive was his experience as a physician who had to deal with man as he is and not as he should be and biologically speaking never can be. Many questions

---

[1] Confirmation of this may be found in the work of the alchemist and mystic John Pordage (1607–1681), "Ein Philosophisches Send-Schreiben vom Stein der Weissheit," printed in Roth-Scholtz, *Deutsches Theatrum chemicum*, I, pp. 557–596. For text, see my "Psychology of the Transference," pars. 507ff.

are put to a doctor which he cannot honestly answer with "should" but only from his knowledge and experience of nature. In these fragments of a nature mystery there is nothing to suggest a misplaced curiosity or perverse interest on Paracelsus's part; they bear witness rather to the strenuous efforts of a physician to find satisfactory answers to psychological questions which the ecclesiastical casuist is inclined to twist in his own favour.

195   This nature mystery was indeed so much at odds with the Church—despite the superficial analogies—that the Hungarian alchemist Nicolaus Melchior Szebeny,[2] court astrologer to Ladislaus II (1471–1516), made the bold attempt to present the *opus alchymicum* in the form of a Mass.[3] It is difficult to prove whether and to what extent the alchemists were aware that they were in conflict with the Church. Mostly they showed no insight into what they were doing. This is true also of Paracelsus—except for a few hints about the "Pagoyum." It is the more understandable that no real self-criticism could come about, since they genuinely believed that they were performing a work well-pleasing to God on the principle "quod natura relinquit imperfectum, ars perficit" (what nature left imperfect, the art perfects). Paracelsus himself was wholly filled with the godliness of his profession as a doctor, and nothing disquieted or disturbed his Christian faith. He took it for granted that his work supplemented the hand of God and that he was the faithful steward of the talent that had been entrusted to him. And as a matter of fact he was right, for the human soul is not something cut off from nature. It is a natural phenomenon like any other, and its problems are just as important as the questions and riddles which are presented by the diseases of the body. Moreover there is scarcely a disease of the body in which psychic factors do not play a part, just as physical ones have to be considered in many psychogenic disturbances. Paracelsus was fully alive to this. In his own peculiar way he took the psychic phenomena into account as perhaps none of the great physicians ever did before or after him. Although his homunculi, *Trarames, Durdales,* nymphs, Melusines, etc., are the grossest superstitions for us so-called moderns, for a man of Paracelsus's time they were nothing of the sort. In those days these figures were living and effective forces. They were projections, of course; but of that, too, Paracelsus seems to have had an

---

[2] Condemned to death under Ferdinand I, and executed in Prague, May 2, 1531. See *Psychology and Alchemy,* par. 480 and n.

[3] "Addam et processum sub forma missae, a Nicolao Cibinensi, Transilvano, ad Ladislaum Ungariae et Bohemiae regem olim missum," *Theatr. chem.,* III (1659), pp. 758ff.

inkling, since it is clear from numerous passages in his writings that he was aware that homunculi and suchlike beings were creatures of the imagination. His more primitive cast of mind attributed a reality to these projections, and this reality did far greater justice to their psychological effect than does our rationalistic assumption of the absolute unreality of projected contents. Whatever their reality may be, functionally at all events they behave just like realities. We should not let ourselves be so blinded by the modern rationalistic fear of superstition that we lose sight completely of those little-known psychic phenomena which surpass our present scientific understanding. Although Paracelsus had no notion of psychology, he nevertheless affords—precisely because of his "benighted superstition"—deep insights into psychic events which the most up-to-date psychology is only now struggling to investigate again. Even though mythology may not be "true" in the sense that a mathematical law or a physical experiment is true, it is still a serious subject for research and contains quite as many truths as a natural science; only, they lie on a different plane. One can be perfectly scientific about mythology, for it is just as good a natural product as plants, animals or chemical elements.

196   Even if the psyche were a product of the will, it would still not be outside nature. No doubt it would have been a greater achievement if Paracelsus had developed his natural philosophy in an age when the psyche had been discredited as an object of scientific study. As it was, he merely included in the scope of his investigations something that was already present, without being obliged to prove its existence anew. Even so his achievement is sufficiently great, despite the fact that we moderns still find it difficult to estimate correctly the full psychological implications of his views. For what, in the end, do we know about the causes and motives that prompted man, for more than a thousand years, to believe in that "absurdity" the transmutation of metals and the simultaneous psychic transformation of the artifex? We have never seriously considered the fact that for the medieval investigator the redemption of the world by God's son and the transubstantiation of the Eucharistic elements were not the last word, or rather, not the last answer to the manifold enigmas of man and his soul. If the *opus alchymicum* claimed equality with the *opus divinum* of the Mass, the reason for this was not grotesque presumption but the fact that a vast, unknown Nature, disregarded by the eternal verities of the Church, was imperiously demanding recognition and acceptance. Paracelsus knew, in advance of modern times, that this Nature was not only chemical and physical but also psychic. Even though his Trarames and whatnot

cannot be demonstrated in a test tube, they nevertheless had their place in his world. And even if, like all the rest of them, he never produced any gold, he was yet on the track of a process of psychic transformation that is incomparably more important for the happiness of the individual than the possession of the red tincture.

A. The Light of the Darkness

197   So when we try to elucidate the riddles of the *Vita longa* we are following the traces of a psychological process that is the vital secret of all seekers after truth. Not all are vouchsafed the grace of a faith that anticipates all solutions, nor is it given to all to rest content with the sun of revealed truth. The light that is lighted in the heart by the grace of the Holy Spirit, that same light of nature, however feeble it may be, is more important to them than the great light which shines in the darkness and which the darkness comprehended not. They discover that in the very darkness of nature a light is hidden, a little spark without which the darkness would not be darkness.[4] Paracelsus was one of these. He was a well-intentioned, humble Christian. His ethics and his professed faith were Christian, but his most secret, deepest passion, his whole creative yearning, belonged to the *lumen naturae*, the divine spark buried in the darkness, whose sleep of death could not be vanquished even by the revelation of God's son. The light from above made the darkness still darker; but the *lumen naturae* is the light of the darkness itself, which illuminates its own darkness, and this light the darkness comprehends. Therefore it turns blackness into brightness, burns away "all superfluities," and leaves behind nothing but "faecem et scoriam et terram damnatam" (dross and scoriae and the rejected earth).

198   Paracelsus, like all the philosophical alchemists, was seeking for something that would give him a hold on the dark, body-bound nature of man, on the soul which, intangibly interwoven with the world and with matter, appeared before itself in the terrifying form of strange, demoniacal figures and secured to be the secret source of life-shortening diseases. The Church might exorcise demons and banish them, but that only alienated man from his own nature, which, unconscious of itself, had clothed itself in these spectral forms. Not separation of the

---

[4] "Pharmaco ignito spolianda densi est corporis umbra" (The drug being ignited, the shadow of the dense body is to be stripped away). Maier, *Symbola aureae mensae*, p. 91.

natures but union of the natures was the goal of alchemy. From the time of Democritus its *leitmotiv* had been: "Nature rejoices in nature, nature conquers nature, nature rules over nature."[5] This principle is pagan in feeling and an expression of nature worship. Nature not only contains a process of transformation—it is itself transformation. It strives not for isolation but for union, for the wedding feast followed by death and rebirth. Paracelsus's "exaltation in May" is this marriage, the "gamonymus" or hierosgamos of light and darkness in the shape of Sol and Luna. Here the opposites unite what the light from above had sternly divided. This is not so much a reversion to antiquity as a continuation of that religious feeling for nature, so alien to Christianity, which is expressed most beautifully in the "Secret Inscription" in the Great Magic Papyrus of Paris:[6]

Greetings, entire edifice of the Spirit of the air, greetings, Spirit that penetratest from heaven to earth, and from earth, which abideth in the midst of the universe, to the uttermost bounds of the abyss, greetings, Spirit that penetratest into me, and shakest me, and departest from me in goodness according to God's will; greetings, beginning and end of irremovable Nature, greetings, thou who revolvest the elements which untiringly render service, greetings, brightly shining sun, whose radiance ministereth to the world, greetings, moon shining by night with disc of fickle brilliance, greetings, all ye spirits of the demons of the air, greetings, ye for whom the greeting is offered in praise, brothers and sisters, devout men and women! O great, greatest, incomprehensible fabric of the world, formed in a circle! Heavenly One, dwelling in the heavens, aetherial spirit, dwelling in the aether, having the form of water, of earth, of fire, of wind, of light, of darkness, star-glittering, damp-fiery-cold Spirit! I praise thee, God of gods, who hast fashioned the world, who hast established the depths upon the invisible support of their firm foundation, who hast separated heaven and earth, and hast encompassed the heavens with golden, eternal wings, and founded the earth upon eternal bases, who hast hung the aether high above the earth, who hast scattered the air with the self-moving wind, who hast laid the waters round about, who callest forth the tempests, the thunder, the lightning, the rain: Destroyer, Begetter of living things, God of the Aeons, great art thou, Lord, God, Ruler of All!

99   Just as this prayer has come down to us embedded in a mass of magical recipes, so does the *lumen naturae* rise up from a world of ko-

---

[5] 'Η φύσις τῇ φύσει τέρπεται, καὶ ἡ φύσις τὴν φύσιν νικᾷ, καὶ ἡ φύσις τὴν φύσιν κρατεῖ. Berthelot, *Alch. grecs*, II, i, 3.

[6] Preisendanz, *Papyri Graecae Magicae*, I. p. 111.

bolds and other creatures of darkness, veiled in magical spells and al-most extinguished in a morass of mystification. Nature is certainly equivocal, and one can blame neither Paracelsus nor the alchemists if, anxiously aware of their responsibilities, they cautiously expressed themselves in parables. This procedure is indeed the more appropriate one in the circumstances. What takes place between light and dark-ness, what unites the opposites, has a share in both sides and can be judged just as well from the left as from the right, without our becom-ing any the wiser: indeed, we can only open up the opposition again. Here only the symbol helps, for, in accordance with its paradoxical nature, it represents the "tertium" that in logic does not exist, but which in reality is the living truth. So we should not begrudge Para-celsus and the alchemists their secret language: deeper insight into the problems of psychic development soon teaches us how much better it is to reserve judgment instead of prematurely announcing to all and sundry what's what. Of course we all have an understandable desire for crystal clarity, but we are apt to forget that in psychic matters we are dealing with processes of experience, that is, with transformations which should never be given hard and fast names if their living move-ment is not to petrify into something static. The protean mythologem and the shimmering symbol express the processes of the psyche far more trenchantly and, in the end, far more clearly than the clearest concept; for the symbol not only conveys a visualization of the process but—and this is perhaps just as important—it also brings a re-experi-encing of it, of that twilight which we can learn to understand only through inoffensive empathy, but which too much clarity only dispels. Thus the symbolic hints of marriage and exaltation in the "true May," when the heavenly flowers bloom and the secret of the inner man is made manifest, by the very choice and sound of the words convey a vision and experience of a climax whose significance could be ampli-fied only by the finest flights of the poets. But the clear and unam-biguous concept would find not the smallest place where it would fit. And yet something deeply significant has been said, for as Paracelsus rightly remarks: "When the heavenly marriage is accomplished, who will deny its superexcellent virtue?"

5

"THE MASS AND THE INDIVIDUATION PROCESS"

From *Psychology and Religion: West and East,*
CW 11, pars. 414–48

14   Looked at from the psychological standpoint, Christ, as the Original Man (Son of Man, second Adam, τέλειος ἄνθρωπος), represents a totality which surpasses and includes the ordinary man, and which corresponds to the total personality that transcends consciousness.[1] We have called this personality the "self." Just as, on the more archaic level of the Zosimos vision, the homunculus is transformed into pneuma and exalted, so the mystery of the Eucharist transforms the soul of the empirical man, who is only a part of himself, into his totality, symbolically expressed by Christ. In this sense, therefore, we can speak of the Mass as the *rite of the individuation process.*

15   Reflections of this kind can be found very early on in the old Christian writings, as for instance in the Acts of John, one of the most important of the apocryphal texts that have come down to us.[2] That part of the text with which we are concerned here begins with a description of a mystical "round dance" which Christ instituted before his crucifixion. He told his disciples to hold hands and form a ring, while he himself stood in the centre. As they moved round in a circle, Christ sang a song of praise, from which I would single out the following characteristic verses:[3]

> I will be saved and I will save, Amen.
> I will be loosed and I will loose,[4] Amen.
> I will be wounded and I will wound, Amen.

---

[1] Cf. my *Aion*, Ch. V.
[2] *The Apocryphal New Testament.* The Acts of John were probably written during the first half of the 2nd cent.
[3] Ibid., pp. 253f., modified.
[4] [Or: I will be freed and I will free.—TRANS.]

I will be begotten and I will beget, Amen.
I will eat and I will be eaten, Amen.

. . .

I will be thought, being wholly spirit, Amen.
I will be washed and I will wash, Amen.
Grace paces the round. I will blow the pipe. Dance
    the round all, Amen.

. . .

The Eight [*group of eight* ǒgdoad] sings praises with us, Amen.
The Twelve paces the round aloft, Amen.
To each and all it is given to dance, Amen.
Who joins not the dance mistakes the event, Amen.

. . .

I will be united and I will unite, Amen.

. . .

A lamp am I to you that perceive me, Amen.
A mirror am I to you that know me, Amen.
A door am I to you that knock on me, Amen.
A way am I to you the wayfarer.

Now as you respond to my dancing, behold yourself in me who speaks . . .

As you dance, ponder what I do, for yours is this human suffering which I will to suffer. For you would be powerless to understand your suffering had I not been sent to you as the Logos by the Father. . . . If you had understood suffering, you would have non-suffering. Learn to suffer, and you shall understand how not to suffer. . . . Understand the Word of Wisdom in me.[5]

416   I would like to interrupt the text here, as we have come to a natural break, and introduce a few psychological remarks. They will help us to understand some further passages that still have to be discussed. Although our text is obviously based on New Testament models, what strikes us most of all is its antithetical and paradoxical style, which has very little in common with the spirit of the Gospels. This feature only appears in a veiled way in the canonical writings, for instance in the parable of the unjust steward (Luke 16), in the Lord's Prayer ("Lead us not into temptation"), in Matthew 10:16 ("Be wise as serpents"), John 10:34 ("Ye are gods"), in the logion of the Codex Bezae to Luke 6:4,[6]

[5] Trans. based on James, pp. 253f., and that of Ralph Manheim from the German of Max Pulver, "Jesus' Round Dance and Crucifixion according to the Acts of St. John," in *The Mysteries*, pp. 179f.
[6] See James, p. 33.

in the apocryphal saying "Whoso is near unto me is near unto the fire," and so on. Echoes of the antithetical style can also be found in Matthew 10:26: ". . . . for nothing is covered that will not be revealed, or hidden that will not be known."

417   Paradox is a characteristic of the Gnostic writings. It does more justice to the *unknowable* than clarity can do, for uniformity of meaning robs the mystery of its darkness and sets it up as something that is *known.* That is a usurpation, and it leads the human intellect into hybris by pretending that it, the intellect, has got hold of the transcendent mystery by a cognitive act and has "grasped" it. The paradox therefore reflects a higher level of intellect and, by not forcibly representing the unknowable as known, gives a more faithful picture of the real state of affairs.

418   These antithetical predications show the amount of *reflection* that has gone into the hymn: it formulates the figure of our Lord in a series of paradoxes, as God and man, sacrificer and sacrificed. The latter formulation is important because the hymn was sung just before Jesus was arrested, that is, at about the moment when the synoptic gospels speak of the Last Supper and John—among other things—of the parable of the vine. John, significantly enough, does not mention the Last Supper, and in the Acts of John its place is taken by the "round dance." But the round table, like the round dance, stands for synthesis and union. In the Last Supper this takes the form of participation in the body and blood of Christ, i.e., there is an ingestion and assimilation of the Lord, and in the round dance there is a circular circumambulation round the Lord as the central point. Despite the outward difference of the symbols, they have a common meaning: Christ is taken into the midst of the disciples. But, although the two rites have this common basic meaning, the outward difference between them should not be overlooked. The classical Eucharistic feast follows the synoptic gospels, whereas the one in the Acts of John follows the Johannine pattern. One could almost say that it expresses, in a form borrowed from some pagan mystery feast, a more immediate relationship of the congregation to Christ, after the manner of the Johannine parable: "I am the vine, ye are the branches. He that abideth in me, and I in him, the same bringeth forth much fruit" (John 15:5). This close relationship is represented by the circle and central point: the two parts are indispensable to each other and equivalent. Since olden times the circle with a centre has been a symbol for the Deity, illustrating the wholeness of God incarnate: the single point in the centre and the series of points constituting the circumference. Ritual circumambulation often bases

itself quite consciously on the cosmic picture of the starry heavens revolving, on the "dance of the stars," an idea that is still preserved in the
comparison of the twelve disciples with the zodiacal constellations, as
also in the depictions of the zodiac that are sometimes found in
churches, in front of the altar or on the roof of the nave. Some such
picture may well have been at the back of the medieval ball-game of
pelota that was played in church by the bishop and his clergy.

419   At all events, the aim and effect of the solemn round dance is to
impress upon the mind the image of the circle and the centre and the
relation of each point along the periphery to that centre.[7] Psychologically this arrangement is equivalent to a mandala and is thus a symbol of the self,[8] the point of reference not only of the individual ego
but of all those who are of like mind or who are bound together by
fate. The self is not an ego but a supraordinate totality embracing the
conscious and the unconscious. But since the latter has no assignable
limits and in its deeper layers is of a collective nature, it cannot be
distinguished from that of another individual. As a result, it continually
creates that ubiquitous *participation mystique* which is the unity of many,
the *one* man in all men. This psychological fact forms the basis for the
archetype of the ἄνθρωπος, the Son of Man, the *homo maximus*, the *vir
unus*, purusha, etc.[9] Because the unconscious, in fact and by definition,
cannot be discriminated as such, the most we can hope to do is to infer
its nature from the empirical material. Certain unconscious contents
are undoubtedly personal and individual and cannot be attributed to
any other individual. But, besides these, there are numerous others

[7] Another idea of the kind is that every human being is a ray of sunlight. This image
occurs in the Spanish poet Jorge Guillén, *Cantico: Fe de Vida*, pp. 24–25 ("Más allá," VI):

> Where could I stray to, where?
> This point is my centre . . .
>
> With this earth and this ocean
> To rise to the infinite:
> One ray more of the sun.
>
> (Trans. by J. M. Cohen.)

[8] Cf. *Aion*, Ch. IV.

[9] The universality of this figure may explain why its epiphanies take so many different
forms. For instance, it is related in the Acts of John (James, p. 251) that Drusiana saw
the Lord once "in the likeness of John" and another time "in that of a youth." The
disciple James saw him as a child, but John as an adult. John saw him first as "a small
man and uncomely," and then again as one reaching to heaven (p. 251). Sometimes his
body felt "material and solid," but sometimes "the substance was immaterial and as if it
existed not at all" (p. 252).

that can be observed in almost identical form in many different individuals in no way connected with one another. These experiences suggest that the unconscious has a collective aspect. It is therefore difficult to understand how people today can still doubt the existence of a collective unconscious. After all, nobody would dream of regarding the instincts or human morphology as personal acquisitions or personal caprices. The unconscious is the universal mediator among men. It is in a sense the all-embracing One, or the one psychic substratum common to all. The alchemists knew it as their Mercurius and they called him the mediator in analogy to Christ.[10] Ecclesiastical doctrine says the same thing about Christ, and so, particularly, does our hymn. Its antithetical statements could, however, be interpreted as referring just as well to Mercurius, if not better. *referring to him selfas*

20   For instance, in the first verse, "I will be saved," it is not clear how far the Lord is able to say such a thing of himself, since he is the saviour (σωτήρ) par excellence. Mercurius, on the other hand, the helpful arcane substance of the alchemists, is the world-soul imprisoned in matter and, like the Original Man who fell into the embrace of Physics, is in need of salvation through the labours of the artifex. Mercurius is set free ("loosed") and redeemed; as *aqua permanens* he is also the classical solvent. "I will be wounded, and I will wound" is clearer: it refers to the wound in Christ's side and to the divisive sword. But Mercurius too, as the arcane substance, is divided or pierced through with the sword (*separatio* and *penetratio*), and wounds himself with the sword or *telum passionis*, the dart of love. The reference to Christ is less clear in the words "I will be begotten, and I will beget." The first statement refers essentially to him in so far as the Son was begotten by the Holy Ghost and not created, but the "begetting" is generally held to be the property of the Holy Ghost and not of Christ as such. It certainly remains a moot point whether Mercurius as the world-soul was begotten or created, but he is unquestionably "vivifying," and in his ithyphallic form as Hermes Kyllenios he is actually the symbol of generation. "Eating" as compared with "being eaten" is not exactly characteristic of Christ, but rather of the devouring dragon, the corrosive Mercurius, who, as the uroboros, also eats himself, like Zosimos's homunculus.

21   "I will be thought," if evangelical at all, is an exclusively Johannine, post-apostolic speculation concerning the nature of the Logos. Hermes was very early considered to be Nous and Logos, and Hermes Trisme-

---

[10] "The Spirit Mercurius," pt. 2, ch. 9.

gistus was actually the Nous of revelation. Mercurius, until well into the seventeenth century, was thought of as the *veritas* hidden in the human body, i.e., in matter, and this truth had to be known by meditation, or by *cogitatio*, reflection. Meditation is an idea that does not occur at all in the New Testament.[11] The *cogitatio* which might possibly correspond to it usually has a negative character and appears as the wicked *cogitatio cordis* of Genesis 6:5 (and 8:21): "Cuncta cogitatio cordis intenta ad malum" (DV: ". . . all the thought of their heart was bent upon evil at all times"; AV: ". . . every imagination of the thoughts of his heart . . ."). In I Peter 4:1 ἔννοια is given as "cogitatio" (DV: ". . . arm yourselves with the same intent"; AV: "same mind"; RSV: "same thought"). "Cogitare" has a more positive meaning in II Corinthians 10:7, where it really means to "bethink oneself," "remember by reflection": "hoc cogitet iterum apud se" ("τοῦτο λογιζέσθω πάλιν ἐφ᾽ ἑαυτοῦ"; DV: "let him reflect within himself"; AV: "let him of himself think, this again"; RSV: "let him remind himself"). But this positive thinking in us is of God (II Cor. 3:5: "non quod sufficientes simus cogitare aliquid a nobis, quasi ex nobis"; "οὐχ ὅτι ἀφ᾽ ἑαυτῶν ἱκανοί ἐσμεν λογίσασθαί τι ὡς ἐξ ἑαυτῶν, ἀλλ᾽ ἡ ἱκανότης ἡμῶν ἐκ τοῦ θεοῦ"; DV: "Not that we are sufficient of ourselves to think anything, as from ourselves, but our sufficiency is from God"). The only place where *cogitatio* has the character of a meditation culminating in enlightenment is Acts 10:19: "Petro autem cogitante de visione, dixit Spiritus ei" ("Τοῦ δὲ Πέτρου διενθυμουμένου περὶ τοῦ ὁράματος εἶπεν τὸ πνεῦμα αὐτῷ"; DV: "But while Peter was pondering over the vision, the spirit said to him . . .").

422   Thinking, in the first centuries of our era, was more the concern of the Gnostics than of the Church, for which reason the great Gnostics, such as Basilides and Valentinus, seem almost like Christian theologians with a bent for philosophy. With John's doctrine of the Logos, Christ came to be regarded simultaneously as the Nous and the object of human thought; the Greek text says literally: "Νοηθῆναι θέλω νοῦς ὢν ὅλος"[12] (I will be thought, being wholly spirit). Similarly, the Acts of Peter say of Christ: "Thou art perceived of the spirit only."[13]

423   The "washing" refers to the *purificatio*, or to baptism, and equally to

---

[11] "Haec meditare" (ταῦτα μελέτα) in I Tim. 4:15 has more the meaning of 'see to' or 'attend to' these things. [Both DV and AV have "meditate on these things," but RSV has "practise these duties."—TRANS.]

[12] Lipsius and Bonnet, eds., *Acta Apostolorum Apocrypha*, I, p. 197.

[13] James, p. 335.

the washing of the dead body. The latter idea lingered on into the eighteenth century, as the alchemical washing of the "black corpse," an *opus mulierum*. The object to be washed was the black *prima materia*: it, the washing material (*sapo sapientum!*), and the washer were—all three of them—the selfsame Mercurius in different guises. But whereas in alchemy the *nigredo* and sin were identical concepts (since both needed washing), in Christian Gnosticism there are only a few hints of Christ's possible identity with the darkness. The λούσασθαι ("I will be washed") in our text is one of them.

424   The "ogdoad," being a double quaternity, belongs to the symbolism of the mandala. It obviously represents the archetype of the round dance in the "supra-celestial place," since it sings in harmony. The same applies to the number Twelve, the zodiacal archetype of the twelve disciples, a cosmic idea that still echoes in Dante's *Paradiso*, where the saints form shining constellations.

425   Anyone who does not join in the dance, who does not make the circumambulation of the centre (Christ and Anthropos), is smitten with blindness and sees nothing. What is described here as an outward event is really a symbol for the inward turning towards the centre in each of the disciples, towards the archetype of man, towards the self— for the dance can hardly be understood as an historical event. It should be understood, rather, as a sort of paraphrase of the Eucharist, an amplifying symbol that renders the mystery more assimilable to con- sciousness, and it must therefore be interpreted as a psychic phenome- non. It is an act of conscious realization on a higher level, establishing a connection between the consciousness of the individual and the su- praordinate symbol of totality.

426   The "Acts of Peter" says of Christ:

> Thou art unto me father, thou my mother, thou my brother, thou my friend, thou my bondsman, thou my steward. Thou art All and All is in thee; thou Art, and there is naught else that is save thee only.
>
> Unto him therefore do ye also, brethren, flee, and if ye learn that in him alone ye exist, ye shall obtain those things whereof he saith unto you: "Which neither eye hath seen nor ear heard, neither have they entered into the heart of man."[14]

427   The words "I will be united" must be understood in this sense, as meaning that subjective consciousness is united with an objective cen- tre, thus producing the unity of God and man represented by Christ.

[14] James, p. 335.

The self is brought into actuality through the concentration of the many upon the centre, and the self wants this concentration. It is the subject and the object of the process. Therefore it is a "lamp" to those who "perceive" it. Its light is invisible if it is not perceived; it might just as well not exist. It is as dependent on being perceived as the act of perception is on light. This brings out once again the paradoxical subject-object nature of the unknowable. Christ, or the self, is a "mirror": on the one hand it reflects the subjective consciousness of the disciple, making it visible to him, and on the other hand it "knows" Christ, that is to say it does not merely reflect the empirical man, it also shows him as a (transcendental) whole. And, just as a "door" opens to one who "knocks" on it, or a "way" opens out to the wayfarer who seeks it, so, when you relate to your own (transcendental) centre, you initiate a process of conscious development which leads to oneness and wholeness. You no longer see yourself as an isolated point on the periphery, but as the One in the centre. Only subjective consciousness is isolated; when it relates to its centre it is integrated into wholeness. Whoever joins in the dance sees himself in the reflecting centre, and his suffering is the suffering which the One who stands in the centre "wills to suffer." The paradoxical identity and difference of ego and self could hardly be formulated more trenchantly.

428   As the text says, you would not be able to understand what you suffer unless there were that Archimedean point outside, the objective standpoint of the self, from which the ego can be seen as a phenomenon. Without the objectivation of the self the ego would remain caught in hopeless subjectivity and would only gyrate round itself. But if you can see and understand your suffering without being subjectively involved, then, because of your altered standpoint, you also understand "how not to suffer," for you have reached a place beyond all involvements ("you have me as a bed, rest upon me"). This is an unexpectedly psychological formulation of the Christian idea of overcoming the world, though with a Docetist twist to it: "Who I am, you shall know when I depart. What now I am seen to be, I am not."[15] These statements are clarified by a vision in which John sees the Lord "standing in the midst of the cave and illuminating it." He says to John:

429   ) John, for the multitude below in Jerusalem I am being crucified and pierced with lances and staves, and vinegar and gall are given me to drink. But to you I speak, and what I say, hear: I put it into your mind to go up on this mountain, that you might hear those things which a disciple must learn from his master

[15] Ibid., p. 254.

and a man from his God. And with these words he showed me a cross of light, and about the cross a great multitude that had no form [μίαν μορφὴν μὴ ἔχοντα], and in the cross there was one form and one appearance. And above [ἐπάνω], the cross I saw the Lord himself, and he had no outward shape [σχῆμα], but only a voice, and a voice not such as we knew, but one sweet and kind and truly [that] of [a] God, which spoke to me: John, one man must hear this from me, for I require one that shall hear. For your sakes this cross of light was named by me now Logos, now, Nous, now Jesus, now Christ, now Door, now Way, now Bread, now Seed [σπόρος], now Resurrection, now Son, now Father, now Pneuma, now Life, now Truth, now Faith [πίστις], now Grace. So is it called for men; but in itself and in its essence, is spoken of to you, it is the Boundary of all things, and the composing of things unstable,[16] and the harmony of wisdom, and the wisdom that is in harmony. For there are [places] of the right and of the left, Powers, Authorities, Archons, Daemons, Workings, Threatenings, Wraths, Devils, Satan, and the Nether Root whence proceeded the nature of whatever comes to be. And so it is this cross which joined all things together through the Word, and which separated the things that are from those that are below, and which caused all things to flow forth from the One.

But this is not the cross of wood which you will see when you go down from here; neither am I he that is on the cross, whom now you do not see, but only hear his voice. I passed for that which I am not, for I am not what I was to many others. But what they will say of me is vile and not worthy of me. Since, then, the place of rest is neither seen nor named, how much less will they see and name me, their Lord!

Now the formless multitude about the cross is of the lower nature. And if those whom you see in the cross have not one form, then not all the parts of him who descended have yet been recollected. But when the nature of man has been taken up and a generation of men that obey my voice draws near to me, he that now hears me shall be united with them and shall no longer be what he now is, but shall stand above them, as I do now. For so long as you call not yourself mine, I am not what I was. But if you understand me, you shall be in your understanding as I am, and I shall be what I was when I have you with me. For this you are through me. . . .

Behold, what you are, I have shown you. But what I am, I alone know, and no man else. Therefore let me have what is mine, but behold what is thine through me. And behold me truly, not as I have said I am, but as you, being akin to me, know me.[17]

---

[16] Ἀνάγγη βιάβα uncertain.
[17] Based on James, pp. 254ff., and the author's modified version of Hennecke, ed., Neu-testamentliche Apokryphen, pp. 186ff.

430   Our text throws some doubt on the traditional view of Docetism. Though it is perfectly clear from the texts that Christ only seemed to have a body, which only secured to suffer, this is Docetism at its grossest. The Acts of John are more subtle, and the argument used is almost epistemological: the historical facts are real enough, but they reveal no more than is intelligible to the senses of the ordinary man. Yet even for the knower of divine secrets the act of crucifixion is a mystery, a symbol that expresses a parallel psychic event in the beholder. In the language of Plato it is an event which occurs in a "supracelestial place," i.e., on a "mountain" and in a "cave" where a cross of light is set up, its many synonyms signifying that it has many aspects and many meanings. It expresses the unknowable nature of the "Lord," the supraordinate personality and τέλειος ἄνθρωπος, and since it is a quaternity, a whole divided into four parts, it is the classic symbol of the self.

431   Understood in this sense, the Docetism of the Acts of John appears more as a completion of the historical event than a devaluation of it. It is not surprising that the common people should have failed to appreciate its subtlety, though it is plain enough from a psychological point of view. On the other hand, the educated public of those days were by no means unfamiliar with the parallelism of earthly and metaphysical happenings, only it was not clear to them that their visionary symbols were not necessarily metaphysical realities but were perceptions of intrapsychic or subliminal processes that I have called "phenomena of assimilation." The contemplation of Christ's sacrificial death in its traditional form and cosmic significance constellated analogous psychic processes which in their turn gave rise to a wealth of symbols, as I have shown elsewhere.[18] This is, quite obviously, what has happened here, and it took the form of a visible split between the historical event down below on earth, as perceived by the senses, and its ideal, visionary reflection on high, the cross appearing on the one hand as a wooden instrument of torture and on the other as a glorious symbol. Evidently the centre of gravity has shifted to the ideal event, with the result that the psychic process is involuntarily given the greater importance. Although the emphasis on the pneuma detracts from the meaning of the concrete event in a rather one-sided and debatable way, it cannot be dismissed as superfluous, since a concrete event by itself can never create meaning, but is largely dependent for this on the manner in which it is understood. Interpretation is necessary before the meaning of a thing can be grasped. The naked facts by themselves "mean" nothing.

[18] Cf. Aion.

So one cannot assert that the Gnostic attempts at interpretation were entirely lacking in merit, even though it went far beyond the framework of early Christian tradition. One could even venture to assert that it was already implicit in that tradition, since the cross and the crucified are practically synonymous in the language of the New Testament.[19]

432   The text shows the cross as the antithesis of the formless multitude: it is, or it has, "form" and its meaning is that of a central point defined by the crossing of two straight lines. It is identical with the Kyrios (Lord) and the Logos, with Jesus and with Christ. How John could "see" the Lord above the cross, when the Lord is described as having no "outward shape," must remain a mystery. He only hears an explanatory voice, and this may indicate that the cross of light is only a visualization of the unknowable, whose voice can be heard apart from the cross. This seems to be confirmed by the remark that the cross was named Logos and so on "for your sakes."

433   The cross signifies order as opposed to the disorderly chaos of the formless multitude. It is, in fact, one of the prime symbols of order, as I have shown elsewhere. In the domain of psychological processes it functions as an organizing centre, and in states of psychic disorder[20] caused by an invasion of unconscious contents it appears as a mandala divided into four. No doubt this was a frequent phenomenon in early Christian times, and not only in Gnostic circles.[21] Gnostic introspection could hardly fail, therefore, to perceive the numinosity of this archetype and be duly impressed by it. For the Gnostics the cross had exactly the same function that the atman or Self has always had for the East. This realization is one of the central experiences of Gnosticism.

434   The definition of the cross or centre as διορισμός, the "boundary" of all things, is exceedingly original, for it suggests that the limits of the universe are not to be found in a nonexistent periphery but in its centre. There alone lies the possibility of transcending this world. All instability culminates in that which is unchanging and quiescent, and in the self all disharmonies are resolved in the "harmony of wisdom."

[19] The quaternity, earlier hinted at in the vision of Ezekiel, is patently manifest in the pre-Christian Book of Enoch. (Cf. "Answer to Job," below, pars. 662ff.) In the Apocalypse of Sophonias [Zephaniah], Christ appears surrounded by a garland of doves (Stern, "Die koptische Apokalypse des Sophonias," p. 124). Cf. also the mosaic of St. Felix at Nola, showing a cross surrounded by doves. There is another in San Clemente, Rome (Wickhoff, "Das Apsismosaik in der Basilica des H. Felix zu Nola," pp. 158ff.; and Rossi, *Musaici Cristiani delle Chiese di Roma anteriori al secolo XV*, pl. XXIX).
[20] Symbolized by the formless multitude.
[21] Cf. "speaking with tongues" and glossolalia.

435   As the centre symbolizes the idea of totality and finality, it is quite appropriate that the text should suddenly start speaking of the dichotomy of the universe, polarized into right and left, brightness and darkness, heaven and the "nether root," the *omnium genetrix*. This is a clear reminder that everything is contained in the centre and that, as a result, the Lord (i.e., the cross) unites and composes all things and is therefore "nirdvanda," free from the opposites, in conformity with Eastern ideas and also with the psychology of this archetypal symbol. The Gnostic Christ-figure and the cross are counterparts of the typical mandalas spontaneously produced by the unconscious. They are *natural symbols* and they differ fundamentally from the dogmatic figure of Christ, in whom all trace of darkness is expressly lacking.

436   In this connection mention should be made of Peter's valedictory words, which he spoke during his martyrdom (he was crucified upside down, at his own request):

O name of the cross, hidden mystery! O grace ineffable that is pronounced in the name of the cross! O nature of man, that cannot be separated from God! O love unspeakable and indivisible, that cannot be shown forth by unclean lips! I grasp thee now, I that am at the end of my earthly course. I will declare thee as thou art, I will not keep silent the mystery of the cross which was once shut and hidden from my soul. You that hope in Christ, let not the cross be for you that which appears; for it is another thing, and different from that which appears, this suffering which is in accordance with Christ's. And now above all, because you that can hear are able to hear it of me, who am at the last and farewell hour of my life, hearken: separate your souls from everything that is of the senses, from everything that appears to be but in truth is not. Lock your eyes, close your ears, shun those happenings which are seen! Then you shall perceive that which was done to Christ, and the whole mystery of your salvation. . . .

Learn the mystery of all nature and the beginning of all things, as it was. For the first man, of whose race I bear the likeness, fell head downwards, and showed forth a manner of birth such as had not existed till then, for it was dead, having no motion. And being pulled downwards, and having also cast his origin upon the earth, he established the whole disposition of things; for, being hanged up in the manner appointed, he showed forth the things of the right as those of the left, and the things of the left as those of the right, and changed about all the marks of their nature, so that things that were not fair were perceived to be fair, and those that were in truth evil were perceived to be good. Wherefore the Lord says in a mystery: "Except ye make the things of the right as those of the left, and those of the left as those of the right, and those that

144

are above as those below, and those that are behind as those that are before, ye shall not have knowledge of the kingdom."

This understanding have I brought you, and the figure in which you now see me hanging is the representation of that first man who came to birth.

437   In this passage, too, the symbolical interpretation of the cross is coupled with the problem of opposites, first in the unusual idea that the creation of the first man caused everything to be turned upside down, and then in the attempt to unite the opposites by identifying them with one another. A further point of significance is that Peter, crucified head downwards, is identical not only with the first created man, but with the cross:

For what else is Christ but the word, the sound of God? So the word is this upright beam on which I am crucified; and the sound is the beam which crosses it, the nature of man; but the nail which holds the centre of the cross-beam to the upright is man's conversion and repentance (μετάνοια).[22]

438   In the light of these passages it can hardly be said that the author of the Acts of John—presumably a Gnostic—has drawn the necessary conclusions from his premises or that their full implications have become clear to him. On the contrary, one gets the impression that the light has swallowed up everything dark. Just as the enlightening vision appears high above the actual scene of crucifixion, so, for John, the enlightened one stands high above the formless multitude. The text says: "Therefore care not for the many, and despise those that are outside the mystery!"[23] This overweening attitude arises from an inflation caused by the fact that the enlightened John has identified with his own light and confused his ego with the self. Therefore he feels superior to the darkness in him. He forgets that light only has a meaning when it illuminates something dark and that his enlightenment is no good to him unless it helps him to recognize his own darkness. If the powers of the left are as real as those of the right, then their union can only produce a third thing that shares the nature of both. Opposites unite in a new energy potential: the "third" that arises out of their union is a figure "free from the opposites," beyond all moral categories. This conclusion would have been too advanced for the Gnostics. Recognizing the danger of Gnostic irrealism, the Church, more practical in these matters, has always insisted on the concretism of the historical events despite the fact that the original New Testament texts pre-

[22] Based on James, pp. 334f.
[23] Ibid., p. 255.

dict the ultimate deification of man in a manner strangely reminiscent of the words of the serpent in the Garden of Eden: "Ye shall be as gods."[24] Nevertheless, there was some justification for postponing the elevation of man's status until after death, as this avoided the danger of Gnostic inflation.[25]

439   Had the Gnostic not identified with the self, he would have been bound to see how much darkness was in him—a realization that comes more naturally to modern man but causes him no less difficulties. Indeed, he is far more likely to assume that he himself is wholly of the devil than to believe that God could ever indulge in paradoxical statements. For all the ill consequences of his fatal inflation, the Gnostic did, however, gain an insight into religion, or into the psychology of religion, from which we can still learn a thing or two today. He looked deep into the background of Christianity and hence into its future developments. This he could do because his intimate connection with pagan Gnosis made him an "assimilator" that helped to integrate the Christian message into the spirit of the times.

440   The extraordinary number of synonyms piled on top of one another in an attempt to define the cross have their analogy in the Naassene and Peratic symbols of Hippolytus, all pointing to this one centre. It is the ἕν τὸ πᾶν of alchemy, which is on the one hand the heart and governing principle of the macrocosm, and on the other hand its reflection in a point, in a microcosm such as man has always been thought to be. He is of the same essence as the universe, and his own mid-point is its centre. This inner experience, shared by Gnostics, alchemists, and mystics alike, has to do with the nature of the unconscious—one could even say that it *is* the experience of the unconscious; for the unconscious, though its objective existence and its influence on consciousness cannot be doubted, is in itself undifferentiable and therefore unknowable. Hypothetical germs of differentiation may be conjectured to exist in it, but their existence cannot be proved, because everything appears to be in a state of mutual contamination. The unconscious gives the impression of multiplicity and unity at once. However overwhelmed we may be by the vast quantity of things differentiated in space and time, we know from the world of the senses that the validity of its laws extends to immense distances. We therefore believe that it is one and the same universe throughout, in its smallest

---

[24] Genesis 3:5.
[25] The possibility of inflation was brought very close indeed by Christ's words: "Ye are gods" (John 10:34).

part as in its greatest. On the other hand the intellect always tries to discern differences, because it cannot discriminate without them. Consequently the unity of the cosmos remains, for it, a somewhat nebulous postulate which it doesn't rightly know what to do with. But as soon as introspection starts penetrating into the psychic background it comes up against the unconscious, which, unlike consciousness, shows only the barest traces of any definite contents, surprising the investigator at every turn with a confusing medley of relationships, parallels, contaminations, and identifications. Although he is forced, for epistemological reasons, to postulate an indefinite number of distinct and separate archetypes, yet he is constantly overcome by doubt as to how far they are really distinguishable from one another. They overlap to such a degree and have such a capacity for combination that all attempts to isolate them conceptually must appear hopeless. In addition the unconscious, in sharpest contrast to consciousness and its contents, has a tendency to personify itself in a uniform way, just as if it possessed only one shape or one voice. Because of this peculiarity, the unconscious conveys an experience of unity, to which are due all those qualities enumerated by the Gnostics and alchemists, and a lot more besides.

141   As can plainly be seen from Gnosticism and other spiritual movements of the kind, people are naïvely inclined to take all the manifestations of the unconscious at their face value and to believe that in them the essence of the world itself, the ultimate truth, has been unveiled. This assumption does not seem to me quite as unwarranted as it may look at first sight, because the spontaneous utterances of the unconscious do after all reveal a psyche which is not identical with consciousness and which is, at times, greatly at variance with it. These utterances occur as a natural psychic activity that can neither be learnt nor controlled by the will. The manifestation of the unconscious is therefore a revelation of the unknown in man. We have only to disregard the dependence of dream language on environment and substitute "eagle" for "aeroplane," "dragon" for "automobile" or "train," "snake-bite" for "injection," and so forth, in order to arrive at the more universal and more fundamental language of mythology. This gives us access to the primordial images that underlie all thinking and have a considerable influence even on our scientific ideas.[26]

142   In these archetypal forms, something, presumably, is expressing itself that must in some way be connected with the mysterious operation of a natural psyche—in other words, with a cosmic factor of the first order.

[26] Cf. Pauli, "The Influence of Archetypal Ideas on Kepler's Scientific Theories."

To save the honour of the objective psyche, which the contemporary hypertrophy of consciousness has done so much to depreciate, I must again emphasize that without the psyche we could not establish the existence of any world at all, let alone know it. But, judging by all we do know, it is certain that the original psyche possesses no consciousness of itself. This only comes in the course of development, a development that falls mostly within the historical epoch.[27] Even today we know of primitive tribes whose level of consciousness is not so far removed from the darkness of the primordial psyche, and numerous vestiges of this state can still be found among civilized people. It is even probable, in view of its potentialities for further differentiation, that our modern consciousness is still on a relatively low level. Nevertheless, its development so far has made it emancipated enough to forget its dependence on the unconscious psyche. It is not a little proud of this emancipation, but it overlooks the fact that although it has apparently got rid of the unconscious it has become the victim of its own verbal concepts. The devil is cast out with Beelzebub. Our dependence on words is so strong that a philosophical brand of "existentialism" had to restore the balance by pointing to a reality that exists in spite of words—at considerable risk, however, of concepts such as "existence," "existential," etc. turning into more words which delude us into thinking that we have caught a reality. One can be—and is—just as dependent on words as on the unconscious. Man's advance towards the Logos was a great achievement, but he must pay for it with loss of instinct and loss of reality to the degree that he remains in primitive dependence on mere words. Because words are substitutes for things, which of course they cannot be in reality, they take on intensified forms, become eccentric, outlandish, stupendous, swell up into what schizophrenic patients call "power words." A primitive word-magic develops, and one is inordinately impressed by it because anything out of the ordinary is felt to be especially profound and significant. Gnosticism in particular affords some very instructive examples of this. Neologisms tend not only to hypostatize themselves to an amazing degree, but actually to replace the reality they were originally intended to express.

443   This rupture of the link with the unconscious and our submission to the tyranny of words have one great disadvantage: the conscious mind becomes more and more the victim of its own discriminating activity,

[27] Cf. the remarkable account of developing consciousness in an ancient Egyptian text, translated, with commentary, by Jacobsohn, entitled "Das Gespräch eines Lebensmüden mit seinem Ba."

the picture we have of the world gets broken down into countless particulars, and the original feeling of unity, which was integrally connected with the unity of the unconscious psyche, is lost. This feeling of unity, in the form of the correspondence theory and the sympathy of all things, dominated philosophy until well into the seventeenth century and is now, after a long period of oblivion, looming up again on the scientific horizon, thanks to the discoveries made by the psychology of the unconscious and by parapsychology. The manner in which the unconscious forcibly obtrudes upon the conscious by means of neurotic disturbances is not only reminiscent of contemporary political and social conditions but even appears as an accompanying phenomenon. In both cases there is an analogous dissociation: in the one case a splitting of the world's consciousness by an "iron curtain," and in the other a splitting of the individual personality. This dissociation extends throughout the entire world, so that a psychological split runs through vast numbers of individuals who, in their totality, call forth the corresponding mass phenomena. In the West it was chiefly the mass factor, and in the East technology, that undermined the old hierarchies. The cause of this development lay principally in the economic and psychological uprootedness of the industrial masses, which in turn was caused by the rapid technological advance. But technology, it is obvious, is based on a specifically rationalistic differentiation of consciousness which tends to repress all irrational psychic factors. Hence there arises, in the individual and nation alike, an unconscious counterposition which in time grows strong enough to burst out into open conflict.

244   The same situation in reverse was played out on a smaller scale and on a spiritual plane during the first centuries of our era, when the spiritual disorientation of the Roman world was compensated by the irruption of Christianity. Naturally, in order to survive, Christianity had to defend itself not only against its enemies but also against the excessive pretensions of some of its adherents, including those of the Gnostics. Increasingly it had to rationalize its doctrines in order to stem the flood of irrationality. This led, over the centuries, to that strange marriage of the originally irrational Christian message with human reason, which is so characteristic of the Western mentality. But to the degree that reason gradually gained the upper hand, the intellect asserted itself and demanded autonomy. And just as the intellect subjugated the psyche, so also it subjugated Nature and begat on her an age of scientific technology that left less and less room for the natural and irrational man. Thus the foundations were laid for an inner opposition which today threatens the world with chaos. To make the reversal com-

plete, all the powers of the underworld now hide behind reason and intellect, and under the mask of rationalistic ideology a stubborn faith seeks to impose itself by fire and sword, vying with the darkest aspects of a church militant. By a strange enantiodromia,[28] the Christian spirit of the West has become the defender of the irrational, since, in spite of having fathered rationalism and intellectualism, it has not succumbed to them so far as to give up its belief in the rights of man, and especially the freedom of the individual. But this freedom guarantees a recognition of the irrational principle, despite the lurking danger of chaotic individualism. By appealing to the eternal rights of man, faith binds itself inalienably to a higher order, not only on account of the historical fact that Christ has proved to be an ordering factor for many hundreds of years, but also because the self effectively compensates chaotic conditions no matter by what name it is known: for the self is the Anthropos above and beyond this world, and in him is contained the freedom and dignity of the individual man. From this point of view, disparagement and vilification of Gnosticism are an anachronism. Its obviously psychological symbolism could serve many people today as a bridge to a more living appreciation of Christian tradition.

445   These historical changes have to be borne in mind if we wish to understand the Gnostic figure of Christ, because the sayings in the Acts of John concerning the nature of the Lord only become intelligible when we interpret them as expressing an experience of the original unity as contrasted with the formless multiplicity of conscious contents. This Gnostic Christ, of whom we hear hints even in the Gospel according to St. John, symbolizes man's original unity and exalts it as the saving goal of his development. By "composing the unstable," by bringing order into chaos, by resolving disharmonies and centering upon the mid-point, thus setting a "boundary" to the multitude and focusing attention upon the cross, consciousness is reunited with the unconscious, the unconscious man is made one with his centre, which is also the centre of the universe, and in this wise the goal of man's salvation and exaltation is reached.

446   Right as this intuition may be, it is also exceedingly dangerous, for it presupposes a coherent ego-consciousness capable of resisting the temptation to identify with the self. Such an ego-consciousness seems to be comparatively rare, as history shows; usually the ego identifies with the inner Christ, and the danger is increased by an *imitatio Christi*

---

[28] [Cf. *Psychological Types*, Def. 18, and *Two Essays on Analytical Psychology*, par. 111.—EDITORS.]

falsely understood. The result is inflation, of which our text affords eloquent proof. In order to exorcise this danger, the Church has not made too much of the "Christ within," but has made all it possibly could of the Christ whom we "have seen, heard, and touched with hands," in other words, with the historical event "below in Jerusalem." This is a wise attitude, which takes realistic account of the primitiveness of man's consciousness, then as now. For the less mindful it is of the unconscious, the greater becomes the danger of its identification with the latter, and the greater, therefore, the danger of inflation, which, as we have experienced to our cost, can seize upon whole nations like a psychic epidemic. If Christ is to be "real" for this relatively primitive consciousness, then he can be so only as an historical figure and a metaphysical entity, but not as a psychic centre in all too perilous proximity to a human ego. The Gnostic development, supported by scriptural authority, pushed so far ahead that Christ was clearly recognized as an inner, psychic fact. This also entailed the relativity of the Christ-figure, as expressively formulated in our text: "For so long as you call not yourself mine, I am not what I was. . . . I shall be what I was when I have you with me." From this it follows unmistakably that although Christ was whole once upon a time, that is, before time and consciousness began, he either lost this wholeness or gave it away to mankind[29] and can only get it back again through man's integration. His wholeness depends on man: "You shall be in your understanding as I am"—this ineluctable conclusion shows the danger very clearly. The ego is dissolved in the self; unbeknown to itself, and with all its inadequacy and darkness, it has become a god and deems itself superior to its unenlightened fellows. It has identified with its own conception of the "higher man," quite regardless of the fact that this figure consists of "Places of the right and left, Authorities, Archons, Daemons" etc., and the devil himself. A figure like this is simply not to be comprehended, an awesome mystery with which one had better not identify if one has any sense. It is sufficient to know that such a mystery exists and that somewhere man can feel its presence, but he should take care not to confuse his ego with it. On the contrary, the confrontation with his own darkness should not only warn him against identification but should inspire him with salutary terror on beholding just what he is

---

[29] This view may be implicit in the *kenosis* passage (Philippians 2:5f.): "Have this mind in you which was also in Christ Jesus, who though he was by nature God, did not consider being equal to God a thing to be clung to, but emptied himself [ἐκένωσεν, *exinanivit*], taking the nature of a slave and being made like unto man" (DV).

capable of becoming. He cannot conquer the tremendous polarity of his nature on his own resources; he can only do so through the terrifying experience of a psychic process that is independent of him, that works *him* rather than he *it*.

447   If such a process exists at all, then it is something that can be experienced. My own personal experience, going back over several decades and garnered from many individuals, and the experience of many other doctors and psychologists, not to mention the statements—terminologically different, but essentially the same—of all the great religions,[30] all confirm the existence of a compensatory ordering factor which is independent of the ego and whose nature transcends consciousness. The existence of such a factor is no more miraculous, in itself, than the orderliness of radium decay, or the attunement of a virus to the anatomy and physiology of human beings,[31] or the symbiosis of plants and animals. What is miraculous in the extreme is that man can have conscious, reflective knowledge of these hidden processes, while animals, plants, and inorganic bodies seemingly lack it. Presumably it would also be an ecstatic experience for a radium atom to know that the time of its decay is exactly determined, or for the butterfly to recognize that the flower has made all the necessary provisions for its propagation.

448   The numinous experience of the individuation process is, on the archaic level, the prerogative of shamans and medicine men; later, of the physician, prophet, and priest; and finally, at the civilized stage, of philosophy and religion. The shaman's experience of sickness, torture, death, and regeneration implies, at a higher level, the idea of being made whole through sacrifice, of being changed by transubstantiation and exalted to the pneumatic man—in a word, of apotheosis. The Mass is the summation and quintessence of a development which began many thousands of years ago and, with the progressive broadening and deepening of consciousness, gradually made the isolated experience of specifically gifted individuals the common property of a larger group. The underlying psychic process remained, of course, hidden from view and was dramatized in the form of suitable "mysteries" and "sacraments," these being reinforced by religious teachings, exercises, meditations, and acts of sacrifice which plunge the celebrant so deeply

---

[30] Including shamanism, whose widespread phenomenology anticipates the alchemist's individuation symbolism on an archaic level. For a comprehensive account see Eliade, *Shamanism*.
[31] Cf. Portmann, "Die Bedeutung der Bilder in der lebendigen Energiewandlung."

into the sphere of the mystery that he is able to become conscious of his intimate connection with the mythic happenings. Thus, in ancient Egypt, we see how the experience of "Osirification,"[32] originally the prerogative of the Pharaohs, gradually passed to the aristocracy and finally, towards the end of the Old Kingdom, to the single individual as well. Similarly, the mystery religions of the Greeks, originally esoteric and not talked about, broadened out into collective experience, and at the time of the Caesars it was considered a regular sport for Roman tourists to get themselves initiated into foreign mysteries. Christianity, after some hesitation, went a step further and made celebration of the mysteries a public institution, for, as we know, it was especially concerned to introduce as many people as possible to the experience of the mystery. So, sooner or later, the individual could not fail to become conscious of his own transformation and of the necessary psychological conditions for this, such as confession and repentance of sin. The ground was prepared for the realization that, in the mystery of transubstantiation, it was not so much a question of magical influence as of psychological processes—a realization for which the alchemists had already paved the way by putting their *opus operatum* at least on a level with the ecclesiastical mystery, and even attributing to it a cosmic significance since, by its means, the divine world-soul could be liberated from imprisonment in matter. As I think I have shown, the "philosophical" side of alchemy is nothing less than a symbolic anticipation of certain psychological insights, and these—to judge by the example of Gerhard Dorn—were pretty far advanced by the end of the sixteenth century.[33] Only our intellectualized age could have been so deluded as to see in alchemy nothing but an abortive attempt at chemistry, and in the interpretative methods of modern psychology a mere "psychologizing," i.e., annihilation, of the mystery. Just as the alchemists knew that the production of their stone was a miracle that could only happen "Deo concedente," so the modern psychologist is aware that he can produce no more than a description, couched in scientific symbols, of a psychic process whose real nature transcends consciousness just as much as does the mystery of life or of matter. At no point has he explained the mystery itself, thereby causing it to fade. He has merely, in accordance with the spirit of Christian tradition, brought it a little nearer to individual consciousness, using the empirical material to set forth the individuation process and show it as an actual and experi-

---

[32] Cf. Neumann, *The Origins and History of Consciousness*, pp. 220ff.
[33] *Aion*, pp. 162ff.

enceable fact. To treat a metaphysical statement as a psychic process is not to say that it is "merely psychic," as my critics assert—in the fond belief that the word "psychic" postulates something known. It does not seem to have occurred to people that when we say "psyche" we are alluding to the densest darkness it is possible to imagine. The ethics of the researcher require him to admit where his knowledge comes to an end. This end is the beginning of true wisdom.

6

"SYMBOLISM OF THE CROSS"
From *Dream Analysis*, pp. 362–66

Dr. Barrett: In man's tendency to anthropomorphize all his conceptions of life, he makes his own figure the form of the cross.

Dr. Jung: So you would say the cross is man as the source of mana? Do you mean something like this? Man certainly experiences himself as a creator in sexuality. Sex is the union of two different principles, the sexual act is the meeting of two opposing directions. The association of the cross and sexuality is shown by the phallic crosses which Dr. Barrett has mentioned, so in as much as life springs from sex, man feels himself a life-giver through sexuality.

Another source of life fertility is the earth. To early primitive man, the earth was flat, and they saw its horizon as a circle. In the more advanced civilization of the North American Indians, the earth is represented as a circle, and they put in the four cardinal points. The observer is naturally always in the centre of that circle or cross. Thus one arrives again at the symbol of the cross within the circle. If the figure of man represents a cross, the circle around it most probably represents the horizon. Or it might also be that it is a magic circle drawn around man as a mana figure. Mana figures are always in a way taboo. I fancy that in some such way the so-called sun-wheel originated. The <u>mana</u> of man, of the earth, of the tree and so on—life in every form—was represented by the cross and the circle, apparently on account of the similarity of the form of man and the tree with a cross, and concerning the earth, on account of the partition of the horizon. (In astrology, the sign of earth is ♁ and of Venus ♀.)

But that would be explaining the symbol through its objectivation, and my question is, why is the life-giver represented by the cross? It not only symbolizes the sun, it symbolizes sex, or the points of the horizon, or the human form, but they do not all necessarily suggest the cross. It is not very clear why it should stand for all these mana objects. Take peculiar electric phenomena, like lightning, polar lights, and so on, they all have to do with electricity, but what is electricity? The cross designates the essence of all these objects, as electricity designates the essence, the force or power in all its different manifestations.

Dr. Barrett: Was there an intuitive idea that the cross would be the right symbol for all this?

Mrs. Baynes: Do you not have to go back to the original vision of the primitive man, to intuition?

Dr. Jung: Yes, it seems to have been one of the most original intuitions of man that the right form to express the source of mana would be the cross. Plato says in the *Timaeus* that when the Demiourgos created the world, he divided it into four parts, and then he sewed them together again, four seams in the form of the cross.[1] Here the origin of the world is connected with the sign of the cross, the original act of giving life. Pythagoras, who was earlier than Plato, says that the fundamental number is four, the *tetraktys*, which was considered by the Pythagoreans as a mystical entity. In Egypt, the Eight was the most sacred company of the gods, the Ogdoads. There the origin of the world is watched by the *four* monkeys and the *four* toads. Horus, the rising sun, has four sons. One finds the four in the paradise legend where four rivers flowed out of Eden[2]—the source of life. So since four is one of the primitive numbers that were first geometrically visualized in a prehistoric age, when abstract counting was not invented, people probably saw the cross in the form of four: ∵ or: ∷. This figure suggests the typical crosses: + and ×. So the number four and the cross are probably identical.

My idea is that the symbol of the cross does not originate from any *external* form, but from an *endopsychic vision* of the primitive man. The peculiar nature of the vision expresses, as nearly as man can grasp it, the essential quality of life's energy as it appeared not only in him but

---

[1] *Timaeus* 36B. See "A Psychological Approach to the Dogma of the Trinity" (1940), CW 11, par. 190 and the related diagram, and *Symbols of Transformation*, pars. 404, 406 (as in 1912 edn.).

[2] In *Aion* (1951), CW 9 ii, par. 353, the four rivers are the Gihon, Pison, Hiddekel, and Euphrates.

also in all his objects. It is an absolutely irrational fact to me that vital energy should have anything to do with a cross or with the number four. I don't know why it is perceived in such a form; I only know that the cross has always meant mana or lifepower.

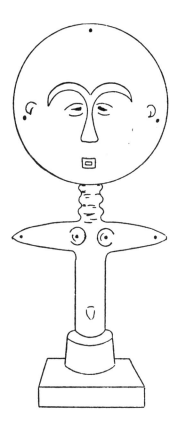

Wooden figure of a god.
From Accra, Gold Coast [present-day Ghana]

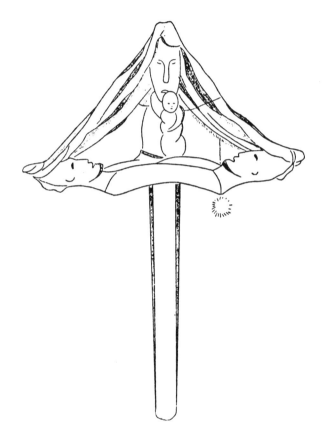

Ceremonial sword of wood.
From the Batak, Sumatra [Indonesia]

Mask (wood). Opaina Indians, Northwestern Brazil

Cap worn to influence the
spirits of the rice.
Celebes [Indonesia]

Design on a clay vessel.
Egypt, 1580–1350 B.C.

7

MYTHIC FEATURES IN CHRISTIAN DOCTRINE

From *Letters*, vol. 2, pp. 201–08, 74–78, 133–38

To Upton Sinclair

[ORIGINAL IN ENGLISH]

Dear Mr. Sinclair, 7 January 1955

Having read your novel *Our Lady*[1] and having enjoyed every page of it, I cannot refrain from bothering you again with a letter. This is the trouble you risk when giving your books to a psychologist who has made it his profession to receive impressions and to have reactions. On the day after I had read the story, I happened to come across the beautiful text of the "Exultet" in the Easter night liturgy:

> *O inaestimabilis dilectio caritatis*
> *Ut servum redimeres, Filium tradidisti!*
> *O certe necessarium Adae peccatum,*
> *Quod Christi morte deletum est!*

[Cont.d p. 162]

This letter was published, with minor changes and some omissions, in *New Republic*, vol. 132, no. 8, issue 2100 (21 Feb. 1955).—As some of Jung's comments will hardly be intelligible to readers unfamiliar with *Our Lady*, a brief summary is given: The heroine of the story is Marya, a widow and grandmother, a peasant woman of ancient Nazareth speaking only Aramaic. Her son Jeshu, who is depicted as a religious and social revolutionary, has gone away on a mission, and in an agony of fear as to his future she consults a sorceress. Under a spell, she awakens in a great city (Los Angeles), moving with the crowd into a stadium where she witnesses what she takes to be a battle: the football game between Notre Dame U., Indiana, and the U. of California. Sitting next to her is a professor of Semitic languages at Notre Dame; on addressing the utterly bewildered woman he learns to his astonishment that she speaks ancient Aramaic. He hears her story and takes her to the bishop, who exorcises the demons and sends her back to Nazareth with no enlightenment whatever. There she rebukes the sorceress, saying: "I asked to see the future of myself and my son: and nothing I saw has anything to do with us."

[1] Emmaus, Pennsylvania, 1938.

O felix culpa
Quae talem ac tantum meruit habere Redemptorem![2]

Although I am peculiarly sensitive to the beauty of the liturgical language and of the feeling expressed therein, something was amiss, as if a corner had been knocked off or a precious stone fallen from its setting. When trying to understand, I instantly remembered the bewildered Marya confronted with the incongruities of the exorcism, her beautiful and simple humanity caught in the coils of a vast historical process which had supplanted her concrete and immediate life by the almost inhuman superstructure of a dogmatic and ritual nature, so strange that, in spite of the identity of names and biographical items, she was not even able to recognize the story of herself and of her beloved son. By the way, a masterful touch! I also remembered your previous novel[3] about the idealistic youth who had almost become a saviour through one of those angelic tricks well known since the time of Enoch (the earthly adventure of Samiasaz[4] and his angelic host). And moreover, I recalled your Jesus biography.[5] Then I knew what it was that caused my peculiarly divided feeling: it was your common sense and realism, reducing the Holy Legend to human proportions and to probable possibilities, that never fails in knocking off a piece of the spiritual architecture or in causing a slight tremor of the Church's mighty structure. The anxiety of the priests to suppress the supposedly satanic attempt at verisimilitude is therefore most convincing, as the devil is particularly dangerous when he tells the truth, as he often does (*vide* the biography of St. Anthony of Egypt by St. Athanasius[6]).

---

[2] The *Missale Romanum* (liturgy of the Roman Catholic Mass), has the following text for Holy Saturday: "Oh unspeakable tenderness of charity! In order to redeem the servant, Thou hast given the son. Oh truly necessary sin of Adam which has been redeemed through the death of Christ. Oh happy guilt which has found so great a Redeemer!"— The term "felix culpa" (happy fault) goes back to St. Augustine.

[3] *What Didymus Did* (London, 1954), the story of a young gardener in a suburb of Los Angeles who is visited by an angel and receives the power to perform miracles. (Didymus, "twin," is the name of the apostle Thomas. Cf. John 11:16.)

[4] In the Book of Enoch, Samiasaz is the leader of the angels who took human wives (Gen. 6:2). Cf. "Answer to Job," CW 11, par. 689.

[5] Cf. Sinclair, 3 Nov. 52: *A Personal Jesus.*

[6] St. Athanasius (*ca.* 293–373), archbishop of Alexandria, wrote a biography of St. Anthony (*ca.* 250–350), the first Christian monk. St. Anthony is noted for his fights with the devil, who appeared to him under manifold disguises. In one story the devil admits defeat by the saint, hoping to seduce him into the sin of pride. A long excerpt from the biography, "Life of St. Anthony," in *The Paradise or Garden of the Holy Fathers* (1904), is in *Psychological Types*, CW 6, par. 82.

It is obviously your *laudabilis intentio* to extract a quintessence of truth from the incomprehensible chaos of historical distortions and dogmatic constructions, a truth of human size and acceptable to common sense. Such an attempt is hopeful and promises success, as the "truth" represented by the Church is so remote from ordinary understanding as to be well-nigh inacceptable. At all events, it conveys nothing any more to the modern mind that wants to understand since it is incapable of blind belief. In this respect, you continue the Strauss-Renan tradition in liberal theology.

I admit it is exceedingly probable that there is a human story at the bottom of it all. But under these conditions I must ask: Why the devil had this simple and therefore satisfactory story to be embellished and distorted beyond recognition? Or why had Jesus taken on unmistakably mythological traits already with the Gospel writers? And why is this process continued even in our enlightened days when the original picture has been obscured beyond all reasonable expectation? Why the Assumptio of 1950 and the Encyclical *Ad caeli Reginam*[7] of Oct. 11, 1954?

The impossibility of a concrete saviour, as styled by the Gospel writers, is and has always been to me obvious and indubitable. Yet I know my contemporaries too well to forget that to them it is news hearing the simple fundamental story. Liberal theology and incidentally your *laudabilis intentio* have definitely their place where they make sense. To me the human story is the inevitable *point de départ*, the self-evident basis of historical Christianity. It is the "small beginnings" of an amazing development. But the human story—I beg your pardon—is just ordinary, well within the confines of everyday life, not exciting and unique and thus not particularly interesting. We have heard it a thousand times and we ourselves have lived it at least in parts. It is the well-known psychological *ensemble* of Mother and beloved Son, and how the legend begins with mother's anxieties and hopes and son's heroic fantasies and helpful friends and foes joining in, magnifying and augmenting little deviations from the truth and thus slowly creating the web called the *reputation of a personality.*

Here you have me—the psychologist—with what the French call his *deformation professionnelle.* He is *blasé,* overfed with the "simple" human story, which does not touch his interest and particularly not his reli-

---

[7] After having promulgated the dogma of the bodily assumption of Mary into heaven in *Munificentissimus Deus,* Nov. 1950, Pius XII confirmed it in his Encyclical *Ad Caeli Reginam,* 11 Oct. 1954, which established a yearly feast in honour of Mary's "royal dignity" as Queen of Heaven and Earth.

gious feeling. The human story is even the thing to get away from, as the small story is neither exciting nor edifying. On the contrary, one wants to hear the great story of gods and heroes and how the world was created and so on. The small stories can be heard where the women wash in the river, or in the kitchen or at the village well, and above all everybody lives them at home. That has been so since the dawn of consciousness. But there was a time in antiquity, about the fourth century B.C. (I am not quite certain about the date. Being actually away on vacation, I miss my library!), when a man Euhemeros[8] made himself a name through a then new theory: The divine and heroic myth is founded upon the small story of an ordinary human chief or petty king of local fame, magnified by a minstrel's fantasy. All-Father Zeus, the mighty "gatherer of clouds," was originally a little tyrant, ruling some villages from his *maison forte* upon a hill, and "nocturnis ululatibus horrenda Prosperpina"[9] was presumably his awe-inspiring mother-in-law. That was certainly a time sick of the old gods and their ridiculous fairy stories, curiously similar to the "enlightenment" of our epoch equally fed up with its "myth" and welcoming any kind of iconoclasm, from the *Encyclopédie*[10] of the XVIIIth century to the Freudian theory reducing the religious "illusion" to the basic "family romance" with its incestuous innuendos in the early XXth century. Unlike your predecessor, you do not insist upon the *chronique scandaleuse* of the Olympians and other ideals, but with a loving hand and with decency like a benevolent pedagogue, you take your reader by the hand: "I am going to tell you a better story, something nice and reasonable, that anybody can accept. I don't repeat these ancient absurdities, these god-awful theologoumena[11] like the Virgin Birth, blood and flesh mysteries, and other wholly superfluous miracle gossip. I show you the touching and simple humanity behind these gruesome inventions of benighted ecclesiastical brains."

This is a kind-hearted iconoclasm far more deadly than the frankly murderous arrows from M. de Voltaire's quiver: all these mythological assertions are so obviously impossible that their refutation is not even needed. These relics of the dark ages vanish like morning mist before

---

[8] Euhemeros, Greek philosopher (*fl.* 4th–3rd cent. B.C.). He taught that the Olympians were originally great kings and war heroes.

[9] "Proserpine striking terror with midnight ululations."—Apuleius, *The Golden Ass*, XI, 2.

[10] *Encycloédie ou Dictionnaire raisonée des sciences, des arts et des métiers*, edited by Diderot (1713–84), became one of the most important influences in the French Enlightenment.

[11] Teachings not part of Church dogma but supported by theologians; more generally, theological formulations of the nature of God.

the rising sun, when the idealistic and charming gardener's boy experiments with miracles of the good old kind, or when your authentic Galilean grandmother "Marya" does not even recognize herself or her beloved son in the picture produced by the magic mirror of Christian tradition.

Yet, why should a more or less ordinary story of a good mother and her well-meaning idealistic boy give rise to one of the most amazing mental or spiritual developments of all times? Who or what is its *agens*? Why could the facts not remain as they were originally? The answer is obvious: The story is so ordinary that there would not have been any reason for its tradition, quite certainly not for its world-wide expansion. The fact that the original situation has developed into one of the most extraordinary myths about a divine *heros*, a God-man and his cosmic fate, is not due to its underlying human story, but to the powerful action of pre-existing mythological motifs attributed to the biographically almost unknown Jesus, a wandering miracle Rabbi in the style of the ancient Hebrew prophets, or of the contemporary teacher John the Baptizer, or of the much later Zaddiks of the Chassidim.[12] The immediate source and origin of the myth projected upon the teacher Jesus is to be found in the then popular Book of Enoch and its central figure of the "Son of Man" and his messianic mission. From the Gospel texts it is even manifest that Jesus identified himself with this "Son of Man." Thus it is the spirit of his time, the collective hope and expectation, which caused this astounding transformation and not at all the more or less insignificant story of the man Jesus. The true *agens* is the archetypal image of the God-man, appearing in Ezekiel's vision[13] for the first time in Jewish history, but in itself a considerably older figure in Egyptian theology, viz., Osiris and Horus.

The transformation of Jesus, i.e., the integration of his human self into a super- or inhuman figure of a deity, accounts for the amazing "distortion" of his ordinary personal biography. In other words: the essence of Christian tradition is by no means the simple man Jesus whom we seek in vain in the Gospels, but the lore of the God-man and his cosmic drama. Even the Gospels themselves make it their special job to prove that their Jesus is the incarnated God equipped with all

[12] The Chassidim (or Hasidim) were a mystical sect of Judaism, founded shortly before the middle of the 18th cent. by the mystic Israel Baal Shem ("Master of the Holy Name"; 1700–1760). The leaders were called Zaddiks (righteous men).
[13] Ezekiel 1:26.

the magic powers of a κύριος τῶν πνευμάτων.[14] That is why they are so liberal with miracle gossip which they naïvely assume proves their point. It is only natural that the subsequent post-apostolic developments even went several points better in this respect, and in our days the process of mythological integration is still expanding and spreading itself even to Jesus' mother, formerly carefully kept down to the human rank and file for at least 500 years of early church history. Boldly breaking through the sacrosanct rule about the definability of a new dogmatic truth, viz., that the said truth is only *definibilis* inasmuch as it was believed and taught in apostolic times, *explicite* or *implicite*, the pope has declared the *Assumptio Mariae* a dogma of the Christian creed. The justification he relies on is the pious belief of the masses for more than 1000 years, which he considers sufficient proof of the work of the Holy Ghost. Obviously the "pious belief" of the masses continues the process of projection, i.e., of transformation of human situations into myth.

But why should there be myth at all? My letter is already too long so that I can't answer this last question any more, but I have written several books about it. I only wanted to explain to you my idea that in trying to extract the quintessence of Christian tradition, you have removed it like Prof. Bultmann in his attempt at "demythologizing" the Gospels. One cannot help admitting that the human story is so very much more probable, but it has little or nothing to do with the problem of the myth containing the essence of Christian religion. You catch your priests most cleverly in the disadvantageous position which they have created for themselves by their preaching a concrete historicity of clearly mythological facts. Nobody reading your admirable novel can deny being deeply impressed by the very dramatic confrontation of the original with the mythological picture, and very probably he will prefer the human story to its mythological "distortion."

But what about the εὐαγγέλιον, the "message" of the God-man and Redeemer and his divine fate, the very foundation of everything that is holy to the Church? There is the spiritual heritage and harvest of 1900 years still to account for, and I am very doubtful whether the reduction to common sense is the correct answer or not. As a matter of fact, I attribute an incomparably greater importance to the dogmatic truth than to the probable human story. The religious need gets nothing out of the latter, and at all events less than from a mere belief in Jesus Christ or any other dogma. Inasmuch as the belief is real and living, it

---

[14] = Lord of the spirits.

works. But inasmuch as it is mere imagination and an effort of the will without understanding, I see little merit in it. Unfortunately, this unsatisfactory condition prevails in modern times, and in so far as there is nothing beyond belief without understanding but doubt and scepticism, the whole Christian tradition goes by the board as a mere fantasy. I consider this event a tremendous loss for which we are to pay a terrific price. The effect becomes visible in the dissolution of ethical values and a complete disorientation of our *Weltanschauung*. The "truths" of natural science or "existential philosophy" are poor surrogates. Natural "laws" are in the main mere abstractions (being statistical averages) instead of reality, and they abolish individual existence as being merely exceptional. But the individual as the only carrier of life and existence is of paramount importance. He cannot be substituted by a group or by a mass. Yet we are rapidly approaching a state in which nobody will accept individual responsibility any more. We prefer to leave it as an odious business to groups and organizations, blissfully unconscious of the fact that the group or mass psyche is that of an animal and wholly inhuman.

What we need is the development of the inner spiritual man, the unique individual whose treasure is hidden on the one hand in the symbols of our mythological tradition, and on the other hand in man's unconscious psyche. It is tragic that science and its philosophy discourage the individual and that theology resists every reasonable attempt to understand its symbols. Theologians call their creed a *symbolum*,[15] but they refuse to call their truth "symbolic." Yet, if it is anything, it is anthropomorphic symbolism and therefore capable of re-interpretation.

Hoping you don't mind my frank discussion of your very inspiring writings,

I remain, with my best wishes for the New Year,

Yours sincerely, C. G. JUNG

P.S. Thank you very much for your kind letter that has reached me just now. I am amazed at the fact that you should have difficulties in finding a publisher.[16] What is America coming to, when her most capable authors cannot reach their public any more? What a time!

---

[15] A *symbolum*, in the theological sense, is the formulation of a basic tenet of Christian faith; the creeds were *symbola*. Cf. "Dogma of the Trinity," CW 11, pars. 210ff.

[16] In his letter S. spoke of his difficulties in finding a publisher for *What Didymus Did*. It was never published in America but only in England.—This postscript was added in handwriting.

To Dorothee Hoch

Dear Dr. Hoch,   3 July 1952

I am very grateful that this time you have met my endeavour with more friendliness and understanding. I certainly admit that personal motives creep in everywhere in an exasperating way, but I still think it is a bit too glib to suspect an objective argument of personal resentment without closer and surer knowledge of the circumstances. Only at the end of a discussion, when all objective elements have run out, may one hazard the question whether personal motives have also had a hand in it. But I won't make any annotations to Knigge's *Umgang mit Menschen.*[1]

You are surprised at my reaction to your avowed faith in a personal meeting with Christ. I thought I ought not to conceal from you that such an avowal has a thoroughly intimidating effect on many people, because they feel (with good reason, I think) that this only happens to one of the elect, who has been singled out from the human community of the unblest, the wayward, the unbelievers, the doubters and the God-forsaken, and, especially if they are religious people, it makes them feel inferior. Many theologians make themselves unpopular on that account and so make the doctor, who is expected to have a better understanding of the ordinary, uninitiated person, appear as a more desirable proposition.

I do, to be sure, maintain that the Bible was written by man and is therefore "mythological," i.e., anthropomorphic. God is certainly made *vivid* enough in it, but not *visible.* That would be a bit too much for our human inadequacy, even if we could see him in his incarnate form. This is the μορφὴ δούλου after the kenosis[2] had taken place, the well-attested pagan figure of the κάταχος[3] and the Old Testament "servant of God,"[4] or the unsuccessful, suffering hero like Oedipus or Prometheus.

The insistence on the uniqueness of Christianity, which removes it from the human sphere and doesn't even allow it a mythological status

---

[1] By Adolf Freiherr von Knigge (1752–96), an immensely popular book (1788) on etiquette and good manners.
[2] = "emptying": cf. Phil. 2:7: ". . . Christ Jesus who . . . emptied himself, taking the form of a servant, being made in the likeness of men" (DV). Cf. also *Mysterium,* par. 29 & n. 195.
[3] = prisoner.
[4] Isaiah 42:1–7, 49:1–6, 50:4–9, 52:13, 53:12.

conditioned by history, has just as disastrous an effect on the layman as the afore-mentioned "avowal." The gospel becomes unreal; all possible points of contact with human understanding are abolished, and it is made thoroughly implausible and unworthy of belief. It is really and truly sterilized, for all the psychic propensities in us which would willingly accept it are brusquely thrust aside or suppressed and devalued. This short-sightedness is neither rational nor Christian and empties the Protestant churches in the most effective way; but it is very *convenient* because then the clergyman doesn't have to bother about whether the congregation understand the gospel or not but can comfortably go on preaching at them as before. Educated people, for instance, would be much more readily convinced of the meaning of the gospel if it were shown them that the myth was always there to a greater or lesser degree, and moreover is actually present in archetypal form in every individual. Then people would understand where, in spite of its having been artificially screened off by the theologians, the gospel really touches them and what it is talking about. Without this link the Jesus legend remains a mere wonder story, and is understood as little as a fairytale that merely serves to entertain. Uniqueness is synonymous with unintelligibility. How do you make head or tail of a ἅπαξ λεγόμενον?[5] If you are not fascinated at the first go, it tells you absolutely nothing. How can you "meet people in their lives" if you talk of things, and especially of unique events, that have *nothing* to do with the human psyche?

You refer me to your sermon. You talk there of rebirth, for instance, something the man of antiquity was thoroughly familiar with, but modern man? He has no inkling of the mysteries, which anyway are discredited by Protestant theology, because for it there is only *one* truth, and whatever else God may have done for man is mere bungling. Does modern man know what "water" and "spirit" signify? Water is *below*, heavy and material; wind above and the "spiritual" breath body. The man of antiquity understood this as a clash of opposites, a *complexio oppositorum*, and felt this conflict to be so impossible that he equated matter with evil outright. Christ forces man into the impossible conflict. He took himself with exemplary seriousness and lived his life to the bitter end, regardless of human convention and in opposition to his own lawful tradition, as the worst heretic in the eyes of the Jews and a madman in the eyes of his family. But we? We imitate Christ and hope he will deliver us from our own fate. Like little lambs we follow

[5] An expression used only once.

169

the shepherd, naturally to good pastures. No talk at all of uniting our Above and Below! On the contrary, Christ and *his* cross deliver us from our conflict, which we simply leave alone. We are Pharisees, faithful to law and tradition, we flee heresy and are mindful only of the *imitatio Christi* but not of our own reality which is laid upon us, the union of opposites in ourselves, preferring to believe that Christ has already achieved this for us. Instead of bearing ourselves, i.e., our own cross, ourselves, we load Christ with our unresolved conflicts. We "place ourselves under *his* cross,"[6] but by golly not under our own. Anyone who does this is a heretic, self-redeemer, "psychoanalyst" and God knows what. The cross of Christ was *borne by himself* and was *his*. To put oneself under somebody else's cross, which has already been carried by him, is certainly easier than to carry your own cross amid the mockery and contempt of the world. That way you remain nicely ensconced in tradition and are praised as devout. This is well-organized Pharisaism and highly un-Christian. Whoever imitates Christ and has the cheek to want to take Christ's cross on himself when he can't even carry his own has in my view not yet learnt the ABC of the Christian message.

Have your congregation understood that they must close their ears to the traditional teachings and go through the darknesses of their own souls and set aside everything in order to become that which every individual bears in himself as his individual task, and that no one can take this burden from him? We continually pray that "this cup may pass from us" and not harm us. Even Christ did so, but without success. Yet we use Christ to secure this success for ourselves. For all these reasons theology wants to know nothing of psychology, because through it we could discover our own cross. But we only want to talk of Christ's cross, and how splendidly his crucifixion has smoothed the way for us and solved our conflicts. We might also discover, among other things, that in every feature Christ's life is a prototype of individuation and hence cannot be imitated: *one can only live one's own life totally in the same way with all the consequences this entails.* This is hard and must therefore be prevented. How this is done is shown among other things by the following example. A devout professor of theology (i.e., a lamb of Christ) once publicly rebuked me for having said "in flagrant contradiction to the word of the Lord" that it is unethical to *"remain"* a child. The "Christian" ought to remain sitting on his father's knee and leave the odious task of individuation to dear little Jesus. Thus naïvely, but with unconscious design, the meaning of the gospel is subverted, and in-

---

[6] These words occur in a sermon of H.'s which she enclosed with her letter.

stead of catechizing ourselves on the meaning of Christ's life we prefer, in *ostensible* agreement with the word of the Lord, to remain infantile and not responsible for ourselves. Thus an exemplary διδάσκαλος τοῦ Ἰσραήλ[7] who can't even read the New Testament properly.[8] No one but me protested because it suits everybody's book. This is only one of many examples of the way we are cheated in all godliness. Without anybody noticing it, Protestantism has become a Judaism *redivivus*.

Denominationalism has likewise become a flight from the conflict: people don't want to be Christians any more because otherwise they would be sitting between two stools in the middle of the schism of the Church. Allegiance to a particular creed is—heaven be praised!—unambiguous, and so they can skulk round the schism with a good conscience and fight "manfully" for a one-sided belief, the other fellow—alas—being always in the wrong. The fact that I as a Christian struggle to unite Catholicism and Protestantism within myself is chalked up against me in true Pharisaic fashion as blatant proof of lack of character. That psychology is needed for such an undertaking seems to be a nuisance of the first order. The resistance to and devaluation of the soul as "only psychic" has become a yardstick for Pharisaic hypocrisy. Yet people should be glad that dogmatic ideas have psychological foundations. If they hadn't, they would remain eternally alien to us and finally wither away, which they are already doing very speedily in Protestantism. But that is what people unconsciously want, because then they wouldn't be reminded of their own cross and could talk all the more uninhibitedly about Christ's cross, which takes them away from their own reality, willed by God himself. Therefore, by entrenching themselves behind a creed, they calmly perpetuate the hellish scandal that the so-called Christians cannot reach agreement even among themselves.

Even if you thought there is anything to my reflections you could hardly preach a sermon about them to your congregation. This "cross" would presumably be a bit too heavy. But Christ accepted a cross that cost him his life. It is fairly easy to live a praiseworthy truth, but difficult to hold one's own as an individual against a collective and be found unpraiseworthy. Is it clear to your congregation that Christ may possibly mean just this?

These reflections came to me as I read the sermon you have kindly

---

[7] = teacher of Israel.
[8] Matthew 18:3: "Except ye . . . *become* as little children, ye shall not enter into the kingdom of heaven."

placed at my disposal. I was particularly affected by your thesis of "total surrender." Is it clear to you what that means: *absolute exposure?* A fate without if's and but's, with no assurance that it will turn out harmlessly, for then one would have ventured nothing and risked nothing for God's sake. It was these rather sombre undertones, so true to reality, that I missed in your sermon. With best greetings,

Yours sincerely, C. G. JUNG

To Father Victor White

[O R I G I N A L   I N   E N G L I S H]

Dear Victor,   24 November 1953

Forget for once dogmatics and listen to what psychology has to say concerning your problem: *Christ as a symbol is far from being invalid,*[1] although he is one side of the self and the devil the other. This pair of opposites is contained in the creator as his right and left hand, as Clemens Romanus says.[2] From the psychological standpoint the experience of God the creator is the perception of an overpowering impulse issuing from the sphere of the unconscious.[3] We don't know whether this influence or compulsion deserves to be called good or evil, although we cannot prevent ourselves from welcoming or cursing it, giving it a bad or a good name, according to our subjective condition. Thus Yahweh has either aspect because he is essentially the creator (*primus motor*) and because he is yet unreflected in his whole nature.

With the *incarnation* the picture changes completely, as it means that God becomes manifest in the form of Man who is conscious and therefore cannot avoid judgment. He simply has to call the one good and the other evil. It is a historical fact that the real devil only came into existence together with Christ.[4] Though Christ was God, as Man

---

[1] In a letter of 8 Nov., W. said that Jung seemed to create a dilemma by maintaining that "Christ is no longer an adequate and valid symbol of the self"—a misunderstanding which Jung tries to correct here. (Most of this letter is published in German in Ges. Werke, XI, Anhang, pp. 681ff.)

[2] Cf. Dr. H., 17 Mar. 51, n. 10.

[3] "Psychology and Religion," CW 11, par. 137: ". . . it is always the overwhelming psychic factor that is called 'God.' "

[4] Jung was, of course, perfectly aware of the fact that the figure of Satan occurs in the OT. What he means is that, Christ being the incarnation of God's goodness, the devil becomes a psychological inevitability as the incarnation of evil—in other words the devil is the personification of Christ's split-off dark side. Cf. *Aion*, CW 9, ii, par. 113.

172

he was detached from God and he watched the devil falling out of heaven,[5] removed from God as he (Christ) was separated from God inasmuch as he was human. In his utter helplessness on the cross, he even confessed that God had forsaken him. The Deus Pater would leave him to his fate as he always "strafes" those whom he has filled before with this abundance by breaking his promise.[6] This is exactly what S. Joannes a cruce describes as the "dark night of the soul." It is the reign of darkness, which is also God, but an ordeal for Man. The Godhead has a double aspect, and as Master Eckhart says: God is not blissful in his mere Godhead, and that is the reason for his incarnation.[7]

But becoming Man, he becomes at the same time a definite being, which is this and not that. Thus the very first thing Christ must do is to sever himself from his shadow and call it the devil (sorry, but the Gnostics of Irenaeus[8] already knew it!).

When a patient in our days is about to emerge from an unconscious condition, he is instantly confronted with his *shadow* and he has to decide for the good, otherwise he goes down the drain. *Nolens volens* he "imitates" Christ and follows his example. The first step on the way to individuation consists in the discrimination between himself and the shadow.

In this stage the Good is the goal of individuation, and consequently Christ represents the self.

The next step is the *problem of the shadow*: in dealing with darkness, you have got to cling to the Good, otherwise the devil devours you. You need every bit of your goodness in dealing with Evil and just there. To keep the light alive in the darkness, that's the point, and only there your candle makes sense.

Now tell me how many people you know who can say with any verisimilitude that they have finished their dealings with the devil and consequently can chuck the Christian symbol overboard?

As a matter of fact, our society has not even begun to face its shadow or to develop those Christian virtues so badly needed in dealing with the powers of darkness. Our society cannot afford the luxury of cutting itself loose from the *imitatio Christi*, even if it should know that the *conflict with the shadow*, i.e., Christ versus Satan, is only the first step on the way to the far-away goal of the unity of the self in God.

It is true however that the *imitatio Christi* leads you into your own very

---

[5] Luke 10:18.
[6] Rev. 3:19.
[7] Cf. *Psychological Types*, CW 6, par. 418.
[8] *Aion*, par. 75, n. 23.

real and *Christlike conflict* with darkness, and the more you are engaged in this war and in these attempts at peacemaking helped by the anima, the more you begin to look forward beyond the Christian aeon to the *Oneness of the Holy Spirit. He is the pneumatic state the creator attains to through the phase of incarnation.* He is the experience of every individual that has undergone the complete abolition of his ego through the absolute opposition expressed by the symbol Christ versus Satan.

The state of the Holy Spirit means a restitution of the original oneness of the unconscious on the level of consciousness. That is alluded to, as I see it, by Christ's logion: "Ye are gods."[9] This state is not quite understandable yet. It is a mere anticipation.

The later development from the Christian aeon to the one of the S. spiritus has been called the *evangelium aeternum* by Gioacchino da Fiori[10] in a time when the great tearing apart had just begun. Such vision seems to be granted by divine grace as a sort of *consolamentum,*[11] so that man is not left in a completely hopeless state during the time of darkness. We are actually in the state of darkness viewed from the standpoint of history. We are still within the Christian aeon and just beginning to realize the age of darkness where we shall need Christian virtues *to the utmost.*

In such a state we could not possibly dismiss Christ as an invalid symbol although we clearly foresee the approach of his opposite. Yet we don't see and feel the latter as the preliminary step toward the future union of the divine opposites, but rather as a menace against everything that is good, beautiful, and holy to us. The *adventus diaboli* does not invalidate the Christian symbol of the self, on the contrary: it complements it. It is a mysterious transmutation of both.

Since we are living in a society that is unconscious of this development and far from understanding the importance of the Christian symbol, we are called upon to hinder its invalidation, although some of us are granted the vision of a future development. But none of us could safely say that he has accomplished the assimilation and integration of the shadow.

---

[9] John 10:34, referring to Psalm 82:6.

[10] Joachim of Flora (*ca.* 1145–1202), Italian mystic and theologian. He taught that there are three periods of world history: the Age of the Law, or of the Father; the Age of the Gospel, or of the Son; and the Age of the Holy Spirit, or of Contemplation. His teachings were condemned by the Fourth Lateran Council, 1215. Cf. *Aion,* pars. 137ff.

[11] The rite of "consoling" or "comforting," the central rite of the Cathars (cf. ibid., pars. 225ff.). It was baptism with the Spirit, considered to be the Paraclete sent by Christ (the "comforter which is the Holy Ghost," John 14:26). The *consolamentum* freed man from original sin.

174

Since the Christian church is the community of all those having surrendered to the principle of the *imitatio Christi*, this institution (i.e., such a mental attitude) is to be maintained until it is clearly understood what the assimilation of the shadow means. Those that foresee, must—as it were—stay behind their vision in order to help and to teach, particularly so if they belong to the church as her appointed servants.

You should not mind if some of your analysands are helped out of the church. It is their destiny and adventure. Others will stay in it anyhow. It does not matter whether the ecclesiastical powers-that-be approve of your vision or not. When the time is fulfilled a new orientation will irresistibly break through, as one has seen in the case of the Conceptio Immaculata[12] and the Assumptio which both deviate from the time-hallowed principle of apostolic authority,[13] a thing unheard-of before. It would be a lack of responsibility and a rather autoerotic attitude if we were to deprive our fellow beings of a vitally necessary symbol before they had a reasonable chance to understand it thoroughly, and all this because it is not complete if envisaged from an anticipated stage we ourselves in our individual lives have not yet made real.

Anybody going ahead is alone or thinks he is lonely at times, no matter whether he is in the church or in the world. Your practical work as *directeur de conscience* brings to you individuals having something in their character that corresponds with certain aspects of your personality (like the many men fitting themselves as stones into the edifice of the tower in the *Shepherd of Hermas*).[14]

Whatever your ultimate decision will be, you ought to realize beforehand that staying in the church makes sense as it is important to make people understand what the symbol of Christ means, and such understanding is indispensable to any further development. There is no way round it, as little as we can eliminate from our life old age, illness, and death, or Buddha's Nidana-chain of evils.[15] The vast majority of people

[12] The dogma of the Immaculate Conception pronounced as "of faith" by Pius IX in the bull *Ineffabilis Deus* (1854).
[13] The principle by which all that the Apostles were supposed to have taught was regarded as infallible, and by which nothing in religious teaching or practice was considered Christian unless it was of Apostolic origin.
[14] An early Christian text ascribed to Hermas, brother of Pope Pius I (*ca.* 140–55), containing lessons to be disseminated for the instruction of the Church. Cf. *Psychological Types*, pars. 381ff., esp. par. 390 for the building of the tower.
[15] The twelve *nidanas* of Buddhism, starting with "ignorance" and ending with "despair," form the *nidana*-chain, the conditions which keep man a prisoner in *samsara*, the endless chain of rebirth.

are still in such an unconscious state that one should almost protect them from the full shock of the real *imitatio Christi*. Moreover we are still in the Christian aeon, threatened with a complete annihilation of our world.

As there are not only the many but also the few, somebody is entrusted with the task of looking ahead and talking of the things to be. That is partially my job, but I have to be very careful not to destroy the things that are. Nobody will be so foolish as to destroy the foundations when he is adding an upper storey to his house, and how can he build it really if the foundations are not yet properly laid? Thus, making the statement that Christ is not a complete symbol of the self, I cannot make it complete by abolishing it. I must keep it therefore in order to build up the symbol of the perfect contradiction in God by adding this darkness to the *lumen de lumine*.[16]

Thus I am approaching the end of the Christian aeon and I am to take up Gioacchino's anticipation and Christ's prediction of the coming of the Paraclete. This archetypal drama is at the same time exquisitely psychological and historical. We are actually living in the time of the splitting of the world and of the invalidation of Christ.

But an anticipation of a faraway future is no way out of the actual situation. It is a mere *consolamentum* for those despairing at the atrocious possibilities of the present time. Christ is still the valid symbol. Only God himself can "invalidate" him through the Paraclete.

Now that is all I can say. It is a long letter and I am tired. If it is not helpful to you, it shows at least what I think.

I have seen X. She is as right as she can be and as she usually is, and just as wrong as her nature permits, altogether as hopeful as a hysterical temperament ever can be.

You have probably heard of the little celebration we had here round the Nag-Hamâdi Gnostic Codex[17] given to the Institute by a generous donor. There was even a note in the *Times*.[18] It was a disproportionate

[16] The Council of Nicaea (325) defined the everlasting Word, "the true light" (John 1:9), as *lumen de lumine*, light of the light.
[17] A Gnostic Papyrus in Coptic found in 1945 near the village of Nag-Hamâdi in Upper Egypt and acquired in 1952 for the C. G. Jung Institute. It is now known as the Codex Jung; its main part consists of the so-called "Gospel of Truth" attributed to Valentinus. This has been published under the editorship of M. Malinine, H. C. Puech, and G. Quispel as *Evangelium Veritatis* (Zurich, 1956). Two further parts: *De Resurrectione* (1963) and *Epistula Jacobi Apocrypha* (1968); the fourth part, *Tractatus Tripartitus*, is still unpublished.
[18] "New Light on a Coptic Codex," *The Times*, 16 Nov. 1953.

affair and neither my doing, nor liking. But I was manoeuvred into saying in the end a few words about the relation between Gnosticism and psychology.[19]

My best wishes![20]

Yours cordially, C. G.

---

[19] Jung's address is in CW 18, pars. 1514ff.

[20] W. answered in a short note of 20 Nov., saying how "immensely grateful" he was for the letter, adding: ". . . the points that 'ring the bell' most immediately are those about the 'autocratic attitude' and about 'an anticipation of a faraway future is no way out.'"

.

PART III

JUNG'S INTERPRETATION OF
CHRISTIAN HISTORY AND ITS FUTURE

1
"INTRODUCTION TO THE RELIGIOUS AND PSYCHOLOGICAL PROBLEMS OF ALCHEMY"

From *Psychology and Alchemy*, vol. 12, pars. 1–43

A pair of alchemists, kneeling by the furnace and praying for God's blessing—*Mutus liber* (1702)

1   For the reader familiar with analytical psychology, there is no need of any introductory remarks to the subject of the following study. But for the reader whose interest is not professional and who comes to this book unprepared, some kind of preface will probably be necessary. The concepts of alchemy and the individuation process are matters that seem to lie very far apart, so that the imagination finds it impossible at first to conceive of any bridge between them. To this reader I owe an explanation, more particularly as I have had one or two experiences since the publication of my recent lectures which lead me to infer a certain bewilderment in my critics.

2   What I now have to put forward as regards the nature of the human psyche is based first and foremost on my observations of people. It has been objected that these observations deal with experiences that are

either unknown or barely accessible. It is a remarkable fact, which we come across again and again, that absolutely everybody, even the most unqualified layman, thinks he knows all about psychology as though the psyche were something that enjoyed the most universal understanding. But anyone who really knows the human psyche will agree with me when I say that it is one of the darkest and most mysterious regions of our experience. There is no end to what can be learned in this field. Hardly a day passes in my practice but I come across something new and unexpected. True enough, my experiences are not commonplaces lying on the surface of life. They are, however, within easy reach of every psychotherapist working in this particular field. It is therefore rather absurd, to say the least, that ignorance of the experiences I have to offer should be twisted into an accusation against me. I do not hold myself responsible for the shortcomings in the lay public's knowledge of psychology.

3   There is in the analytical process, that is to say in the dialectical discussion between the conscious mind and the unconscious, a development or an advance towards some goal or end, the perplexing nature of which has engaged my attention for many years. Psychological treatment may come to an *end* at any stage in the development without one's always or necessarily having the feeling that a *goal* has also been reached. Typical and temporary terminations may occur (1) after receiving a piece of good advice; (2) after making a fairly complete but nevertheless adequate confession; (3) after having recognized some hitherto unconscious but essential psychic content whose realization gives a new impetus to one's life and activity; (4) after a hard-won separation from the childhood psyche; (5) after having worked out a new and rational mode of adaptation to perhaps difficult or unusual circumstances and surroundings; (6) after the disappearance of painful symptoms; (7) after some positive turn of fortune such as an examination, engagement, marriage, divorce, change of profession, etc.; (8) after having found one's way back to the church or creed to which one previously belonged, or after a conversion; and finally, (9) after having begun to build up a practical philosophy of life (a "philosophy" in the classical sense of the word).

4   Although the list could admit of many more modifications and additions, it ought to define by and large the main situations in which the analytical or psychotherapeutic process reaches a temporary or sometimes even a definitive end. Experience shows, however, that there is a relatively large number of patients for whom the outward termination of work with the doctor is far from denoting the end of the analytical

process. It is rather the case that the dialectical discussion with the unconscious still continues, and follows much the same course as it does with those who have not given up their work with the doctor. Occasionally one meets such patients again after several years and hears the often highly remarkable account of their subsequent development. It was experiences of this kind which first confirmed me in my belief that there is in the psyche a process that seeks its own goal independently of external factors, and which freed me from the worrying feeling that I myself might be the sole cause of an unreal—and perhaps unnatural—process in the psyche of the patient. This apprehension was not altogether misplaced inasmuch as no amount of argument based on any of the nine categories mentioned above—not even a religious conversion or the most startling removal of neurotic symptoms—can persuade certain patients to give up their analytical work. It was these cases that finally convinced me that the treatment of neurosis opens up a problem which goes far beyond purely medical considerations and to which medical knowledge alone cannot hope to do justice.

5   Although the early days of analysis now lie nearly half a century behind us, with their pseudo-biological interpretations and their depreciation of the whole process of psychic development, memories die hard and people are still very fond of describing a lengthy analysis as "running away from life," "unresolved transference," "auto-eroticism"—and by other equally unpleasant epithets. But since there are two sides to everything, it is legitimate to condemn this so-called "hanging on" as negative to life only if it can be shown that it really does contain nothing positive. The very understandable impatience felt by the doctor does not prove anything in itself. Only through infinitely patient research has the new science succeeded in building up a profounder knowledge of the nature of the psyche, and if there have been certain unexpected therapeutic results, these are due to the self-sacrificing perseverance of the doctor. Unjustifiably negative judgments are easily come by and at times harmful; moreover they arouse the suspicion of being a mere cloak for ignorance if not an attempt to evade the responsibility of a thorough-going analysis. For since the analytical work must inevitably lead sooner or later to a fundamental discussion between "I" and "You" and "You" and "I" on a plane stripped of all human pretences, it is very likely, indeed it is almost certain, that not only the patient but the doctor as well will find the situation "getting under his skin." Nobody can meddle with fire or poison without being affected in some vulnerable spot; for the true physician does not stand outside his work but is always in the thick of it.

6   This "hanging on," as it is called, may be something undesired by both parties, something incomprehensible and even unendurable, without necessarily being negative to life. On the contrary, it can easily be a positive "hanging on," which, although it constitutes an apparently insurmountable obstacle, represents just for that reason a unique situation that demands the maximum effort and therefore enlists the energies of the whole man. In fact, one could say that while the patient is unconsciously and unswervingly seeking the solution to some ultimately insoluble problem, the art and technique of the doctor are doing their best to help him towards it. "Ars totum requirit hominem!" exclaims an old alchemist. It is just this *homo totus* whom we seek. The labours of the doctor as well as the quest of the patient are directed towards that hidden and as yet unmanifest "whole" man, who is at once the greater and the future man. But the right way to wholeness is made up, unfortunately, of fateful detours and wrong turnings. It is a *longissima via*, not straight but snakelike, a path that unites the opposites in the manner of the guiding caduceus, a path whose labyrinthine twists and turns are not lacking in terrors. It is on this *longissima via* that we meet with those experiences which are said to be "inaccessible." Their inaccessibility really consists in the fact that they cost us an enormous amount of effort: they demand the very thing we most fear, namely the "wholeness" which we talk about so glibly and which lends itself to endless theorizing, though in actual life we give it the widest possible berth.[1] It is infinitely more popular to go in for "compartment psychology," where the left-hand pigeon-hole does not know what is in the right.

7   I am afraid that we cannot hold the unconsciousness and impotence of the individual entirely responsible for this state of affairs: it is due also to the general psychological education of the European. Not only is this education the proper concern of the ruling religions, it belongs to their very nature—for religion excels all rationalistic systems in that it alone relates to the outer and inner man in equal degree. We can accuse Christianity of arrested development if we are determined to excuse our own shortcomings; but I do not wish to make the mistake of blaming religion for something that is due mainly to human incompetence. I am speaking therefore not of the deepest and best understanding of Christianity but of the superficialities and disastrous misunderstandings that are plain for all to see. The demand made by the *imitatio*

---

[1] It is worth noting that a Protestant theologian, writing on homiletics, had the courage to demand wholeness of the preacher from the ethical point of view. He substantiates his argument by referring to my psychology. See Händler, *Die Predigt.*

Christi that we should follow the ideal and seek to become like it—ought logically to have the result of developing and exalting the inner man. In actual fact, however, the ideal has been turned by superficial and formalistically-minded believers into an external object of worship, and it is precisely this veneration for the object that prevents it from reaching down into the depths of the psyche and giving the latter a wholeness in keeping with the ideal. Accordingly the divine mediator stands outside as an image, while man remains fragmentary and untouched in the deepest part of him. Christ can indeed be imitated even to the point of stigmatization without the imitator coming anywhere near the ideal or its meaning. For it is not a question of an imitation that leaves a man unchanged and makes him into a mere artifact, but of realizing the ideal on one's own account—*Deo concedente*—in one's own individual life. We must not forget, however, that even a mistaken imitation may sometimes involve a tremendous moral effort which has all the merits of a total surrender to some supreme value, even though the real goal may never be reached and the value is represented externally. It is conceivable that by virtue of this total effort a man may even catch a fleeting glimpse of his wholeness, accompanied by the feeling of grace that always characterizes this experience.

8   The mistaken idea of a merely outward *imitatio Christi* is further exacerbated by a typically European prejudice which distinguishes the Western attitude from the Eastern. Western man is held in thrall by the "ten thousand things"; he sees only particulars, he is ego-bound and thing-bound, and unaware of the deep root of all being. Eastern man, on the other hand, experiences the world of particulars, and even his own ego, like a dream; he is so rooted essentially in the "Ground," which attracts him so powerfully that his relations with the world are relativized to a degree that is often incomprehensible to us. The Western attitude, with its emphasis on the object, tends to fix the ideal—Christ—in its outward aspect and thus to rob it of its mysterious relation to the inner man. It is this prejudice, for instance, which impels the Protestant interpreters of the Bible to interpret ἐντὸς ὑμῶν (referring to the Kingdom of God) as "among you" instead of "within you." I do not mean to say anything about the validity of the Western attitude: we are sufficiently convinced of its rightness. But if we try to come to a real understanding of Eastern man—as the psychologist must—we find it hard to rid ourselves of certain misgivings. Anyone who can square it with his conscience is free to decide this question as he pleases, though he may be unconsciously setting himself up as an *arbiter mundi*. I for my part prefer the precious gift of doubt, for the reason that it does not violate the virginity of things beyond our ken.

9   Christ the ideal took upon himself the sins of the world. But if the ideal is wholly outside then the sins of the individual are also outside, and consequently he is more of a fragment than ever, since superficial misunderstanding conveniently enables him, quite literally, to "cast his sins upon Christ" and thus to evade his deepest responsibilities—which is contrary to the spirit of Christianity. Such formalism and laxity were not only one of the prime causes of the Reformation, they are also present within the body of Protestantism. If the supreme value (Christ) and the supreme negation (sin) are outside, then the soul is void: its highest and lowest are missing. The Eastern attitude (more particularly the Indian) is the other way about: everything, highest and lowest, is in the (transcendental) Subject. Accordingly the significance of the Atman, the Self, is heightened beyond all bounds. But with Western man the value of the self sinks to zero. Hence the universal depreciation of the soul in the West. Whoever speaks of the reality of the soul or psyche[2] is accused of "psychologism." Psychology is spoken of as if it were "only" psychology and nothing else. The notion that there can be psychic factors which correspond to divine figures is regarded as a devaluation of the latter. It smacks of blasphemy to think that a religious experience is a psychic process; for, so it is argued, a religious experience "is not *only* psychological." Anything psychic is *only* Nature and therefore, people think, nothing religious can come out of it. At the same time such critics never hesitate to derive all religions—with the

---

[2] [The translation of the German word *Seele* presents almost insuperable difficulties on account of the lack of a single English equivalent and because it combines the two words "psyche" and "soul" in a way not altogether familiar to the English reader. For this reason some comment by the Editors will not be out of place.

[In previous translations, and in this one as well, "psyche"—for which Jung in the German original uses either *Psyche* or *Seele*—has been used with reference to the totality of *all* psychic processes (cf. Jung, *Psychological Types*, Def. 48); i.e., it is a comprehensive term. "Soul," on the other hand, as used in the technical terminology of analytical psychology, is more restricted in meaning and refers to a "function complex" or partial personality and never to the whole psyche. It is often applied specifically to "anima" and "animus"; e.g., in this connection it is used in the composite word "soul-image" (*Seelenbild*). This conception of the soul is more primitive than the Christian one with which the reader is likely to be more familiar. In its Christian context it refers to "the transcendental energy in man" and "the spiritual part of man considered in its moral aspect or in relation to God." (Cf. definition in *The Shorter Oxford English Dictionary*)

[In the above passage in the text (and in similar passages), "soul" is used in a nontechnical sense (i.e., it does not refer to "animus" or "anima"), nor does it refer to the transcendental conception, but to a psychic (phenomenological) fact of a highly numinous character. This usage is adhered to except when the context shows clearly that the term is used in the Christian or Neoplatonic sense.—EDITORS.]

186

exception of their own—from the nature of the psyche. It is a telling fact that two theological reviewers of my book *Psychology and Religion*—one of them Catholic, the other Protestant—assiduously overlooked my demonstration of the psychic origin of religious phenomena.

10   Faced with this situation, we must really ask: How do we know so much about the psyche that we can say "only" psychic? For this is how Western man, whose soul is evidently "of little worth," speaks and thinks. If much were in his soul he would speak of it with reverence. But since he does not do so we can only conclude that there is nothing of value in it. Not that this is necessarily so always and everywhere, but only with people who put nothing into their souls and have "all God outside." (A little more Meister Eckhart would be a very good thing sometimes!)

11   An exclusively religious projection may rob the soul of its values so that through sheer inanition it becomes incapable of further development and gets stuck in an unconscious state. At the same time it falls victim to the delusion that the cause of all misfortune lies outside, and people no longer stop to ask themselves how far it is their own doing. So insignificant does the soul seem that it is regarded as hardly capable of evil, much less of good. But if the soul no longer has any part to play, religious life congeals into externals and formalities. However we may picture the relationship between God and soul, one thing is certain: that the soul cannot be "nothing but."[3] On the contrary it has the dignity of an entity endowed with consciousness of a relationship to Deity. Even if it were only the relationship of a drop of water to the sea, that sea would not exist but for the multitude of drops. The immortality of the soul insisted upon by dogma exalts it above the transitoriness of mortal man and causes it to partake of some supernatural quality. It thus infinitely surpasses the perishable, conscious individual in significance, so that logically the Christian is forbidden to regard the soul as a "nothing but."[4] As the eye to the sun, so the soul corresponds to God. Since our conscious mind does not comprehend the soul it is ridiculous to speak of the things of the soul in a patronizing or depreciatory manner. Even the believing Christian does not know God's hid-

---

[3] [The term "nothing but" (*nichts als*), which occurs frequently in Jung to denote the habit of explaining something unknown by reducing it to something apparently known and thereby devaluing it, is borrowed from William James, *Pragmatism*, p. 16: "What is higher is explained by what is lower and treated for ever as a case of 'nothing but'— nothing but something else of a quite inferior sort."]

[4] The dogma that man is formed in the likeness of God weighs heavily in the scales in any assessment of man—not to mention the Incarnation.

den ways and must leave him to decide whether he will work on man from outside or from within, through the soul. So the believer should not boggle at the fact that there are *somnia a Deo missa* (dreams sent by God) and illuminations of the soul which cannot be traced back to any external causes. It would be blasphemy to assert that God can manifest himself everywhere save only in the human soul. Indeed the very intimacy of the relationship between God and the soul precludes from the start any devaluation of the latter.[5] It would be going perhaps too far to speak of an affinity; but at all events the soul must contain in itself the facility of relationship to God, i.e., a correspondence, otherwise a connection could never come about.[6] *This correspondence is, in psychological terms, the archetype of the God-image.*

12   Every archetype is capable of endless development and differentiation. It is therefore possible for it to be more developed or less. In an outward form of religion where all the emphasis is on the outward figure (hence where we are dealing with a more or less complete projection), the archetype is identical with externalized ideas but remains unconscious as a psychic factor. When an unconscious content is replaced by a projected image to that extent, it is cut off from all participation in and influence on the conscious mind. Hence it largely forfeits its own life, because prevented from exerting the formative influence on consciousness natural to it; what is more, it remains in its original form—unchanged, for nothing changes the unconscious. At a certain point it even develops a tendency to regress to lower and more archaic levels. It may easily happen, therefore, that a Christian who believes in all the sacred figures is still undeveloped and unchanged in his inmost soul because he has "all God outside" and does not experience him in the soul. His deciding motives, his ruling interests and impulses, do not spring from the sphere of Christianity but from the unconscious and undeveloped psyche, which is as pagan and archaic as ever. Not the individual alone but the sum total of individual lives in a nation proves the truth of this contention. The great events of our world as planned and executed by man do not breathe the spirit of Christianity but rather of unadorned paganism. These things originate in a psychic condition that has remained archaic and has not been

---

[5] The fact that the devil too can take possession of the soul does not diminish its significance in the least.

[6] It is therefore psychologically quite unthinkable for God to be simply the "wholly other," for a "wholly other" could never be one of the soul's deepest and closest intimacies—which is precisely what God is. The only statements that have psychological validity concerning the God-image are either paradoxes or antinomies.

even remotely touched by Christianity. The Church assumes, not altogether without reason, that the fact of *semel credidisse* (having once believed) leaves certain traces behind it; but of these traces nothing is to be seen in the broad march of events. Christian civilization has proved hollow to a terrifying degree: it is all veneer, but the inner man has remained untouched and therefore unchanged. His soul is out of key with his external beliefs; in his soul the Christian has not kept pace with external developments. Yes, everything is to be found outside—in image and in word, in Church and Bible—but never inside. Inside reign the archaic gods, supreme as of old; that is to say the inner correspondence with the outer God-image is undeveloped for lack of psychological culture and has therefore got stuck in heathenism. Christian education has done all that is humanly possible, but it has not been enough. Too few people have experienced the divine image as the innermost possession of their own souls. Christ only meets them from without, never from within the soul; that is why dark paganism still reigns there, a paganism which, now in a form so blatant that it can no longer be denied and now in all too threadbare disguise, is swamping the world of so-called Christian civilization.

13   With the methods employed hitherto we have not succeeded in Christianizing the soul to the point where even the most elementary demands of Christian ethics can exert any decisive influence on the main concerns of the Christian European. The Christian missionary may preach the gospel to the poor naked heathen, but the spiritual heathen who populate Europe have as yet heard nothing of Christianity. Christianity must indeed begin again from the very beginning if it is to meet its high educative task. So long as religion is only faith and outward form, and the religious function is not experienced in our own souls, nothing of any importance has happened. It has yet to be understood that the *mysterium magnum* is not only an actuality but is first and foremost rooted in the human psyche. The man who does not know this from his own experience may be a most learned theologian, but he has no idea of religion and still less of education.

14   Yet when I point out that the soul possesses by nature a religious function,[7] and when I stipulate that it is the prime task of all education (of adults) to convey the archetype of the God-image, or its emanations and effects, to the conscious mind, then it is precisely the theologian who seizes me by the arm and accuses me of "psychologism." But were it not a fact of experience that supreme values reside in the soul (quite

[7] Tertullian, *Apologeticus*, xvii: "Anima naturaliter christiana."

apart from the ἀντίμιμον πνεῦμα who is also there), psychology would not interest me in the least, for the soul would then be nothing but a miserable vapour. I know, however, from hundredfold experience that it is nothing of the sort, but on the contrary contains the equivalents of everything that has been formulated in dogma and a good deal more, which is just what enables it to be an eye destined to behold the light. This requires limitless range and unfathomable depth of vision. I have been accused of "deifying the soul." Not I but God himself has deified it! *I* did not attribute a religious function to the soul, I merely produced the facts which prove that the soul is *naturaliter religiosa*, i.e., possesses a religious function. I did not invent or insinuate this function, it produces itself of its own accord without being prompted thereto by any opinions or suggestions of mine. With a truly tragic delusion these theologians fail to see that it is not a matter of proving the existence of the light, but of blind people who do not know that their eyes could see. It is high time we realized that it is pointless to praise the light and preach it if nobody can see it. It is much more needful to teach people the art of seeing. For it is obvious that far too many people are incapable of establishing a connection between the sacred figures and their own psyche: they cannot see to what extent the equivalent images are lying dormant in their own unconscious. In order to facilitate this inner vision we must first clear the way for the faculty of seeing. How this is to be done without psychology, that is, without making contact with the psyche, is frankly beyond my comprehension.[8]

15   Another equally serious misunderstanding lies in imputing to psychology the wish to be a new and possibly heretical doctrine. If a blind man can gradually be helped to see it is not to be expected that he will at once discern new truths with an eagle eye. One must be glad if he sees anything at all, and if he begins to understand what he sees. Psychology is concerned with the act of seeing and not with the construction of new religious truths, when even the existing teachings have not yet been perceived and understood. In religious matters it is a well-known fact that we cannot understand a thing until we have experienced it inwardly, for it is in the inward experience that the connection between the psyche and the outward image or creed is first revealed as a relationship or correspondence like that of *sponsus* and *sponsa*. Accordingly when I say as a psychologist that God is an archetype, I mean by that the "type" in the psyche. The word "type" is, as we know, de-

---

[8] Since it is a question here of human effort, I leave aside acts of grace which are beyond man's control.

rived from τύπος, "blow or "imprint": thus an archetype presupposes an imprinter. Psychology as the science of the soul has to confine itself to its subject and guard against overstepping its proper boundaries by metaphysical assertions or other professions of faith. Should it set up a God, even as a hypothetical cause, it would have implicitly claimed the possibility of proving God, thus exceeding its competence in an absolutely illegitimate way. Science can only be science; there are no "scientific" professions of faith and similar *contradictiones in adiecto*. We simply do not know the ultimate derivation of the archetype any more than we know the origin of the psyche. The competence of psychology as an empirical science only goes so far as to establish, on the basis of comparative research, whether for instance the imprint found in the psyche can or cannot reasonably termed a "God-image." Nothing positive or negative has thereby been asserted about the possible existence of God, any more than the archetype of the "hero" posits the actual existence of a hero.

16   Now if my psychological researches have demonstrated the existence of certain psychic types and their correspondence with well-known religious ideas, then we have opened up a possible approach to those experienceable contents which manifestly and undeniably form the empirical foundations of all religious experience. The religious-minded man is free to accept whatever metaphysical explanations he pleases about the origin of these images; not so the intellect, which must keep strictly to the principles of scientific interpretation and avoid trespassing beyond the bounds of what can be known. Nobody can prevent the believer from accepting God, Purusha, the Atman, or Tao as the Prime Cause and thus putting an end to the fundamental disquiet of man. The scientist is a scrupulous worker; he cannot take heaven by storm. Should he allow himself to be seduced into such an extravagance he would be sawing off the branch on which he sits.

17   The fact is that with the knowledge and actual experience of these inner images a way is opened for reason and feeling to gain access to those other images which the teachings of religion offer to mankind. Psychology thus does just the opposite of what it is accused of: it provides possible approaches to a better understanding of these things, it opens people's eyes to the real meaning of dogmas, and, far from destroying, it throws open an empty house to new inhabitants. I can corroborate this from countless experiences: people belonging to creeds of all imaginable kinds, who had played the apostate or cooled off in their faith, have found a new approach to their old truths, not a few Catholics among them. Even a Parsee found the way back to the Zoroastrian fire-temple, which should bear witness to the objectivity of my point of view.

18   But this objectivity is just what my psychology is most blamed for: it is said not to decide in favour of this or that religious doctrine. Without prejudice to my own subjective convictions I should like to raise the question: Is it not thinkable that when one refrains from setting oneself up as an *arbiter mundi* and, deliberately renouncing all subjectivism, cherishes on the contrary the belief, for instance, that God has expressed himself in many languages and appeared in diverse forms and that all these statements are *true*—is it not thinkable, I say, that this too is a decision? The objection raised, more particularly by Christians, that it is impossible for contradictory statements to be true, must permit itself to be politely asked: Does one equal three? How can three be one? Can a mother be a virgin? And so on. Has it not yet been observed that all religious statements contain logical contradictions and assertions that are impossible in principle, that this is in fact the very essence of religious assertion? As witness to this we have Tertullian's avowal: "And the Son of God is dead, which is worthy of belief because it is absurd. And when buried He rose again, which is certain because it is impossible."[9] If Christianity demands faith in such contradictions it does not seem to me that it can very well condemn those who assert a few paradoxes more. Oddly enough the paradox is one of our most valuable spiritual possessions, while uniformity of meaning is a sign of weakness. Hence a religion becomes inwardly impoverished when it loses or waters down its paradoxes; but their multiplication enriches because only the paradox comes anywhere near to comprehending the fulness of life. Non-ambiguity and non-contradiction are one-sided and thus unsuited to express the incomprehensible.

19   Not everyone possesses the spiritual strength of a Tertullian. It is evident not only that he had the strength to sustain paradoxes but that they actually afforded him the highest degree of religious certainty. The inordinate number of spiritual weaklings makes paradoxes dangerous. So long as the paradox remains unexamined and is taken for granted as a customary part of life, it is harmless enough. But when it occurs to an insufficiently cultivated mind (always, as we know, the most sure of itself) to make the paradoxical nature of some tenet of faith the object of its lucubrations, as earnest as they are impotent, it is not long before such a one will break out into iconoclastic and scornful laughter, pointing to the manifest absurdity of the mystery. Things have gone rapidly downhill since the Age of Enlightenment, for, once this petty reasoning mind, which cannot endure any paradoxes, is awak-

[9] Tertullian, *De carne Christi*, 5 (Migne, *P.L.*, vol. 2, col. 751).

ened, no sermon on earth can keep it down. A new task then arises: to lift this still undeveloped mind step by step to a higher level and to increase the number of persons who have at least some inkling of the scope of paradoxical truth. If this is not possible, then it must be admitted that the spiritual approaches to Christianity are as good as blocked. We simply do not understand any more what is meant by the paradoxes contained in dogma; and the more external our understanding of them becomes the more we are affronted by their irrationality, until finally they become completely obsolete, curious relics of the past. The man who is stricken in this way cannot estimate the extent of his spiritual loss, because he has never experienced the sacred images as his inmost possession and has never realized their kinship with his own psychic structure. But it is just this indispensable knowledge that the psychology of the unconscious can give him, and its scientific objectivity is of the greatest value here. Were psychology bound to a creed it would not and could not allow the unconscious of the individual that free play which is the basic condition for the production of archetypes. It is precisely the spontaneity of archetypal contents that convinces, whereas any prejudiced intervention is a bar to genuine experience. If the theologian really believes in the almighty power of God on the one hand and in the validity of dogma on the other, why then does he not trust God to speak in the soul? Why this fear of psychology? Or is, in complete contradiction to dogma, the soul itself a hell from which only demons gibber? Even if this were really so it would not be any the less convincing; for as we all know the horrified perception of the reality of evil has led to at least as many conversions as the experience of good.

20   The archetypes of the unconscious can be shown empirically to be the equivalents of religious dogmas. In the hermeneutic language of the Fathers the Church possesses a rich store of analogies with the individual and spontaneous products to be found in psychology. What the unconscious expresses is far from being merely arbitrary or opinionated; it is something that happens to be "just-so," as is the case with every other natural being. It stands to reason that the expressions of the unconscious are natural and not formulated dogmatically; they are exactly like the patristic allegories which draw the whole of nature into the orbit of their amplifications. If these present us with some astonishing *allegoriae Christi*, we find much the same sort of thing in the psychology of the unconscious. The only difference is that the patristic allegory *ad Christum spectat*—refers to Christ—whereas the psychic archetype is simply itself and can therefore be interpreted according to

time, place, and milieu. In the West the archetype is filled out with the dogmatic figure of Christ; in the East, with Purusha, the Atman, Hiranyagarbha, the Buddha, and so on. The religious point of view, understandably enough, puts the accent on the imprinter, whereas scientific psychology emphasizes the *typos*, the imprint—the only thing it can understand. The religious point of view understands the imprint as the working of an imprinter; the scientific point of view understands it as the symbol of an unknown and incomprehensible content. Since the *typos* is less definite and more variegated than any of the figures postulated by religion, psychology is compelled by its empirical material to express the *typos* by means of a terminology not bound by time, place, or milieu. If, for example, the *typos* agreed in every detail with the dogmatic figure of Christ, and if it contained no determinant that went beyond that figure, we would be bound to regard the *typos* as at least a faithful copy of the dogmatic figure, and to name it accordingly. The *typos* would then coincide with Christ. But as experience shows, this is not the case, seeing that the unconscious, like the allegories employed by the Church Fathers, produces countless other determinants that are not explicitly contained in the dogmatic formula; that is to say, non-Christian figures such as those mentioned above are included in the *typos*. But neither do these figures comply with the indeterminate nature of the archetype. It is altogether inconceivable that there could be any definite figure capable of expressing archetypal indefiniteness. For this reason I have found myself obliged to give the corresponding archetype the psychological name of the "self"—a term on the one hand definite enough to convey the essence of human wholeness and on the other hand indefinite enough to express the indescribable and indeterminable nature of this wholeness. The paradoxical qualities of the term are a reflection of the fact that wholeness consists partly of the conscious man and partly of the unconscious man. But we cannot define the latter or indicate his boundaries. Hence in its scientific usage the term "self" refers neither to Christ nor to the Buddha but to the totality of the figures that are its equivalent, and each of these figures is a symbol of the self. This mode of expression is an intellectual necessity in scientific psychology and in no sense denotes a transcendental prejudice. On the contrary, as we have said before, this objective attitude enables one man to decide in favour of the determinant Christ, another in favour of the Buddha, and so on. Those who are irritated by this objectivity should reflect that science is quite impossible without it. Consequently by denying psychology the right to objectivity they are making an untimely attempt to extinguish the life-light of a science. Even if such a preposterous attempt were to succeed, it would only widen the already catastrophic gulf between the secular mind on the one hand and Church and religion on the other.

21   It is quite understandable for a science to concentrate more or less exclusively on its subject—indeed, that is its absolute *raison d'être*. Since the concept of the self is of central interest in psychology, the latter naturally thinks along lines diametrically opposed to theology: for psychology the religious figures point to the self, whereas for theology the self points to its—theology's—own central figure. In other words, theology might possibly take the psychological self as an allegory of Christ. This opposition is, no doubt, very irritating, but unfortunately inevitable, unless psychology is to be denied the right to exist at all. I therefore plead for tolerance. Nor is this very hard for psychology since as a science it makes no totalitarian claims.

22   The Christ-symbol is of the greatest importance for psychology in so far as it is perhaps the most highly developed and differentiated symbol of the self, apart from the figure of the Buddha. We can see this from the scope and substance of all the pronouncements that have been made about Christ: they agree with the psychological phenomenology of the self in unusually high degree, although they do not include all aspects of this archetype. The almost limitless range of the self might be deemed a disadvantage as compared with the definiteness of a religious figure, but it is by no means the task of science to pass value judgments. Not only is the self indefinite but—paradoxically enough— it also includes the quality of definiteness and even of uniqueness. This is probably one of the reasons why precisely those religions founded by historical personages have become world religions, such as Christianity, Buddhism, and Islam. The inclusion in a religion of a unique human personality—especially when conjoined to an indeterminable divine nature—is consistent with the absolute individuality of the self, which combines uniqueness with eternity and the individual with the universal. The self is a union of opposites *par excellence*, and this is where it differs essentially from the Christ-symbol. The androgyny of Christ is the utmost concession the Church has made to the problem of opposites. The opposition between light and good on the one hand and darkness and evil on the other is left in a state of open conflict, since Christ simply represents good, and his counterpart the devil, evil. This opposition is the real world problem, which at present is still unsolved. The self, however, is absolutely paradoxical in that it represents in every respect thesis and antithesis, and at the same time synthesis. (Psychological proofs of this assertion abound, though it is impossible for me to quote them here *in extenso*. I would refer the knowledgeable reader to the symbolism of the mandala.)

195

23   Once the exploration of the unconscious has led the conscious mind to an experience of the archetype, the individual is confronted with the abysmal contradictions of human nature, and this confrontation in turn leads to the possibility of a direct experience of light and darkness, of Christ and the devil. For better or worse there is only a bare possibility of this, and not a guarantee; for experiences of this kind cannot of necessity be induced by any human means. There are factors to be considered which are not under our control. Experience of the opposites has nothing whatever to do with intellectual insight or with empathy. It is more what we would call fate. Such an experience can convince one person of the truth of Christ, another of the truth of the Buddha, to the exclusion of all other evidence.

24   Without the experience of the opposites there is no experience of wholeness and hence no inner approach to the sacred figures. For this reason Christianity rightly insists on sinfulness and original sin, with the obvious intent of opening up the abyss of universal opposition in every individual—at least from the outside. But this method is bound to break down in the case of a moderately alert intellect: dogma is then simply no longer believed and on top of that is thought absurd. Such an intellect is merely one-sided and sticks at the *ineptia mysterii*. It is miles from Tertullian's antinomies; in fact, it is quite incapable of enduring the suffering such a tension involves. Cases are not unknown where the rigorous exercises and proselytizings of the Catholics, and a certain type of Protestant education that is always sniffing out sin, have brought about psychic damage that leads not to the Kingdom of Heaven but to the consulting room of the doctor. Although insight into the problem of opposites is absolutely imperative, there are very few people who can stand it in practice—a fact which has not escaped the notice of the confessional. By way of a reaction to this we have the palliative of "moral probabilism," a doctrine that has suffered frequent attack from all quarters because it tries to mitigate the crushing effect of sin.[10] Whatever one may think of this phenomenon one thing is

---

[10] Zöckler ("Probabilismus," p. 67) defines it as follows: "Probabilism is the name generally given to that way of thinking which is content to answer scientific questions with a greater or lesser degree of probability. The moral probabilism with which alone we are concerned here consists in the principle that acts of ethical self-determination are to be guided not by conscience but according to what is probably right, i.e., according to whatever has been recommended by any representative or doctrinal authority." The Jesuit probabilist Escobar (d. 1669) was, for instance, of the opinion that if the penitent should plead a probable opinion as the motive of his action, the father-confessor would he obliged to absolve him even if he were not of the same opinion. Escobar quotes a

certain: that apart from anything else it holds within it a large humanity and an understanding of human weakness which compensate for the world's unbearable antinomies. The tremendous paradox implicit in the insistence on original sin on the one hand and the concession made by probabilism on the other is, for the psychologist, a necessary consequence of the Christian problem of opposites outlined above— for in the self good and evil are indeed closer than identical twins! The reality of evil and its incompatibility with good cleave the opposites asunder and lead inexorably to the crucifixion and suspension of everything that lives. Since "the soul is by nature Christian" this result is bound to come as infallibly as it did in the life of Jesus: we all have to be "crucified with Christ," i.e., suspended in a moral suffering equivalent to veritable crucifixion. In practice this is only possible up to a point, and apart from that is so unbearable and inimical to life that the ordinary human being can afford to get into such a state only occasionally, in fact as seldom as possible. For how could he remain ordinary in face of such suffering! A more or less probabilistic attitude to the problem of evil is therefore unavoidable. Hence the truth about the self—the unfathomable union of good and evil—comes out concretely in the paradox that although sin is the gravest and most pernicious thing there is, it is still not so serious that it cannot be disposed of with "probabilist" arguments. Nor is this necessarily a lax or frivolous proceeding but simply a practical necessity of life. The confessional proceeds like life itself, which successfully struggles against being engulfed in an irreconcilable contradiction. Note that at the same time the conflict remains in full force, as is once more consistent with the antinomial character of the self, which is itself both conflict and unity.

25 Christianity has made the antinomy of good and evil into a world problem and, by formulating the conflict dogmatically, raised it to an absolute principle. Into this as yet unresolved conflict the Christian is cast as a protagonist of good, a fellow player in the world drama. Understood in its deepest sense, being Christ's follower involves a suffering that is unendurable to the great majority of mankind. Consequently the

---

number of Jesuit authorities on the question of how often one is bound to love God in a lifetime. According to one opinion, loving God once shortly before death is sufficient; another says once a year or once every three or four years. He himself comes to the conclusion that it is sufficient to love God once at the first awakening of reason, then once every five years, and finally once in the hour of death. In his opinion the large number of different moral doctrines forms one of the main proofs of God's kindly providence, "because they make the yoke of Christ so light" (Zöckler, p. 68). Cf. also Harnack, *History of Dogma*, VII, pp. 101ff.

example of Christ is in reality followed either with reservation or not at all, and the pastoral practice of the Church even finds itself obliged to "lighten the yoke of Christ." This means a pretty considerable reduction in the severity and harshness of the conflict and hence, in practice, a relativism of good and evil. Good is equivalent to the unconditional imitation of Christ and evil is its hindrance. Man's moral weakness and sloth are what chiefly hinder the imitation, and it is to these that probabilism extends a practical understanding which may sometimes, perhaps, come nearer to Christian tolerance, mildness, and love of one's neighbour than the attitude of those who see in probabilism a mere laxity. Although one must concede a number of cardinal Christian virtues to the probabilist endeavour, one must still not overlook the fact that it obviates much of the suffering involved in the imitation of Christ and that the conflict of good and evil is thus robbed of its harshness and toned down to tolerable proportions. This brings about an approach to the psychic archetype of the self, where even these opposites seem to be united—though, as I say, it differs from the Christian symbolism, which leaves the conflict open. For the latter there is a rift running through the world: light wars against night and the upper against the lower. The two are not one, as they are in the psychic archetype. But, even though religious dogma may condemn the idea of two being one, religious practice does, as we have seen, allow the natural psychological symbol of the self at one with itself an approximate means of expression. On the other hand, dogma insists that three are one, while denying that four are one. Since olden times, not only in the West but also in China, uneven numbers have been regarded as masculine and even numbers as feminine. The Trinity is therefore a decidedly masculine deity, of which the androgyny of Christ and the special position and veneration accorded to the Mother of God are not the real equivalent.

26   With this statement, which may strike the reader as peculiar, we come to one of the central axioms of alchemy, namely the saying of Maria Prophetissi: "One becomes two, two becomes three, and out of the third comes the one as the fourth." As the reader has already seen from its title, this book is concerned with the psychological significance of alchemy and thus with a problem which, with very few exceptions, has so far eluded scientific research. Until quite recently science was interested only in the part that alchemy played in the history of chemistry, concerning itself very little with the part it played in the history of philosophy and religion. The importance of alchemy for the historical development of chemistry is obvious, but its cultural importance is still so little known that it seems almost impossible to say in a few words

wherein that consisted. In this introduction, therefore, I have attempted to outline the religious and psychological problems which are germane to the theme of alchemy. The point is that alchemy is rather like an undercurrent to the Christianity that ruled on the surface. It is to this surface as the dream is to consciousness, and just as the dream compensates the conflicts of the conscious mind, so alchemy endeavours to fill in the gaps left open by the Christian tension of opposites. Perhaps the most pregnant expression of this is the axiom of Maria Prophetissa quoted above, which runs like a *leitmotiv* throughout almost the whole of the lifetime of alchemy, extending over more than seventeen centuries. In this aphorism the even numbers which signify the feminine principle, earth, the regions under the earth, and evil itself, are interpolated between the uneven numbers of the Christian dogma. They are personified by the *serpens mercurii*, the dragon that creates and destroys itself and represents the *prima materia*. This fundamental idea of alchemy points back to the תְּהוֹם (Tehom),[11] to Tiamat with her dragon attribute, and thus to the primordial matriarchal world which, in the theomachy of the Marduk myth,[12] was overthrown by the masculine world of the father. The historical shift in the world's consciousness towards the masculine is compensated at first by the chthonic femininity of the unconscious. In certain pre-Christian religions the differentiation of the masculine principle had taken the form of the father-son specification, a change which was to be of the utmost importance for Christianity. Were the unconscious merely complementary, this shift of consciousness would have been accompanied by the production of a mother and daughter, for which the necessary material lay ready to hand in the myth of Demeter and Persephone. But, as alchemy shows, the unconscious chose rather the Cybele-Attis type in the form of the *prima materia* and the *filius macrocosmi*, thus proving that it is not complementary but compensatory. This goes to show that the unconscious does not simply act *contrary* to the conscious mind but *modifies* it more in the manner of an opponent or partner. The son type does not call up a daughter as a complementary image from the depths of the "chthonic" unconscious—it calls up another son. This remarkable fact would seem to be connected with the incarnation in our earthly human nature of a purely spiritual God, brought about by

---

[11] Cf. Genesis 1:2.

[12] The reader will find a collection of these myth motifs in Lang, *Hat ein Gott die Welt erschaffen?* Unfortunately philological criticism will have much to take exception to in this book, interesting though it is for its Gnostic trend.

199

the Holy Ghost impregnating the womb of the Blessed Virgin. Thus the higher, the spiritual, the masculine inclines to the lower, the earthly, the feminine; and accordingly, the mother, who was anterior to the world of the father, accommodates herself to the masculine principle and, with the aid of the human spirit (alchemy or "the philosophy"), produces a son—not the antithesis of Christ but rather his chthonic counterpart, not a divine man but a fabulous being conforming to the nature of the primordial mother. And just as the redemption of man the microcosm is the task of the "upper" son, so the "lower" son has the function of a *salvator macrocosmi*.

27   This, in brief, is the drama that was played out in the obscurities of alchemy. It is superfluous to remark that these two sons were never united, except perhaps in the mind and innermost experience of a few particularly gifted alchemists. But it is not very difficult to see the "purpose" of this drama: in the Incarnation it looked as though the masculine principle of the father-world were approximating to the feminine principle of the mother-world, with the result that the latter felt impelled to approximate in turn to the father-world. What it evidently amounted to was an attempt to bridge the gulf separating the two worlds as compensation for the open conflict between them.

28   I hope the reader will not be offended if my exposition sounds like a Gnostic myth. We are moving in those psychological regions where, as a matter of fact, Gnosis is rooted. The message of the Christian symbol is Gnosis, and the compensation effected by the unconscious is Gnosis in even higher degree. Myth is the primordial language natural to these psychic processes, and no intellectual formulation comes anywhere near the richness and expressiveness of mythical imagery. Such processes are concerned with the primordial images, and these are best and most succinctly reproduced by figurative language.

29   The process described above displays all the characteristic features of psychological compensation. We know that the mask of the unconscious is not rigid—it reflects the face we turn towards it. Hostility lends it a threatening aspect, friendliness softens its features. It is not a question of mere optical reflection but of an autonomous answer which reveals the self-sufficing nature of that which answers. Thus the *filius philosophorum* is not just the reflected image, in unsuitable material, of the son of God; on the contrary, this son of Tiamat reflects the features of the primordial maternal figure. Although he is decidedly hermaphroditic he has a masculine name—a sign that the chthonic underworld, having been rejected by the spirit and identified with evil, has a tendency to compromise. There is no mistaking the fact that he is a concession to the spiritual and masculine principle, even though he

carries in himself the weight of the earth and the whole fabulous nature of primordial animality.

30   This answer of the mother-world shows that the gulf between it and the father-world is not unbridgeable, seeing that the unconscious holds the seed of the unity of both. The essence of the conscious mind is discrimination; it must, if it is to be aware of things, separate the opposites, and it does this *contra naturam*. In nature the opposites seek one another—*les extrêmes se touchent*—and so it is in the unconscious, and particularly in the archetype of unity, the self. Here, as in the deity, the opposites cancel out. But as soon as the unconscious begins to manifest itself they split asunder, as at the Creation; for every act of dawning consciousness is a creative act, and it is from this psychological experience that all our cosmogonic symbols are derived.

31   Alchemy is pre-eminently concerned with the seed of unity which lies hidden in the chaos of Tiamat and forms the counterpart to the divine unity. Like this, the seed of unity has a trinitarian character in Christian alchemy and a triadic character in pagan alchemy. According to other authorities it corresponds to the unity of the four elements and is therefore a quaternity. The overwhelming majority of modern psychological findings speaks in favour of the latter view. The few cases I have observed which produced the number three were marked by a systematic deficiency in consciousness, that is to say, by an unconsciousness of the "inferior function." The number three is not a natural expression of wholeness, since four represents the minimum number of determinants in a whole judgment. It must nevertheless be stressed that side by side with the distinct leanings of alchemy (and of the unconscious) towards quaternity there is always a vacillation between three and four which comes out over and over again. Even in the axiom of Maria Prophetissa the quaternity is muffled and alembicated. In alchemy there are three as well as four *regimina* or procedures, three as well as four colours. There are always four elements, but often three of them are grouped together, with the fourth in a special position—sometimes earth, sometimes fire. Mercurius[13] is of course *quadratus*, but he is also a

---

[13] In alchemical writings the word "Mercurius" is used with a very wide range of meaning, to denote not only the chemical element mercury or quicksilver, Mercury (Hermes) the god, and Mercury the planet, but also—and primarily—the secret "transforming substance" which is at the same time the "spirit" indwelling in all living creatures. These different connotations will become apparent in the course of the book. It would be misleading to use the English "Mercury" and "mercury," because there are innumerable passages where neither word does justice to the wealth of implications. It has therefore been decided to retain the Latin "Mercurius" as in the German text, and to use the personal pronoun (since "Mercurius" is personified), the word "quicksilver" being em-

three-headed snake or simply a triunity. This uncertainty has a duplex character—in other words, the central ideas are ternary as well as quaternary. The psychologist cannot but mention the fact that a similar puzzle exists in the psychology of the unconscious: the least differentiated or "inferior" function is so much contaminated with the collective unconscious that, on becoming conscious, it brings up among others the archetype of the self as well—τὸ ἕν τέταρτον, as Maria Prophetissa says. Four signifies the feminine, motherly, physical; three the masculine, fatherly, spiritual. Thus the uncertainty as to three or four amounts to a wavering between the spiritual and the physical—a striking example of how every human truth is a last truth but one.

32   I began my introduction with human wholeness as the goal to which the psychotherapeutic process ultimately leads. This question is inextricably bound up with one's philosophical or religious assumptions. Even when, as frequently happens, the patient believes himself to be quite unprejudiced in this respect, the assumptions underlying his thought, mode of life, morale, and language are historically conditioned down to the last detail, a fact of which he is often kept unconscious by lack of education combined with lack of self-criticism. The analysis of his situation will therefore lead sooner or later to a clarification of his general spiritual background going far beyond his personal determinants, and this brings up the problems I have attempted to sketch in the preceding pages. This phase of the process is marked by the production of symbols of unity, the so-called mandalas, which occur either in dreams or in the form of concrete visual impressions, often as the most obvious compensation of the contradictions and conflicts of the conscious situation. It would hardly be correct to say that the gaping "rift"[14] in the Christian order of things is responsible for this, since it is easy to show that Christian symbolism is particularly concerned with healing, or attempting to heal, this very wound. It would be more correct to take the open conflict as a symptom of the psychic situation of Western man, and to deplore his inability to assimilate the whole range of the Christian symbol. As a doctor I cannot demand anything of my patients in this respect, also I lack the Church's means of grace. Consequently I am faced with the task of taking the only path open to me: the archetypal images—which in a certain sense correspond to the dogmatic images—must be brought into conscious-

ployed only where the chemical element (Hg) is plainly meant. [*Author's note for the English edn.*]

[14] Przywara, *Deus semper maior*, I, pp. 71ff.

ness. At the same time I must leave my patient to decide in accordance with his assumptions, his spiritual maturity, his education, origins, and temperament, so far as this is possible without serious conflicts. As a doctor it is my task to help the patient to cope with life. I cannot presume to pass judgment on his final decisions, because I know from experience that all coercion—be it suggestion, insinuation, or any other method of persuasion—ultimately proves to be nothing but an obstacle to the highest and most decisive experience of all, which is to be alone with his own self, or whatever else one chooses to call the objectivity of the psyche. The patient must be alone if he is to find out what it is that supports him when he can no longer support himself. Only this experience can give him an indestructible foundation.

33   I would be only too delighted to leave this anything but easy task to the theologian, were it not that it is just from the theologian that many of my patients come. They ought to have hung on to the community of the Church, but they were shed like dry leaves from the great tree and now find themselves "hanging on" to the treatment. Something in them clings, often with the strength of despair, as if they or the thing they cling to would drop off into the void the moment they relaxed their hold. They are seeking firm ground on which to stand. Since no outward support is of any use to them they must finally discover it in themselves—admittedly the most unlikely place from the rational point of view, but an altogether possible one from the point of view of the unconscious. We can see this from the archetype of the "lowly origin of the redeemer."

34   The way to the goal seems chaotic and interminable at first, and only gradually do the signs increase that it is leading anywhere. The way is not straight but appears to go round in circles. More accurate knowledge has proved it to go in spirals: the dream-motifs always return after certain intervals to definite forms, whose characteristic it is to define a centre. And as a matter of fact the whole process revolves about a central point or some arrangement round a centre, which may in certain circumstances appear even in the initial dreams. As manifestations of unconscious processes the dreams rotate or circumambulate round the centre, drawing closer to it as the amplifications increase in distinctness and in scope. Owing to the diversity of the symbolical material it is difficult at first to perceive any kind of order at all. Nor should it be taken for granted that dream sequences are subject to any governing principle. But, as I say, the process of development proves on closer inspection to be cyclic or spiral. We might draw a parallel between such spiral courses and the processes of growth in plants; in fact the plant

motif (tree, flower, etc.) frequently recurs in these dreams and fantasies and is also spontaneously drawn or painted.[15] In alchemy, the tree
is the symbol of Hermetic philosophy.

35   The first of the following two studies—that which composes Part
II—deals with a series of dreams which contain numerous symbols of
the centre or goal. The development of these symbols is almost the
equivalent of a healing process. The centre or goal thus signifies *salvation* in the proper sense of the word. The justification for such a terminology comes from the dreams themselves, for these contain so many
references to religious phenomena that I was able to use some of them
as the subject of my book *Psychology and Religion.* It seems to me beyond
all doubt that these processes are concerned with the religion-creating
archetypes. Whatever else religion may be, those psychic ingredients of
it which are empirically verifiable undoubtedly consist of unconscious
manifestations of this kind. People have dwelt far too long on the fundamentally sterile question of whether the assertions of faith are true
or not. Quite apart from the impossibility of ever proving or refuting
the truth of a metaphysical assertion, the very existence of the assertion
is a self-evident fact that needs no further proof, and when a *consensus
gentium* allies itself thereto the validity of the statement is proved to just
that extent. The only thing about it that we can verify is the psychological phenomenon, which is incommensurable with the category of objective rightness or truth. No phenomenon can ever be disposed of by
rational criticism, and in religious life we have to deal with phenomena
and facts and not with arguable hypotheses.

36   During the process of treatment the dialectical discussion leads logically to a meeting between the patient and his shadow, that dark half
of the psyche which we invariably get rid of by means of projection:
either by burdening our neighbours—in a wider or narrower sense—
with all the faults which we obviously have ourselves, or by casting our
sins upon a divine mediator with the aid of *contritio* or the milder *attritio.*[16] We know of course that without sin there is no repentance and
without repentance no redeeming grace, also that without original sin
the redemption of the world could never have come about; but we
assiduously avoid investigating whether in this very power of evil God

---

[15] See the illustrations in Jung, "Concerning Mandala Symbolism."

[16] *Contritio* is "perfect" repentance; *attritio* "imperfect" repentance (*contritio imperfecta*, to
which category *contritio naturalis* belongs). The former regards sin as the opposite of the
highest good; the latter reprehends it not only on account of its wicked and hideous
nature but also from fear of punishment.

might not have placed some special purpose which it is most important for us to know. One often feels driven to some such view when, like the psychotherapist, one has to deal with people who are confronted with their blackest shadow.[17] At any rate the doctor cannot afford to point, with a gesture of facile moral superiority, to the tablets of the law and say, "Thou shalt not." He has to examine things objectively and weigh up possibilities, for he knows, less from religious training and education than from instinct and experience, that there is something very like a *felix culpa*. He knows that one can miss not only one's happiness but also one's final guilt, without which a man will never reach his wholeness. Wholeness is in fact a charisma which one can manufacture neither by art nor by cunning; one can only grow into it and endure whatever its advent may bring. No doubt it is a great nuisance that mankind is not uniform but compounded of individuals whose psychic structure spreads them over a span of at least ten thousand years. Hence there is absolutely no truth that does not spell salvation to one person and damnation to another. All universalisms get stuck in this terrible dilemma. Earlier on I spoke of Jesuit probabilism: this gives a better idea than anything else of the tremendous catholic task of the Church. Even the best-intentioned people have been horrified by probabilism, but, when brought face to face with the realities of life, many of them have found their horror evaporating or their laughter dying on their lips. The doctor too must weigh and ponder, not whether a thing is for or against the Church but whether it is for or against life and health. On paper the moral code looks clear and neat enough; but the same document written on the "living tables of the heart" is often a sorry tatter, particularly in the mouths of those who talk the loudest. We are told on every side that evil is evil and that there can be no hesitation in condemning it, but that does not prevent evil from being the most problematical thing in the individual's life and the one which demands the deepest reflection. What above all deserves our keenest attention is the question "Exactly *who* is the doer?" For the answer to this question ultimately decides the value of the deed. It is true that

---

[17] A religious terminology comes naturally, as the only adequate one in the circumstances, when we are faced with the tragic fate that is the unavoidable concomitant of wholeness. "My fate" means a daemonic will to precisely that fate—a will not necessarily coincident with my own (the ego will). When it is opposed to the ego, it is difficult not to feel a certain "power" in it, whether divine or infernal. The man who submits to his fate calls it the will of God; the man who puts up a hopeless and exhausting fight is more apt to see the devil in it. In either event this terminology is not only universally understood but meaningful as well.

society attaches greater importance at first to what is done, because it is immediately obvious; but in the long run the right deed in the hands of the wrong man will also have a disastrous effect. No one who is far-sighted will allow himself to be hoodwinked by the right deed of the wrong man, any more than by the wrong deed of the right man. Hence the psychotherapist must fix his eye not on what is done but on how it is done, because therein is decided the whole character of the doer. Evil needs to be pondered just as much as good, for good and evil are ultimately nothing but ideal extensions and abstractions of doing, and both belong to the chiaroscuro of life. In the last resort there is no good that cannot produce evil and no evil that cannot produce good.

37   The encounter with the dark half of the personality, or "shadow," comes about of its own accord in any moderately thorough treatment. This problem is as important as that of sin in the Church. The open conflict is unavoidable and painful. I have often been asked, "And what do you *do* about it?" I do nothing; there is nothing I can do except wait, with a certain trust in God, until, out of a conflict borne with patience and fortitude, there emerges the solution destined—although I cannot foresee it—for that particular person. Not that I am passive or inactive meanwhile: I help the patient to understand all the things that the unconscious produces during the conflict. The reader may believe me that these are no ordinary products. On the contrary, they are among the most significant things that have ever engaged my attention. Nor is the patient inactive; he must do the right thing, and do it with all his might, in order to prevent the pressure of evil from becoming too powerful in him. He needs "justification by works," for "justification by faith" alone has remained an empty sound for him as for so many others. Faith can sometimes be a substitute for lack of experience. In these cases what is needed is real work. Christ espoused the sinner and did not condemn him. The true follower of Christ will do the same, and, since one should do unto others as one would do unto oneself, one will also take the part of the sinner who is oneself. And as little as we would accuse Christ of fraternizing with evil, so little should we reproach ourselves that to love the sinner who is oneself is to make a pact with the devil. Love makes a man better, hate makes him worse—even when that man is oneself. The danger in this point of view is the same as in the imitation of Christ; but the Pharisee in us will never allow himself to be caught talking to publicans and whores. I must emphasize of course that psychology invented neither Christianity nor the imitation of Christ. I wish everybody could be freed from the burden of their sins by the Church. But he to whom she cannot render this service must bend very low in the imitation of Christ in order to

206

take the burden of his cross upon him. The ancients could get along with the Greek wisdom of the ages: Μηδὲν ἄγαν, τῷ καιρῷ πάντα πρόσεστι καλά (Exaggerate nothing, all good lies in right measure). But what an abyss still separates us from reason!

38   Apart from the moral difficulty there is another danger which is not inconsiderable and may lead to complications, particularly with individuals who are pathologically inclined. This is the fact that the contents of the personal unconscious (i.e., the shadow) are indistinguishably merged with the archetypal contents of the collective unconscious and drag the latter with them when the shadow is brought into consciousness. This may exert an uncanny influence on the conscious mind; for activated archetypes have a disagreeable effect even—or I should perhaps say, particularly—on the most cold-blooded rationalist. He is afraid that the lowest form of conviction, namely superstition, is, as he thinks, forcing itself on him. But superstition in the truest sense only appears in such people if they are pathological, not if they can keep their balance. It then takes the form of the fear of "going mad"—for everything that the modern mind cannot define it regards as insane. It must be admitted that the archetypal contents of the collective unconscious can often assume grotesque and horrible forms in dreams and fantasies, so that even the most hard-boiled rationalist is not immune from shattering nightmares and haunting fears. The psychological elucidation of these images, which cannot be passed over in silence or blindly ignored, leads logically into the depths of religious phenomenology. The history of religion in its widest sense (including therefore mythology, folklore, and primitive psychology) is a treasure-house of archetypal forms from which the doctor can draw helpful parallels and enlightening comparisons for the purpose of calming and clarifying a consciousness that is all at sea. It is absolutely necessary to supply these fantastic images that rise up so strange and threatening before the mind's eye with some kind of context so as to make them more intelligible. Experience has shown that the best way to do this is by means of comparative mythological material.

39   Part II of this volume gives a large number of such examples. The reader will be particularly struck by the numerous connections between individual dream symbolism and medieval alchemy. This is not, as one might suppose, a prerogative of the case in question, but a general fact which only struck me some ten years ago when first I began to come to grips with the ideas and symbolism of alchemy.

40   Part III contains an introduction to the symbolism of alchemy in relation to Christianity and Gnosticism. As a bare introduction it is naturally far from being a complete exposition of this complicated and

obscure subject—indeed, most of it is concerned only with the *lapis*-Christ parallel. True, this parallel gives rise to a comparison between the aims of the *opus alchymicum* and the central ideas of Christianity, for both are of the utmost importance in understanding and interpreting the images that appear in dreams and in assessing their psychological effect. This has considerable bearing on the practice of psychotherapy, because more often than not it is precisely the more intelligent and cultured patients who, finding a return to the Church impossible, come up against archetypal material and thus set the doctor problems which can no longer be mastered by a narrowly personalistic psychology. Nor is a mere knowledge of the psychic structure of a neurosis by any means sufficient; for once the process has reached the sphere of the collective unconscious we are dealing with healthy material, i.e., with the universal basis of the individually varied psyche. Our understanding of these deeper layers of the psyche is helped not only by a knowledge of primitive psychology and mythology, but to an even greater extent by some familiarity with the history of our modern consciousness and the stages immediately preceding it. On the one hand it is a child of the Church; on the other, of science, in whose beginnings very much lies hid that the Church was unable to accept—that is to say, remnants of the classical spirit and the classical feeling for nature which could not be exterminated and eventually found refuge in the natural philosophy of the Middle Ages. As the "spiritus metallorum" and the astrological components of destiny the old gods of the planets lasted out many a Christian century.[18] Whereas in the Church the increasing differentiation of ritual and dogma alienated consciousness from its natural roots in the unconscious, alchemy and astrology were ceaselessly engaged in preserving the bridge to nature, i.e., to the unconscious psyche, from decay. Astrology led the conscious mind back again and again to the knowledge of Heimarmene, that is, the dependence of character and destiny on certain moments in time; and alchemy afforded numerous "hooks" for the projection of those archetypes which could not be fitted smoothly into the Christian process. It is true that alchemy always stood on the verge of heresy and that certain decrees leave no doubt as to the Church's attitude towards it,[19] but on the other hand it was effectively protected by the obscurity of its

---

[18] Paracelsus still speaks of the "gods" enthroned in the *mysterium magnum* (*Philosophia ad Athenienses*, p. 403), and so does the 18th-cent. treatise of Abraham Eleazar, *Uraltes chymisches Werk*, which was influenced by Paracelsus.

[19] Cf. Sanchez, *Opus morale*, Decalog. 2, 49n., 51; and Pignatelli, *Consultationes canonicae*, canon ix.

symbolism, which could always be explained as harmless allegory. For many alchemists the allegorical aspect undoubtedly occupied the foreground to such an extent that they were firmly convinced that their sole concern was with chemical substances. But there were always a few for whom laboratory work was primarily a matter of symbols and their psychic effect. As the texts show, they were quite conscious of this, to the point of condemning the naïve goldmakers as liars, frauds, and dupes. Their own standpoint they proclaimed with propositions like "Aurum nostrum non est aurum vulgi." Although their labours over the retort were a serious effort to elicit the secrets of chemical transformation, it was at the same time—and often in overwhelming degree—the reflection of a parallel psychic process which could be projected all the more easily into the unknown chemistry of matter since that process is an unconscious phenomenon of nature, just like the mysterious alteration of substances. What the symbolism of alchemy expresses is the whole problem of the evolution of personality described above, the so-called individuation process.

41   Whereas the Church's great buttress is the imitation of Christ, the alchemist, without realizing it and certainly without wanting it, easily fell victim, in the loneliness and obscure problems of his work, to the promptings and unconscious assumptions of his own mind, since, unlike the Christians, he had no clear and unmistakable models on which to rely. The authors he studied provided him with symbols whose meaning he thought he understood in his own way; but in reality they touched and stimulated his unconscious. Ironical towards themselves, the alchemists coined the phrase "obscurum per obscurius." But with this method of explaining the obscure by the more obscure they only sank themselves deeper in the very process from which the Church was struggling to redeem them. While the dogmas of the Church offered analogies to the alchemical process, these analogies, in strict contrast to alchemy, had become detached from the world of nature through their connection with the historical figure of the Redeemer. The alchemical four in one, the philosophical gold, the *lapis angularis*, the *aqua divina*, became, in the Church, the four-armed cross on which the Only-Begotten had sacrificed himself once in history and at the same time for all eternity. The alchemists ran counter to the Church in preferring to seek through knowledge rather than to find through faith, though as medieval people they never thought of themselves as anything but good Christians. Paracelsus is a classical example in this respect. But in reality they were in much the same position as modern man, who prefers immediate personal experience to belief in traditional ideas, or rather has it forced upon him. Dogma is not arbitrarily

invented nor is it a unique miracle, although it is often described as miraculous with the obvious intent of lifting it out of its natural context. The central ideas of Christianity are rooted in Gnostic philosophy, which, in accordance with psychological laws, simply *had* to grow up at a time when the classical religions had become obsolete. It was founded on the perception of symbols thrown up by the unconscious individuation process which always sets in when the collective dominants of human life fall into decay. At such a time there is bound to be a considerable number of individuals who are possessed by archetypes of a numinous nature that force their way to the surface in order to form new dominants. This state of possession shows itself almost without exception in the fact that the possessed identify themselves with the archetypal contents of their unconscious, and, because they do not realize that the role which is being thrust upon them is the effect of new contents still to be understood, they exemplify these concretely in their own lives, thus becoming prophets and reformers. In so far as the archetypal content of the Christian drama was able to give satisfying expression to the uneasy and clamorous unconscious of the many, the *consensus omnium* raised this drama to a universally binding truth—not of course by an act of judgment, but by the irrational fact of possession, which is far more effective. Thus Jesus became the tutelary image or amulet against the archetypal powers that threatened to possess everyone. The glad tidings announced: "It has happened, but it will not happen to you inasmuch as you believe in Jesus Christ, the Son of God!" Yet it could and it can and it will happen to everyone in whom the Christian dominant has decayed. For this reason there have always been people who, not satisfied with the dominants of conscious life, set forth—under cover and by devious paths, to their destruction or salvation—to seek direct experience of the eternal roots, and, following the lure of the restless unconscious psyche, find themselves in the wilderness where, like Jesus, they come up against the son of darkness, the ἀντίμιμον πνεῦμα. Thus an old alchemist—and he a cleric!—prays: "Horridas nostrae mentis purga tenebras, accende lumen sensibus!" (Purge the horrible darknesses of our mind, light a light for our senses!) The author of this sentence must have been undergoing the experience of the *nigredo*, the first stage of the work, which was felt as "melancholia" in alchemy and corresponds to the encounter with the shadow in psychology.

42   When, therefore, modern psychotherapy once more meets with the activated archetypes of the collective unconscious, it is merely the repetition of a phenomenon that has often been observed in moments of

great religious crisis, although it can also occur in individuals for whom the ruling ideas have lost their meaning. An example of this is the *descensus ad inferos* depicted in *Faust*, which, consciously or unconsciously, is an *opus alchymicum.*

43   The problem of opposites called up by the shadow plays a great—indeed, the decisive—role in alchemy, since it leads in the ultimate phase of the work to the union of opposites in the archetypal form of the *hierosgamos* or "chymical wedding." Here the supreme opposites, male and female (as in the Chinese *yang* and *yin*), are melted into a unity purified of all opposition and therefore incorruptible. The prerequisite for this, of course, is that the artifex should not identify himself with the figures in the work but should leave them in their objective, impersonal state. So long as the alchemist was working in his laboratory he was in a favourable position, psychologically speaking, for he had no opportunity to identify himself with the archetypes as they appeared, since they were all projected immediately into the chemical substances. The disadvantage of this situation was that the alchemist was forced to represent the incorruptible substance as a chemical product—an impossible undertaking which led to the downfall of alchemy, its place in the laboratory being taken by chemistry. But the psychic part of the work did not disappear. It captured new interpreters, as we can see from the example of *Faust*, and also from the signal connection between our modern psychology of the unconscious and alchemical symbolism.

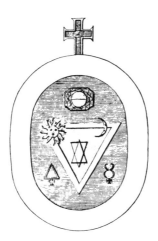

Symbol of the alchemical work.
—*Hermaphroditisches Sonn- und Mondskind* (1752)

211

2

"THE SIGN OF THE FISHES"

From *Aion*, CW 9ii, pars. 127–49

127   The figure of Christ is not as simple and unequivocal as one could wish. I am not referring here to the enormous difficulties arising out of a comparison of the Synoptic Christ with the Johannine Christ, but to the remarkable fact that in the hermeneutic writings of the Church Fathers, which go right back to the days of primitive Christianity, Christ has a number of symbols or "allegories" in common with the devil. Of these I would mention the lion, snake (*coluber*, 'viper'), bird (devil) = *nocturna avis*), raven (Christ = *nycticorax*, 'night-heron'), eagle, and fish. It is also worth noting that Lucifer, the Morning Star, means Christ as well as the devil.[1] Apart from the snake, the fish is one of the oldest allegories. Nowadays we would prefer to call them symbols, because these synonyms always contain more than mere allegories, as is particularly obvious in the case of the fish symbol. It is unlikely that Ἰχθῦς is simply an anagrammatic abbreviation of Ἰ[ησοῦς] Χ[ριστὸς] Θ[εοῦ] Υ[ἱὸς] Σ[ωτήρ],[2] but rather the symbolical designation for something

---

[1] Early collections of such allegories in the *Ancoratus* of Epiphanius, and in Augustine, *Contra Faustum*. For *nycticorax* and *aquila* see Eucherius, *Liber formularum spiritalis intelligentiae*, cap. 5 (Migne, *P.L.*, vol. 50, col. 740).

[2] Augustine (*City of God*, trans. by J. Healey, II, p. 196) relates how the former proconsul Flaccianus, with whom he had a conversation about Jesus, produced a book containing the songs of the Erythraean Sibyl, and showed him the passage where the above words, forming the acrostic Ἰχθῦς, are themselves the acrostic for a whole poem, an apocalyptic prophecy of the Sibyls:

> "Iudicii signum tellus sudore madescet,
> E coelo Rex adveniet per saecla futurus:
> Scilicet in carne praesens ut iudicet orbem.
> Unde Deum cernent incredulus atque fidelis
> Celsum cum Sanctis, aevi iam termino in ipso.
> Sic animae cum carne aderunt quas iudicat ipse . . ."
> (In sign of doomsday the whole earth shall sweat.
> Ever to reign a king in heavenly seat
> Shall come to judge all flesh. The faithful and

CHRISTIAN HISTORY AND ITS FUTURE

far more complex. (As I have frequently pointed out in my other writings, I do not regard the symbol as an allegory or a sign, but take it in its proper sense as the best possible way of describing and formulating an object that is not completely knowable. It is in this sense that the creed is called a "symbolum.") The order of the words gives one more the impression that they were put together for the purpose of explaining an already extant and widely disseminated "Ichthys."[3] For the fish symbol, in the Near and Middle East especially, has a long and colourful prehistory, from the Babylonian fish-god Oannes and his priests who clothed themselves in fish-skins, to the sacred fish-meals in the cult of the Phoenician goddess Derceto-Atargatis and the obscurities of the Abercius inscription.[4] The symbol ranges from the redeemer-fish of Manu in farthest India to the Eucharistic fish-feast celebrated by the "Thracian riders" in the Roman Empire.[5] For our purpose it is hardly necessary to go into this voluminous material more closely. As Doelger and others have shown, there are plenty of occasions for fish symbolism within the original, purely Christian world of ideas. I need only mention the regeneration in the font, in which the baptized swim like fishes.[6]

128   In view of this wide distribution of the fish symbol, its appearance at a particular place or at a particular moment in the history of the world is no cause for wonder. But the sudden activation of the symbol, and its identification with Christ even in the early days of the Church, lead one to conjecture a second source. This source is astrology, and it seems that Friedrich Muenter[7] was the first to draw attention to it. Jer-

---

Unfaithful too before this God shall stand,
Seeing him high with saints in time's last end.
Corporeal shall he sit, and thence extend
His doom on souls . . .) (Ibid., p. 437.)

The Greek original is in *Oracula Sibyllina,* ed. John Geffcken, p. 142. [For Augustine's explanation of the discrepancy in the acrostic, see Healey trans., II. p. 196.—EDITORS.]
[3] Cf. Jeremias, *The Old Testament in the Light of the Ancient East,* I, p. 76, n. 2.
[4] From this inscription I will cite only the middle portion, which says: "Everywhere I had a travelling companion, since I had Paul sitting in the chariot. But everywhere Faith drew me onward, and everywhere he set before me for food a fish from the source, exceeding great and pure, which a holy virgin had caught. And he offered this fish to the friends to eat, having good wine, a mixed drink with bread." See Ramsay, "The Cities and Bishoprics of Phrygia," p. 424.
[5] Cf. the material in Goodenough, *Jewish Symbols in the Greco-Roman Period,* V, pp. 13ff.
[6] Doelger, 'ΙΧΘΥΣ: *Das Fischsymbol in frühchristlicher Zeit.*
[7] *Sinnbilder und Kunstvorstellungen der alten Christen* (1825), p. 49. Muenter mentions Abrabanel (sic) here, "who in all probability drew on older sources."

emias[8] adopts the same view and mentions that a Jewish commentary on Daniel, written in the fourteenth century, expected the coming of the Messiah in the sign of the Fishes. This commentary is mentioned by Muenter in a later publication[9] as stemming from Don Isaac Abarbanel, who was born in Lisbon in 1437 and died in Venice in 1508.[10] It is explained here that the House of the Fishes ($\times$) is the house of justice and of brilliant splendour ($\mathtext{4}$ in $\times$). Further, that in *anno mundi* 2365,[11] a great conjunction of Saturn ($\hbar$) and Jupiter ($\mathtext{4}$) took place in Pisces.[12] These two great planets, he says, are also the most important for the destiny of the world, and especially for the destiny of the Jews. The conjunction took place three years before the birth of Moses. (This is of course legendary.) Abarbanel expects the coming of the Messiah when there is a conjunction of Jupiter and Saturn in Pisces. He was not the first to express such expectations. Four hundred years earlier we find similar pronouncements; for instance, Rabbi Abraham ben Hiyya, who died about 1136, is said to have decreed that the Messiah was to be expected in 1464, at the time of the great conjunction in Pisces; and the same is reported of Solomon ben Gabirol (1020–70).[13] These astrological ideas are quite understandable when one considers that Saturn is the star of Israel, and that Jupiter means the "king" (of justice). Among the territories ruled by the Fishes, the house of Jupiter, are Mesopotamia, Bactria, the Red Sea, and Palestine.[14] Chiun (Saturn) is mentioned in Amos 5:26 as "the star of your god."[15] James of Sarug (d. 521) says the Israelites worshipped Saturn. The Sabaeans called him the "god of the Jews."[16] The Sabbath is Saturday,

---

[8] Op. cit., p. 76.

[9] *Der Stern der Weisen* (1827), pp. 54ff.

[10] Isaac Abravanel (Abarbanel) ben Jehuda, *Má'yene ha-Yeshú'ah* ("Sources of Salvation"—A Commentary on Daniel. Ferrara, 1551).

[11] Corresponding to 1396 B.C.

[12] Actually the conjunction took place in Sagittarius ($\nearrow$). The *coniunctiones magnae* of the water trigon ($\mathfrak{S}$, $\mathfrak{M}$, $\times$) fall in the years 1800 to 1600 and 1000 to 800 B.C.

[13] Anger, "Der Stern der Weisen und das Geburtsjahr Christi," p. 396, and Gerhardt, *Der Stern des Messias*, pp. 54f.

[14] Gerhardt, p. 57. Ptolemy and, following him, the Middle Ages associate Palestine with Aries.

[15] "Ye have borne Siccuth your king and Chiun your images, the star of your god, which ye made to yourselves" (RV). Stephen refers to this in his defence (Acts 7:43): "And you took unto you the tabernacle of Moloch and the star of your god Remphan." "Rempham" ('Ρομφά), is a corruption of Kewan (Chiun).

[16] Dozy and de Goeje, "Nouveaux documents pour l'étude de la religion des Harraniens," p. 350.

Saturn's Day. Albumasar[17] testifies that Saturn is the star of Israel.[18] In medieval astrology Saturn was believed to be the abode of the devil.[19] Both Saturn and Ialdabaoth, the demiurge and highest archon, have lion's faces. Origen elicits from the diagram of Celsus that Michael, the first angel of the Creator, has "the shape of a lion."[20] He obviously stands in the place of Ialdabaoth, who is identical with Saturn, as Origen points out.[21] The demiurge of the Naassenes is a "fiery god, the fourth by number."[22] According to the teachings of Apelles, who had connections with Marcion, there was a "third god who spoke to Moses, a fiery one, and there was also a fourth, the author of evil."[23] Between the god of the Naassenes and the god of Apelles there is evidently a close relationship, and also, it appears, with Yahweh, the demiurge of the Old Testament.

129   Saturn is a "black" star,[24] anciently reputed a "maleficus." "Dragons, serpents, scorpions, vipères, renards, chats et souris, oiseaux nocturnes et autres engeances sournoises sont le lot de Saturne," says Bouché-Leclercq.[25] Remarkably enough, Saturn's animals also include the ass,[26] which on that account was rated a theriomorphic form of the Jewish god. A pictorial representation of it is the well-known mock crucifixion on the Palatine.[27] Similar traditions can be found in

[17] Abu Ma'shar, d. 885.

[18] Gerhardt, p. 57. Also Pierre d'Ailly, *Concordantia astronomie cum theologia*, etc., fol. g4 (Venice, 1490): "But Saturn, as Messahali says, has a meaning which concerns the Jewish people or their faith."

[19] Reitzenstein, *Poimandres*, p. 76.

[20] *Contra Celsum*, VI, 30 (trans. by H. Chadwick, p. 345).

[21] Ibid., VI, 31: "But they say that this angel like unto a lion has a necessary connection with the star Saturn." Cf. *Pistis Sophia*, trans. by Mead, p. 47, and Bousset, *Hauptprobleme der Gnosis*, pp. 352ff.

[22] Hippolytus, *Elenchos*, V, 7, 30 (Legge trans., I, p. 128).

[23] Ibid., VII, 38, 1 (cf. Legge trans., II, p. 96).

[24] Hence the image of Saturn worshipped by the Sabaeans was said to be made of lead or black stone. (Chwolsohn, *Die Ssabier und der Ssabismus*, II, p. 383.)

[25] *L'Astrologie greque*, p. 317.

[26] Bouché-Leclercq (p. 318) conjectures one of the known classical "etymologies," namely an *onos* (ass) contained in *Kronos* (Saturn), based on a joke aimed at the Megarian philosopher Diodoros. But the reason for the Saturn-ass analogy probably lies deeper, that is, in the nature of the ass itself, which was regarded as a "cold, intractable, slow-witted, long-lived animal." (From the Greek bestiary cited by Bouché-Leclercq.) In Polemon's bestiary I find the following description of the wild ass: "Given to flight, timid, stupid, untamed, lustful, jealous, killing its females" (*Scriptores physiognomici graeci et latini*, I, p. 182).

[27] A possible model might be the Egyptian tradition of the martyrdom of Set, depicted at Denderah. He is shown tied to the "slave's post," has an ass's head, and Horus stands before him with a knife in his hand. (Mariette, *Dendérah*, plates vol. IV, pl. 56.)

Plutarch,[28] Diodorus, Josephus,[29] and Tacitus.[30] Sabaoth, the seventh archon, has the form of an ass.[31] Tertullian is referring to these rumours when he says: "You are under the delusion that our God is an ass's head," and that "we do homage only to an ass."[32] As we have indicated, the ass is sacred to the Egyptian Set.[33] In the early texts, however, the ass is the attribute of the sun-god and only later became an emblem of the underworldly Apep and of evil (Set).[34]

130 According to medieval tradition, the religion of the Jews originated in a conjunction of Jupiter with Saturn, Islam in ♃ ☌ ♀, Christianity in ♃ ☌ ☿, and the Antichrist in ♃ ☌ ☾.[35] Unlike Saturn, Jupiter is a beneficent star. In the Iranian view Jupiter signifies life, Saturn death.[36] The conjunction of the two therefore signifies the *union of extreme opposites.* In the year 7 B.C. this famed conjunction took place no less than three times in the sign of the Fishes. The greatest approximation occurred on May 29 of that year, the planets being only 0.21 degrees apart, less than half the width of the full moon.[37] The conjunction took place in the middle of the commissure, "near the bend in the line of the Fishes." From the astrological point of view this conjunction must appear especially significant, because the approximation of the two

[28] *Quaestiones convivales,* IV, 5.

[29] *Contra Apionem,* II, 7–8 (80ff.). (Cf. trans. by H. St. J. Thackeray and R. Marcus, I, pp. 325ff.)

[30] *The Histories,* trans. by W. H. Fyfe, II, pp. 204ff.

[31] Epiphanius, *Panarium,* ed. Oehler, I, p. 184.

[32] *Apologeticus adversus gentes,* XVI (Migne, *P.L.,* vol. 1, cols. 364–65; cf. trans. by S. Thelwall, I, pp. 84f.).

[33] Plutarch, *De Iside et Osiride,* in *Moralia,* pp. 77, 123. In ch. 31 Plutarch states that the legend of Set's flight on an ass and of the fathering of his two sons Hierosolymus and Judaeus is not Egyptian, but pertained to the Ἰουδαϊκά.

[34] In the Papyrus of Ani (ed. E. A. W. Budge, p. 248) a hymn to Ra says: "May I advance upon the earth; may I smite the Ass; may I crush the evil one (Sebau); may I destroy Apep in his hour."

[35] Albumasar, Lib. II, *De magnis coniunctionibus,* tract. I, diff. 4, p. a8ʳ (1489): "If (Jupiter) is in conjunction with Saturn, it signifies that the faith of the citizens thereof is Judaism. . . . And if the moon is in conjunction with Saturn it signifies doubt and revolution and change, and this by reason of the speed of the corruption of the moon and the rapidity of its motion and the shortness of its delay in the sign." Cf. also Pierre d'Ailly, *Concordantia,* etc., fol. d8ʳ. J. H. Heidegger (*Quaestiones ad textum Lucae VII, 12–17,* 1655) says in ch. IX that Abu Mansor (= Albumasar), in his sixth tractate, in the *Introductio maior,* connects the life of Christ, like that of Mahomet, with the stars. Cardan ascribes ☿ ☌ ♃ to Christianity, ☿ ☌ ♄ to Judaism, ☿ ☌ ♂ to Islam, and according to him ☿ ☌ ♀ signifies idolatry ("Commentarium in Ptolemaeum De astrorum Judiciis," p. 188).

[36] Christensen, *Le Premier Homme et le premier roi dans l'histoire légendaire des Iraniens,* part 1, p. 24.

[37] Gerhardt, *Stern des Messias,* p. 74.

planets was exceptionally large and of an impressive brilliance. In addition, seen heliocentrically, it took place near the equinoctial point, which at that time was located between ♈ and ♓, that is, between fire and water.[38] The conjunction was characterized by the important fact that Mars was in opposition (♂ ☍ ♃ ♄), which means, astrologically, that the planet correlated with the instincts stood in a hostile relationship to it, which is peculiarly characteristic of Christianity. If we accept Gerhardt's calculation that the conjunction took place on May 29, in the year 7 B.C., then the position of the sun—especially important in a man's nativity—at Christ's birth would be in the double sign of the *Twins*.[39] One thinks involuntarily of the ancient Egyptian pair of hostile brothers, Horus and Set, the sacrificer and the sacrificed (cf. n. 27, on Set's "martyrdom"), who in a sense prefigure the drama of the Christian myth. In the Egyptian myth it is the evil one who is sacrificed on the "slave's post."[40] But the pair of brothers Heru-ur (the "older Horus") and Set are sometimes pictured as having one body with two heads. The planet Mercury is correlated with Set, and this is interesting in view of the tradition that Christianity originated in a conjunction of Jupiter with Mercury. In the New Kingdom (XIXth dynasty) Set ap-

[38] Calculated on the basis of Peters and Knobel, *Ptolemy's Catalogue of Stars*.

[39] Medieval astrologers cast a number of ideal horoscopes for Christ. Albumasar and Albertus Magnus took Virgo as the ascendent; Pierre d'Ailly (1356–1420), on the other hand, took Libra, and so did Cardan. Pierre d'Ailly says: "For Libra is the human sign, that is, of the Liberator of men, [the sign] of a prudent and just and spiritual man" (*Concordantia*, etc., cap. 2). Kepler, in his *Discurs von der grossen Conjunction* (1623; p. 701), says that God himself marked "such great conjunctions as these with extraordinary and marvellous stars visible in high heaven, also with notable works of his divine Providence." He continues: "Accordingly he appointed the birth of his Son Christ our Saviour exactly at the time of the great conjunction in the signs of the Fishes and the Ram, near the equinoctial point." Seen heliocentrically, the conjunction took place just in front of the equinoctial point, and this give it a special significance astrologically. Pierre d'Ailly (*Concordantia*, etc., fol. b^r) says: "But a great conjunction is that of Saturn and Jupiter in the beginning of the Ram." These conjunctions occur every 20 years and take place every 200 years in the same trigon. But the same position can only recur every 800 years. The most significant positions are those between two trigons. Albumasar (*De magnis coniunc.*, tract. 3, diff. 1, fol. D 8^r) says they manifest themselves "in changes of parties and offices and in changes of the laws and . . . in the coming of prophets and of prophesying and of miracles in parties and offices of state."

[40] Crucifixion was a well-known punishment for slaves. The Cross with a snake on it, instead of the Crucified, is often found in medieval times [*Psychology and Alchemy*, fig. 217], and also in the dreams and fantasy-images of modern people who know nothing of this tradition. A characteristic dream of this sort is the following: *The dreamer was watching a Passion play in the theatre. On the way to Golgotha, the actor taking the part of the Saviour suddenly changed into a snake or crocodile.*

pears as Sutech in the Nile delta. In the new capital built by Rameses II, one district was dedicated to Amon, the other to Sutech.[41] It was here that the Jews were supposed to have done slave-labour.

131   In considering the double aspect of Christ, mention might be made of the legend of Pistis Sophia (3rd cent.), which also originated in Egypt. Mary says to Jesus:

> When thou wert a child, before the spirit had descended upon thee, when thou wert in the vineyard with Joseph, the spirit came down from the height, and came unto me in the house, like unto thee, and I knew him not, but thought that he was thou. And he said unto me, "Where is Jesus, my brother, that I may go to meet him?" And when he had said this unto me, I was in doubt, and thought it was a phantom tempting me. I seized him and bound him to the foot of the bed which was in my house, until I had gone to find you in the field, thee and Joseph; and I found you in the vineyard, where Joseph was putting up the vine-poles. And it came to pass, when thou didst hear me saying this thing unto Joseph, that thou didst understand, and thou wert joyful, and didst say, "Where is he, that I may see him?" And it came to pass, when Joseph heard thee say these words, that he was disturbed. We went up together, entered into the house and found the spirit bound to the bed, and we gazed upon thee and him, and found that thou wert like unto him. And he that was bound to the bed was unloosed, he embraced thee and kissed thee, and thou also didst kiss him, and you became one.[42]

132   It appears from the context of this fragment that Jesus is the "truth sprouting from the earth," whereas the spirit that resembled him is "justice [$\delta\iota\varkappa\alpha\iota\sigma\sigma\acute{\nu}\nu\eta$] looking down from heaven." The text says: "Truth is the power which issued from thee when thou wast in the lower regions of chaos. For this cause thy power hath said through David, 'Truth hath sprouted out of the earth,' because thou wert in the lower regions of chaos."[43] Jesus, accordingly, is conceived as a double personality, part of which rises up from the chaos or *hyle*, while the other part descends as pneuma from heaven.

133   One could hardly find the $\phi\nu\lambda\sigma\varkappa\rho\acute{\iota}\nu\eta\sigma\iota\varsigma$, or 'discrimination of the natures' that characterizes the Gnostic Redeemer, exemplified more graphically than in the astrological determination of time. The astrological statements that were quite possible in antiquity all point to the

---

[41] Erman, *Die Religion der Ägypter*, p. 137.
[42] *Pistis Sophia*, Mead trans., pp. 118f., slightly modified.
[43] Cf. the fish that Augustine says was "drawn from the deep."

prominent double aspect[44] of the birth that occurred at this particular moment of time, and one can understand how plausible was the astrological interpretation of the Christ-Antichrist myth when it entered into manifestation at the time of the Gnostics. A fairly old authority, earlier anyway than the sixth century, which bears striking witness to the antithetical nature of the Fishes is the Talmud. This says:

Four thousand two hundred and ninety-one years after the Creation [A.D. 530], the world will be orphaned. There will follow the war of the *tanninim* [sea-monsters], the war of Gog and Magog,[45] and then the Messianic era; only after seven thousand years will the Holy One, blessed be He, set up his world anew. R. Abba, the son of Raba, said, It was taught: after five thousand years.[46]

The Talmud commentator Solomon ben Isaac, alias Rashi (1039–1105), remarks that the *tanninim* are fishes, presumably basing himself on an older source, since he does not give this as his own opinion, as he usually does. This remark is important, firstly because it takes the battle of the fishes as an eschatological event (like the fight between

---

[44] In this connection mention should be made of the "Saviour of the twins" (σωτῆρες) in *Pistis Sophia* (Mead trans., pp. 2, 17, and elsewhere).

[45] Also mentioned in the *Chronique* of Tabari (I, ch. 23, p. 67). There Antichrist is the king of the Jews, who appears with Gog and Magog. This may be an allusion to Rev. 20:7f.: "And when the thousand years are expired, Satan shall be loosed out of his prison, and shall go out to deceive the nations which are in the four corners of the earth, Gog and Magog, to gather them together to battle" (AV).

Graf von Wackerbarth (*Merkwürdige Geschichte der weltberühmten Gog und Magog*, p. 19) relates from an English "History of the World," which came out in German in 1760, that the Arab writers say the "Yajui" were "of more than ordinary size," whereas the "Majui" were "not more than three spans high." This story, despite the obscurity of its origins, points to the antithetical nature of Gog and Magog, who thus form a parallel to the Fishes. Augustine interprets "the nations which are in the four corners of the earth, Gog and Magog" as, respectively (Gog), *tectum*, 'roof' or 'house,' and (Magog) *de tecto*, 'he that comes out of the house': "Ut illae sint tectum, ipse de tecto." That is to say the nations are the house, but the devil dwells in the house and comes out of it. (*City of God*, Healey trans., II, p. 286.) On Augustine is based the *Compendium theologicae veritatis* (Venice, 1492), which was attributed in turn to Albertus Magnus, Hugh of Strasbourg, and John of Paris. It is our main source for the Antichrist legend. With reference to Augustine it says (Libell. 7, cap. 11) that Gog means "occultatio" (concealment), Magog "detectio" (revelation). This corroborates the antithetical nature of Gog and Magog at least for the Middle Ages. It is another instance of the motif of the hostile brothers, or of duplication. Albumasar (tract. 4, diff. 12, f. 8ʳ) calls the sixth "clima" (inclination towards the Pole) that of Gog and Magog, and correlates it with Gemini and Virgo.

[46] *Nezikin* VI, Sanhedrin II (*BT*, p. 658). R. Hanan ben Tahlifa, into whose mouth this prophecy is put, is mentioned in the list of Amoraim (teachers of the Talmud) and lived in the 2nd cent. A.D.

Behemoth and Leviathan), and secondly because it is probably the oldest testimony to the antithetical nature of the fishes. From about this
period, too—the eleventh century—comes the apocryphal text of a
Johannine Genesis in which the two fishes are mentioned, this time in
unmistakably astrological form.[46a] Both documents fall within the critical epoch that opened with the second millennium of the Christian
era, about which I shall have more to say in due course.

134   The year 531 is characterized astronomically by a conjunction of ♃
and ♄ in Gemini. This sign stands for a pair of brothers, and they too
have a somewhat antithetical nature. The Greeks interpreted them as
the Dioscuri ('boys of Zeus'), the sons of Leda who were begotten by
the swan and hatched out of an egg. Pollux was immortal, but Castor
shared the human lot. Another interpretation takes them as representing Apollo and Heracles or Apollo and Dionysus. Both interpretations
suggest a certain polarity. Astronomically, at any rate, the air sign Gemini stands in a quartile and therefore unfavourable aspect to the conjunction that took place in the year 7 B.C. The inner polarity of ♊ may
perhaps shed light on the prophecy about the war of the *tanninim*,
which Rashi interprets as fishes. From the dating of Christ's birth it
would appear, as said, that the sun was in Gemini. The motif of the
brothers is found very early in connection with Christ, for instance
among the Jewish Christians and Ebionites.[47]

135   From all this we may risk the conjecture that the Talmudic prophecy
was based on astrological premises.

136   The precession of the equinoxes was a fact well known to the astrologers of antiquity. Origen, helped out by the observations and calcula-
tions of Hipparchus,[48] uses it as a cogent argument against an astrology
based on the so-called "morphomata" (the actual constellations).[49] Naturally this does not apply to the distinction already drawn in ancient

[46a] Cf. infra, pars. 225ff.
[47] Epiphanius, *Panarium*, XXX (Oehler edn., I, pp, 240ff.).
[48] Hipparchus is supposed to have discovered the precession. Cf. Boll, *Sphaera*, p. 199, n.
1.
[49] Origen, *Commentaria in Genesim*, tom. III, i, 14, 11 (Migne, *P.G.*, vol. 12, col. 79):
"There is indeed a theory that the zodiacal circle, just like the planets, is carried back
from setting to rising [or: from west to east], within a century by one degree; . . . since
the twelfth part [1 zodion] is one thing when conceived in the mind, another when
perceived by the senses; yet from that which is conceived only in the mind, and can
scarcely, or not even scarcely, be held for certain, the truth of the matter appears." The
Platonic year was then reckoned as 36,000 years. Tycho Brahe reckoned it at 24,120
years. The constant for the precession is 50.3708 seconds and the total cycle (360°) takes
25,725.6 years.

astrology between the morphomata and the ζωδιά νοητά (the fictive signs of the zodiac).[50] If we take the 7,000 years mentioned in the prophecy as *anno mundi* 7000, the year denoted would be A.D. 3239. By then the spring-point will have moved from its present position 18 degrees into Aquarius, the next aeon, that of the Water Carrier. As an astrologer of the second or third century would be acquainted with the precession, we may surmise that these dates were based on astrological considerations. At all events the Middle Ages were much concerned with the calculation of *coniunctiones maximae* and *magnae*, as we know from Pierre d'Ailly and Cardan.[51] Pierre d'Ailly reckoned that the first *coniunctio maxima* (♃ ♂ ♄ in ♈) after the creation of the world took place in 5027 B.C., while Cardan relegated the tenth conjunction to A.D. 3613.[52] Both of them assumed the lapse of too large an interval between conjunctions in the same sign. The correct astronomical interval is about 795 years. Cardan's conjunction would accordingly take place in the year A.D. 3234. For astrological speculation this date is naturally of the greatest importance.

137   As to the 5,000 years, the date we get is A.D. 1239. This was an epoch noted for its spiritual instability, revolutionary heresies and chiliastic expectations, and at the same time it saw the founding of the mendicant orders, which injected new life into monasticism. One of the most powerful and influential voices to announce the coming of a "new age of the spirit" was Joachim of Flora (d. 1202), whose teachings were condemned by the Fourth Lateran Council in 1215. He expected the opening of the seventh seal in the fairly near future, the advent of the "everlasting gospel" and the reign of the "intellectus spiritualis," the age of the Holy Ghost. This third aeon, he says, had already begun with St. Benedict, the founder of the Benedictine Order (the first monastery was supposed to have been built a few years after 529). One of Joachim's followers, the Franciscan friar Gerard of Borgo San Donnino, proclaimed in his *Introductorius in evangelium aeternum*, which appeared in 1254 in Paris, that Joachim's three main treatises were in fact the everlasting gospel, and that in the year 1260 this would replace the gospel of Jesus Christ.[53] As we know, Joachim saw monasticism as

[50] Bouché-Leclercq, p. 591, n. 2; *Antiskia*; Boll, *Sphaera*.
[51] The theory of the conjunctions was set down in writing by the Arabs about the middle of the 9th cent., more particularly by Messahala. Cf. Strauss, *Die Astrologie des Johannes Kepler*.
[52] With his estimate of 960 years between two *coniunctiones maximae*, Pierre d'Ailly would also arrive at A.D. 3613.
[53] This period around the year 1240 would, from the astrological standpoint, be charac-

the true vehicle of the Holy Ghost and for this reason he dated the secret inception of the new era from the lifetime of St. Benedict, whose founding of the Benedictine Order revived monasticism in the West.

138   To Pierre d'Ailly the time of Pope Innocent III (1198–1216) had already seemed significant. About the year 1189, he says, the revolutions of Saturn were once again completed ("completae anno Christi 1189 vel circiter"). He complains that the Pope had condemned a treatise of Abbot Joachim,[54] and also the heretical doctrine of Almaricus.[55] This last is the theological philosopher Amalric of Bene (d. 1204), who took part in the widespread Holy Ghost movement of that age. It was then, too, he says, that the Dominican and Franciscan mendicant orders came into existence, "which was a great and wonderful thing for the Christian church." Pierre d'Ailly thus lays stress on the same phenomena that struck us as being characteristic of the time, and further regards this epoch as having been foretold in astrology.

139   The date for the founding of the monastery of Monte Cassino brings us very close to the year 530, which the Talmud prophesied would be a critical one. In Joachim's view not only does a new era begin then, but a new "status" of the world—the age of monasticism and the reign of the Holy Ghost. Its beginning still comes within the domain of the Son, but Joachim surmises in a psychologically correct manner that a new status—or, as we would say, a new attitude—would appear first as a more or less latent preliminary stage, which would then be followed by the *fructificatio*, the flower and the fruit. In Joachim's day the fruition was still in abeyance, but one could observe far and wide an uncommon agitation and commotion of men's spirits. Everyone felt the rushing wind of the pneuma; it was an age of new and unprecedented ideas which were blazoned abroad by the Cathari, Patarenes, Concorricci, Waldenses, Poor Men of Lyons, Beghards, Brethren of the Free Spirit, "Bread through God,"[56] and whatever else these movements were called. Their visible beginnings all lay in the early years of the eleventh

---

terized by the great conjunction of Jupiter and Saturn in Libra, in 1246. Libra is another double sign with a pneumatic nature (air trigon), like Gemini, and for this reason it was taken by Pierre d'Ailly as Christ's ascendent.

[54] At the Lateran Council, 1215. Cf. Denzinger and Bannwart, *Enchiridion symbolorum*, pp. 190ff.

[55] "His teaching is to be held not so much heretical as insane," says the decree.

[56] Hahn, *Geschichte der Ketzer im Mittelalter*, II, p. 779: ". . . some who under the name of a false and pretended religious order, whom the common folk call Beghards and Schwestrones or 'Brod durch Gott'; but they call themselves Little Brethren and Sisters of the fellowship of the Free Spirit and of Voluntary Poverty."

century. The contemporary documents amassed by Hahn throw a revealing light on the ideas current in these circles:

Item, they believe themselves to be God by nature without distinction . . .
and that they are eternal. . . .
Item, that they have no need of God or the Godhead.
Item, that they constitute the kingdom of heaven.
Item that they are immutable in the new rock, that they rejoice in naught
and are troubled by naught.
Item, that a man is bound to follow his inner instinct rather than the truth of
the Gospel which is preached every day. . . .
They say that they believe the Gospel to contain poetical matters which are
not true.[57]

140   These few examples may suffice to show what kind of spirit animated
these movements. They were made up of people who identified themselves (or were identified) with God, who deemed themselves super-
men, had a critical approach to the gospels, followed the promptings
of the inner man, and understood the kingdom of heaven to be within.
In a sense, therefore, they were modern in their outlook, but they had
a religious inflation instead of the rationalistic and political psychosis
that is the affliction of our day. We ought not to impute these extremist
ideas to Joachim, even though he took part in that great movement of
the spirit and was one of its outstanding figures. One must ask oneself
what psychological impulse could have moved him and his adherents
to cherish such bold expectations as the substitution of the "everlasting
gospel" for the Christian message or the supersession of the second
Person in the Godhead by the third, who would reign over the new era.
This thought is so heretical and subversive that it could never have
occurred to him had he not felt himself supported and swept along by
the revolutionary currents of the age. He felt it as a revelation of the
Holy Ghost, whose life and procreative power no church could bring to
a stop. The numinosity of this feeling was heightened by the temporal
coincidence—"synchronicity"—of the epoch he lived in with the be-

[57] "Item credunt se esse Deum per naturam sine distinctione . . . se esse acternos . . .
"Item quod nullo indigent nec Deo nec Deitate.
"Item quod sunt ipsum regnum coelorum.
"Item quod sunt etiam immutabiles in nova rupe, quod de nullo gaudent, et de nullo
turbantur.
"Item quod homo magis tenetur sequi instinctum interiorem quam veritatem Evangelii
quod cottidie praedicatur . . . dicunt, se credere ibi (in Evangelio) esse poëtica quae non
sunt vera." (Hahn, II, pp. 779f.)

ginning of the sphere of the "antichristian" fish in Pisces. In consequence, one might feel tempted to regard the Holy Ghost movement
and Joachim's central ideas as a direct expression of the antichristian
psychology that was then dawning. At any rate the Church's condemnation is thoroughly understandable, for in many ways his attitude to the
Church of Jesus Christ comes very close to open insurrection, if not
downright apostasy. But if we allow some credence to the conviction of
these innovators that they were moved by the Holy Ghost, then another
interpretation becomes not only possible but even probable.

141   That is to say, just as Joachim supposed that the status of the Holy
Ghost had secretly begun with St. Benedict, so we might hazard the
conjecture that a new status was secretly anticipated in Joachim himself. Consciously, of course, he thought he was bringing the status of
the Holy Ghost into reality, just as it is certain that St. Benedict had
nothing else in mind than to put the Church on a firm footing and
deepen the meaning of the Christian life through monasticism. But,
unconsciously—and this is psychologically what probably happened—
Joachim could have been seized by the archetype of the spirit. There is
no doubt that his activities were founded on a numinous experience,
which is, indeed, characteristic of all those who are gripped by an archetype. He understood the spirit in the dogmatic sense as the third
Person of the Godhead, for no other way was possible, but not in the
sense of the empirical archetype. This archetype is not of uniform
meaning, but was originally an ambivalent dualistic figure[58] that broke
through again in the alchemical concept of spirit after engendering
the most contradictory manifestations within the Holy Ghost movement itself. The Gnostics in their day had already had clear intimations
of this dualistic figure. It was therefore very natural, in an age which
coincided with the beginning of the second Fish and which was, so to
speak, forced into ambiguity, that an espousal of the Holy Ghost in its
Christian form should at the same time help the archetype of the spirit
to break through in all its characteristic ambivalence. It would be unjust to class so worthy a personage as Joachim with the bigoted advocates of that revolutionary and anarchic turbulence, which is what the
Holy Ghost movement turned into in so many places. We must suppose, rather, that he himself unwittingly ushered in a new "status," a
religious attitude that was destined to bridge and compensate the
frightful gulf that had opened out between Christ and Antichrist in the
eleventh century. The antichristian era is to blame that the spirit be-

---

[58] Cf. "The Phenomenology of the Spirit in Fairytales," pars. 396ff.

came non-spiritual and that the vitalizing archetype gradually degenerated into rationalism, intellectualism, and doctrinairism, all of which leads straight to the tragedy of modern times now hanging over our heads like a sword of Damocles. In the old formula for the Trinity, as Joachim knew it, the dogmatic figure of the devil is lacking, for then as now he led a questionable existence somewhere on the fringes of theological metaphysics, in the shape of the *mysterium iniquitatis*. Fortunately for us, the threat of his coming had already been foretold in the New Testament—for the less he is recognized the more dangerous he is. Who would suspect him under those high-sounding names of his, such as public welfare, lifelong security, peace among the nations, etc.? He hides under idealisms, under -isms in general, and of these the most pernicious is doctrinairism, that most unspiritual of all the spirit's manifestations. The present age must come to terms drastically with the facts as they are, with the absolute opposition that is not only tearing the world asunder politically but has planted a schism in the human heart. We need to find our way back to the original, living spirit which, because of its ambivalence, is also a mediator and uniter of opposites,[59] an idea that preoccupied the alchemists for many centuries.

142   If, as seems probable, the aeon of the fishes is ruled by the archetypal motif of the hostile brothers, then the approach of the next Platonic month, namely Aquarius, will constellate the problem of the union of opposites. It will then no longer be possible to write off evil as the mere privation of good; its real existence will have to be recognized. This problem can be solved neither by philosophy, nor by economics, nor by politics, but only by the individual human being, via his experience of the living spirit, whose fire descended upon Joachim, one of many, and, despite all contemporary misunderstandings, was handed onward into the future. The solemn proclamation of the *Assumptio Mariae* which we have experienced in our own day is an example of the way symbols develop through the ages. The impelling motive behind it did not come from the ecclesiastical authorities, who had given clear proof of their hesitation by postponing the declaration for nearly a hundred years,[60] but from the Catholic masses, who have in-

[59] "The Spirit Mercurius," pars. 284ff., and "A Psychological Approach to the Dogma of the Trinity," pars. 257ff.
[60] [Although Mary's Immaculate Conception was declared *de fide* by Pope Pius IX in 1854, by the bull *Ineffabilis Deus*, her Assumption was not defined as part of divine revelation until 1950.—EDITORS.]

sisted more and more vehemently on this development. Their insistence is, at bottom, the urge of the archetype to realize itself.[61]

143   The repercussions of the Holy Ghost movement spread, in the years that followed, to four minds of immense significance for the future. These were Albertus Magnus (1193–1280); his pupil Thomas Aquinas, the philosopher of the Church and an adept in alchemy (as also was Albertus); Roger Bacon (*c.* 1214–*c.* 1294), the English forerunner of inductive science; and finally Meister Eckhart (*c.* 1260–1327), the independent religious thinker, now enjoying a real revival after six hundred years of obscurity. Some people have rightly seen the Holy Ghost movement as the forerunner of the Reformation. At about the time of the twelfth and thirteenth centuries we find also the beginnings of Latin alchemy, whose philosophical and spiritual content I have tried to elucidate in my book *Psychology and Alchemy*. The image mentioned above (par. 139) of "immutability in the new rock" bears a striking resemblance to the central idea of philosophical alchemy, the *lapis philosophorum*, which is used as a parallel to Christ, the "rock," the "stone," the "cornerstone." Priscillian (4th cent.) says: "We have Christ for a rock, Jesus for a cornerstone."[62] An alchemical text speaks of the "rock which is smitten thrice with Moses' rod, so that the waters flow forth freely."[63] The *lapis* is called a "sacred rock" and is described as having four parts.[64] St. Ambrose says the water from the rock is a prefiguration of the blood that flowed from Christ's side.[65] Another alchemical text mentions the "water from the rock" as the equivalent of the universal solvent, the *aqua permanens*.[66] Khunrath, in his somewhat florid language, even speaks of the "Petroleum sapientum."[67] By the Naassenes,

---

[61] [Cf. "Psychology and Religion, par. 122, and "Answer to Job," pars. 748ff.]

[62] *Opera*, ed. G. Schepps, p. 24.

[63] Cf. *Aurora Consurgens* (ed. von Franz), p. 127: "this great and wide sea smote the rock and the metallic waters flowed forth."

[64] *Musaeum hermeticum* (1678), p. 212: "Our stone is called the sacred rock, and is understood or signified in four ways." Cf. Ephesians 3:18. The Pyramid Text of Pepi I mentions a god of resurrection with four faces: "Homage to thee, O thou who hast four faces. . . . Thou art endowed with a soul, and thou dost rise (like the sun) in thy boat . . . carry thou this Pepi with thee in the cabin of thy boat, for this Pepi is the son of the Scarab." (Budge, *Gods of the Egyptians*, I, p. 85.)

[65] *Explanationes in Psalmos*, XXXVIII: "In the shadow there was water from the rock, as it were the blood of Christ."

[66] Mylius, *Philosophia reformata* (1622). p. 112: "Whence the philosopher brought forth water from the rock and oil out of the flinty stone."

[67] *Von hylealischen Chaos* (1597), p. 272.

Adam was called the "rock" and the "cornerstone."[68] Both these allegories of Christ are mentioned by Epiphanius in his *Ancoratus*, and also by Firmicus Maternus.[69] This image, common to ecclesiastical and alchemical language alike, goes back to I Corinthians 10:4 and I Peter 2:4.

144 The new rock, then, takes the place of Christ, just as the everlasting gospel was meant to take the place of Christ's message. Through the descent and indwelling of the Holy Ghost the υἱότῆς, sonship, is infused into every individual, so that everybody who possesses the Holy Ghost will be a new rock, in accordance with I Peter 2:5: "Be you also as living stones built up."[70] This is a logical development of the teaching about the Paraclete and the filiation, as stated in Luke 6:35: "You shall be sons of the Highest," and John 10:34: "Is it not written in your law: I said, you are gods?" The Naassenes, as we know, had already made use of these allusions and thus anticipated a whole tract of historical development—a development that led via monasticism to the Holy Ghost movement, via the *Theologia Germanica* direct to Luther, and via alchemy to modern science.

145 Let us now turn back to the theme of Christ as the fish. According to Doelger, the Christian fish symbol first appeared in Alexandria around A.D. 200;[71] similarly, the baptismal bath was described as a *piscina* (fish-

[68] Hippolytus. *Elenchos*, V, 7, 34f. (Legge trans., I, p. 129). Reference is also made here to the "stone cut from the mountain without hands" (Daniel 2:45), a metaphor used by the alchemists.

[69] *De errore profanarum religionum*, 20, 1.

[70] Cf. the building of the seamless tower (church) with "living stones" in the "Shepherd" of Hermas.

[71] Doelger, ΙΧΘΥΣ: *Das Fischsymbol*, I, p. 18. Though the Abercius inscription, which dates from the beginning of the 3rd cent. (after A.D. 216), is of importance in this connection, it is of doubtful Christian origin. Dieterich (*Die Grabschrift des Aberkios*), in the course of a brilliant argument, demonstrates that the "holy shepherd" mentioned in the inscription is Attis, the Lord of the sacred Ram and the thousand-eyed shepherd of glittering stars. One of his special forms was Elogabal of Emera, the god of the emperor Heliogabalus, who caused the *hieros gamos* of his god to be celebrated with Urania of Carthage, also called *Virgo coelestis*. Heliogabalus was a *gallus* (priest) of the Great Mother, whose fish only the priests might eat. The fish had to be caught by a virgin. It is conjectured that Abercius had this inscription written in commemoration of his journey to Rome to the great *hieros gamos*, sometime after A.D. 216. For the same reasons there are doubts about the Christianity of the Pectorios inscription at Autun, in which the fish figures too: Ἔσθιε πν . . . , ιχθὺν ἔχων παλάμαις Ἰχθύϊ χόρταξ ἄρα λιλαίω δέσποτα σῶτερ: "Eat . . . (reading uncertain), holding the fish in the hands. Nourish now with the fish, I yearn, Lord Saviour." Probable reading: πινάων instead of πεινάων. Cf. Cabrol and Leclercq, *Dictionnaire d'archéologie chrétienne*, XIII, cols. 2884ff., "Pectorios." The first three distichs of the inscription make the acrostic Ichthys. Dating is uncertain (3rd–5th cent.). Cf. Doelger, I, pp. 12ff.

pond) quite early. This presupposes that the believers were fishes, as is in fact suggested by the gospels (for instance Matt. 4:19). There Christ wants to make Peter and Andrew "fishers of men," and the miraculous draught of fishes (Luke 5:10) is used by Christ himself as a paradigm for Peter's missionary activity.

146 A direct astrological aspect of Christ's birth is given us in Matthew 2:1ff. The Magi from the East were star-gazers who, beholding an extraordinary constellation, inferred an equally extraordinary birth. This anecdote proves that Christ, possibly even at the time of the apostles, was viewed from the astrological standpoint or was at least brought into connection with astrological myths. The latter alternative is fully confirmed when we consider the apocalyptic utterances of St. John. Since this exceedingly complex question has been discussed by those who are more qualified than I, we can support our argument on the well-attested fact that glimpses of astrological mythology may be caught behind the stories of the worldly and otherworldly life of the Redeemer.[72]

147 Above all it is the connections with the age of the Fishes which are attested by the fish symbolism, either contemporaneously with the gospels themselves ("fishers of men," fishermen as the first disciples, miracle of loaves and fishes), or immediately afterwards in the post-apostolic era. The symbolism shows Christ and those who believe in him as fishes, fish as the food eaten at the Agape,[73] baptism as immersion in a fish-pond, etc. At first sight, all this points to no more than the fact that the fish symbols and mythologems which have always existed had assimilated the figure of the Redeemer; in other words, it was a symptom of Christ's assimilation into the world of ideas prevailing at that time. But, to the extent that Christ was regarded as the new aeon, it would be clear to anyone acquainted with astrology that he was born as the first fish of the Pisces era, and was doomed to die as the last ram[74] (ἀρνίον,

---

[72] I refer particularly to Boll, *Aus der Offenbarung Johannis*. The writings of Arthur Drews have treated the astrological parallels with—one can well say—monomaniacal thoroughness, not altogether to the advantage of this idea. See *Der Sternenhimmel in der Dichtung und Religion der alten Völker und des Christentums.*

[73] Religious meal. According to Tertullian (*Adversus Marcionem*, I, cap. XIV; Migne, *P.L.*, vol. 2, col. 262) the fish signifies "the holier food." Cf. also Goodenough, *Jewish Symbols*, V, pp. 41ff.

[74] Origen, *In Genesim hom.* VIII, 9 (Migne, *P.G.*, vol. 12, col. 208): "We said . . . that Isaac bore the form of Christ, but that the *ram* also seems no less to bear the form of Christ." Augustine (*City of God*, XVI, 32, 1) asks: "Who was that ram by the offering whereof was made a complete sacrifice in typical blood . . . who was prefigured thereby but Jesus . . . ?" For the Lamb as Aries in the Apocalypse see Boll, *Aus der Offenbarung Johannis.*

lamb) of the declining Aries era.[75] Matthew 27:15ff. hands down this mythologem in the form of the old sacrifice of the seasonal god. Significantly enough, Jesus's partner in the ceremony is called Barabbas, "son of the father." There would be some justification for drawing a parallel between the tension of opposites in early Christian psychology and the fact the zodiacal sign for Pisces (♓) frequently shows two fishes moving in opposite directions, but only if it could be proved that their contrary movement dates from pre-Christian times or is at least contemporary with Christ. Unfortunately, I know of no pictorial representation from this period that would give us any information about the position of the fishes. In the fine bas-relief of the zodiac from the Little Metropolis in Athens, Pisces and Aquarius are missing. There is one representation of the fishes, near the beginning of our era, that is certainly free from Christian influence. This is the globe of the heavens from the Farnese Atlas in Naples. The first fish, depicted north of the equator, is vertical, with its head pointing to the celestial Pole; the second fish, south of the equator, is horizontal, with its head pointing West. The picture follows the astronomical configuration and is therefore naturalistic.[76] The zodiac from the temple of Hathor at Denderah (1st cent. B.C.) shows the fishes, but they both face the same way. The planisphere of Timochares,[77] mentioned by Hipparchus, has only *one* fish where Pisces should be. On coins and gems from the time of the emperors, and also on Mithraic monuments,[78] the fishes are shown either facing the same way or moving in opposite directions.[79] The polarity which the fishes later acquired may perhaps be due to the fact that the astronomical constellation shows the first (northerly) fish as vertical, and the second (southerly) fish as horizontal. They move al-

[75] Eisler, *Orpheus—The Fisher*, pp. 51ff. There is also a wealth of material in Eisler's paper "Der Fisch als Sexualsymbol," though it contains little that would help to interpret the fish-symbol, since the question puts the cart before the horse. It has long been known that *all the instinctual forces of the psyche* are involved in the formation of symbolic images, hence sexuality as well. Sex is not "symbolized" in these images, but leaps to the eye, as Eisler's material clearly shows. In whatsoever a man is involved, there his sexuality will appear too. The indubitably correct statement that St. Peter's is made of stone, wood, and metal hardly helps us to interpret its meaning, and the same is true of the fish symbol if one continues to be astonished that this image, like all others, has its manifest sexual components. With regard to the terminology, it should be noted that something known is never "symbolized," but can only be expressed *allegorically* or *semiotically*.
[76] Thiele, *Antike Himmelsbilder*, p. 29.
[77] Boll, *Sphaera*, Pl. I, and Eisler, *The Royal Art of Astrology*, Pl. 5, following p. 164.
[78] Gaedechens, *Der Marmorne Himmelsglobus*.
[79] Cumont, *Textes et monuments*, II.

most at right angles to one another and hence form a cross. This coun-termovement, which was unknown to the majority of the oldest sources, was much emphasized in Christian times, and this leads one to suspect a certain tendentiousness.[80]

48   Although no connection of any kind can be proved between the figure of Christ and the inception of the astrological age of the fishes, the simultaneity of the fish symbolism of the Redeemer with the astro-logical symbol of the new aeon seems to me important enough to war-rant the emphasis we place upon it. If we try to follow up the compli-cated mythological ramifications of this parallel, we do so with intent to throw light on the multifarious aspects of an archetype that manifests itself on the one hand in a *personality*, and on the other hand syn-chronistically, in a moment of time determined in advance, before Christ's birth. Indeed, long before that, the archetype had been written in the heavens by projection, so as then, "when the time was fulfilled," to coincide with the symbols produced by the new era. The fish, appro-priately enough, belongs to the winter rainy season, like Aquarius and Capricorn (αἰγόκερως, the goat-fish).[81] As a zodiacal sign, therefore, it is not in the least remarkable. It becomes a matter for astonishment only when, through the precession of the equinoxes, the spring-point moves into this sign and thus inaugurates an age in which the "fish" was used as a name for the God who became a man, who was born as a fish and was sacrificed as a ram, who had fishermen for disciples and wanted to make them fishers of men, who fed the multitude with mi-raculously multiplying fishes, who was himself eaten as a fish, the "ho-lier food," and whose followers are little fishes, the "pisciculi." Assume, if you like, that a fairly widespread knowledge of astrology would ac-count for at least some of this symbolism in certain Gnostic-Christian circles.[82] But this assumption does not apply when it comes to eyewit-

---

[80] See the two fishes in Lambspringk's symbols (*Mus. herm.*, p. 343), representing at the same time the opposites to be united. Aratus (*Phaenomena*, Mair trans., p. 401) mentions only the higher position of the northern fish as compared with the southern one, with-out emphasizing their duality or opposition. Their double character is, however, stressed in modern astrological speculation. (E. M. Smith, *The Zodia*, p. 279.) Senard (*Le Zodia-que*, p. 446) says: "The fish . . . swimming from above downwards symbolizes the move-ment of involution of Spirit in Matter; that . . . which swims from below upwards, the movement of evolution of the Spirit-Matter composite returning to its Unique Principle."
[81] Capricorn ♑ or ♑.
[82] A clear reference to astrology can be found in *Pistis Sophia*, where Jesus converses with the "ordainers of the nativity": "But Jesus answered and said to Mary: If the ordainers of the nativity find Heimarmene and the Sphere turned to the left in accordance with their first circulation, then their words will be true, and they will say what must come to pass.

ness accounts in the synoptic gospels. There is no evidence of any such thing. We have no reason whatever to suppose that those stories are disguised astrological myths. On the contrary, one gets the impression that the fish episodes are entirely natural happenings and that there is nothing further to be looked for behind them. They are "Just So" stories, quite simple and natural, and one wonders whether the whole Christian fish symbolism may not have come about equally fortuitously and without premeditation. Hence one could speak just as well of the seemingly fortuitous coincidence of this symbolism with the name of the new aeon, the more so as the age of the fishes seems to have left no very clear traces in the cultures of the East. I could not maintain with any certainty that this is correct, because I know far too little about Indian and Chinese astrology. As against this, the fact that the traditional fish symbolism makes possible a verifiable prediction that had already been made in the New Testament is a somewhat uncomfortable proposition to swallow.

149   The northerly, or easterly, fish, which the spring-point entered at about the beginning of our era,[83] is joined to the southerly, or westerly, fish by the so-called commissure. This consists of a band of faint stars forming the middle sector of the constellation, and the spring-point gradually moved along its southern edge. The point where the ecliptic intersects with the meridian at the tail of the second fish coincides roughly with the sixteenth century, the time of the Reformation, which as we know is so extraordinarily important for the history of Western symbols. Since then the spring-point has moved along the southern edge of the second fish, and will enter Aquarius in the course of the third millennium.[84] Astrologically interpreted, the designation of Christ as one of the fishes identifies him with the first fish, the vertical one. Christ is followed by the Antichrist, at the end of time. The beginning

---

But if they find Heimarmene or the Sphere turned to the right, then they will not say anything true, because I have changed their influences and their squares and their triangles and their octants." (Cf. Mead trans., p. 29.)

[83] The meridian of the star "O" in the commissure passed through the spring-point in A.D. 11, and that of the star "a 113" in 146 B.C. Calculated on the basis of Peters and Knobel, *Ptolemy's Catalogue of Stars.*

[84] Since the delimitation of the constellations is known to be somewhat arbitrary, this date is very indefinite. It refers to the actual constellation of fixed stars, not to the *zodion noeton*, i.e., the zodiac divided into sectors of 30° each. Astrologically the beginning of the next aeon, according to the starting-point you select, falls between A.D. 2000 and 2200. Starting from star "O" and assuming a Platonic month of 2,143 years, one would arrive at A.D. 2154 for the beginning of the Aquarian Age, and at A.D. 1997 if you start from star "a 113." The latter date agrees with the longitude of the stars in Ptolemy's Almagest.

of the enantiodromia would fall, logically, midway between the two
fishes. We have seen that this is so. The time of the Renaissance begins
in the immediate vicinity of the second fish, and with it comes that
spirit which culminates in the modern age.[85]

[85] Modern astrological speculation likewise associates the Fishes with Christ: "The fishes
. . . the inhabitants of the waters, are fitly an emblem of those whose life being hid with
Christ in God, come out of the waters of judgment without being destroyed [an allusion
to the fishes which were *not* drowned in the Deluge!—C.G.J.] and shall find their true
sphere where life abounds and death is not: where, for ever surrounded with the living
water and drinking from its fountain, they 'shall not perish, but have everlasting life.' . . .
Those who shall dwell for ever in the living water are one with Jesus Christ the Son of
God, the Living One." (Smith, *The Zodia*, pp. 280f.)

3

"ANSWER TO JOB"

From *Psychology and Religion: West and East,*
CW 11, pars. 688–758

688   Jesus first appears as a Jewish reformer and prophet of an exclusively
good God. In so doing he saves the threatened religious continuity,
and in this respect he does in fact prove himself a σωτήρ, a saviour. He
preserves mankind from loss of communion with God and from getting lost in mere consciousness and rationality. That would have
brought something like a dissociation between consciousness and the
unconscious, an unnatural and even pathological condition, a "loss of
soul" such as has threatened man from the beginning of time. Again
and again and in increasing measure he gets into danger of overlooking the necessary irrationalities of his psyche, and of imagining that he
can control everything by will and reason alone, and thus paddle his
own canoe. This can be seen most clearly in the great socio-political
movements, such as Socialism and Communism: under the former the
state suffers, and under the latter, man.

689   Jesus, it is plain, translated the existing tradition into his own personal reality, announcing the glad tidings: "God has good pleasure in
mankind. He is a loving father and loves you as I love you, and has sent
me as his son to ransom you from the old debt." He offers himself as
an expiatory sacrifice that shall effect the reconciliation with God. The
more desirable a real relationship of trust between man and God, the
more astonishing becomes Yahweh's vindictiveness and irreconcilability
towards his creatures. From a God who is a loving father, who is actually Love itself, one would expect understanding and forgiveness. So it
comes as a nasty shock when this supremely good God only allows the
purchase of such an act of grace through a human sacrifice, and, what
is worse, through the killing of his own son. Christ apparently overlooked this anticlimax; at any rate all succeeding centuries have accepted it without opposition. One should keep before one's eyes the
strange fact that the God of goodness is so unforgiving that he can only

be appeased by a human sacrifice! This is an insufferable incongruity which modern man can no longer swallow, for he must be blind if he does not see the glaring light it throws on the divine character, giving the lie to all talk about love and the Summum Bonum.

690   Christ proves to be a mediator in two ways: he helps men against God and assuages the fear which man feels towards this being. He holds an important position midway between the two extremes, man and God, which are so difficult to unite. Clearly the focus of the divine drama shifts to the mediating God-man. He is lacking neither in humanity nor in divinity, and for this reason he was long ago characterized by totality symbols, because he was understood to be all-embracing and to unite all opposites. The quaternity of the Son of Man, indicating a more differentiated consciousness, was also ascribed to him (*vide* Cross and tetramorph). This corresponds by and large to the pattern in Enoch, but with one important deviation: Ezekiel and Enoch, the two bearers of the title "Son of Man," were ordinary human beings, whereas Christ by his descent,[1] conception, and birth is a hero and half-god in the classical sense. He is virginally begotten by the Holy Ghost and, as he is not a creaturely human being, has no inclination to sin. The infection of evil was in his case precluded by the preparations for the Incarnation. Christ therefore stands more on the divine than on the human level. He incarnates God's good will to the exclusion of all else and therefore does not stand exactly in the middle, because the essential thing about the creaturely human being, sin, does not touch him. Sin originally came from the heavenly court and entered into creation with the help of Satan, which enraged Yahweh to such an extent that in the end his own son had to be sacrificed in order to placate him. Strangely enough, he took no steps to remove Satan from his entourage. In Enoch a special archangel, Phanuel, was charged with the task of defending Yahweh from Satan's insinuations, and only at the end of the world shall Satan, in the shape of a star,[2] be bound hand and foot, cast into the abyss, and destroyed. (This is not the case in the Book of Revelation, where he remains eternally alive in his natural element.)

691   Although it is generally assumed that Christ's unique sacrifice broke

---

[1] As a consequence of her immaculate conception Mary is already different from other mortals, and this fact is confirmed by her assumption.

[2] Presumably the "morning star" (cf. Revelation 2:28 and 22:16). This is the planet Venus in her psychological implications and not, as one might think, either of the two *malefici*, Saturn and Mars.

the curse of original sin and finally_placated God, Christ nevertheless seems to have had certain misgivings in this respect. What will happen to man, and especially to his own followers, when the sheep have lost their shepherd, and when they miss the one who interceded for them with the father? He assures his disciples that he will always be with them, nay more, that he himself abides within them. Nevertheless this does not seem to satisfy him completely, for in addition he promises to send them from the father another παράκλητος (advocate, "Counsellor"), in his stead, who will assist them by word and deed and remain with them forever.[3] One might conjecture from this that the "legal position" has still not been cleared up beyond a doubt, or that there still exists a factor of uncertainty. *interessant*

692   The sending of the Paraclete has still another aspect. This Spirit of Truth and Wisdom is the Holy Ghost by whom Christ was begotten. He is the spirit of physical and spiritual procreation who from now on shall make his abode in creaturely man. Since he is the Third Person of the Deity, this is as much as to say that God *will be begotten in creaturely man.* This implies a tremendous change in man's status, for he is now raised to sonship and almost to the position of a man-god. With this the prefiguration in Ezekiel and Enoch, where, as we saw, the title "Son of Man" was already conferred on the creaturely man, is fulfilled. But that puts man, despite his continuing sinfulness, in the position of the mediator, the unifier of God and creature. Christ probably had this incalculable possibility in mind when he said: ". . . he who believes in me, will also do the works that I do; and greater works than these will he do,"[4] and, referring to the sixth verse of the Eighty-second Psalm, "I say, 'You are gods, sons of the Most High, all of you,'" he added, "and scripture cannot be broken."[5]

693   The future indwelling of the Holy Ghost in man amounts to a continuing incarnation of God. Christ, as the begotten son of God and pre-existing mediator, is a first-born and a divine paradigm which will be followed by further incarnations of the Holy Ghost in the empirical man. But man participates in the darkness of the world, and therefore, with Christ's death, a critical situation arises which might well be a cause for anxiety. When God became man all darkness and evil were carefully kept outside. Enoch's transformation into the Son of Man took place entirely in the realm of light, and to an even greater extent

[3] John 14:16.
[4] John 14:12.
[5] 10:35.

237

this is true of the incarnation in Christ. It is highly unlikely that the bond between God and man was broken with the death of Christ; on the contrary, the continuity of this bond is stressed again and again and is further confirmed by the sending of the Paraclete. But the closer this bond becomes, the closer becomes the danger of a collision with evil. On the basis of a belief that had existed quite early, the expectation grew up that the light manifestation would be followed by an equally dark one, and Christ by an Antichrist. Such an opinion is the last thing one would expect from the metaphysical situation, for the power of evil is supposedly overcome, and one can hardly believe that a loving father, after the whole complicated arrangement of salvation in Christ, the atonement and declaration of love for mankind, would again let loose his evil watch-dog on his children in complete disregard of all that had gone before. Why this wearisome forbearance towards Satan? Why this stubborn projection of evil on man, whom he has made so weak, so faltering, and so stupid that we are quite incapable of resisting his wicked sons? Why not pull up evil by the roots?

694   God, with his good intentions, begot a good and helpful son and thus created an image of himself as the good father—unfortunately, we must admit, again without considering that there existed in him a knowledge that spoke a very different truth. Had he only given an account of his action to himself, he would have seen what a fearful dissociation he had got into through his incarnation. Where, for instance, did his darkness go—that darkness by means of which Satan always manages to escape his well-earned punishment? Does he think he is completely changed and that his amorality has fallen from him? Even his "light" son, Christ, did not quite trust him in this respect. So now he sends to men the "spirit of truth," with whose help they will discover soon enough what happens when God incarnates only in his light aspect and believes he is goodness itself, or at least wants to be regarded as such. An enantiodromia in the grand style is to be expected. This may well be the meaning of the belief in the coming of the Antichrist, which we owe more than anything else to the activity of the "spirit of truth."

695   Although the Paraclete is of the greatest significance metaphysically, it was, from the point of view of the organization of the Church, most undesirable, because, as is authoritatively stated in scripture, the Holy Ghost is not subject to any control. In the interests of continuity and the Church the uniqueness of the incarnation and of Christ's work of redemption has to be strongly emphasized, and for the same reason the continuing indwelling of the Holy Ghost is discouraged and ignored as much as possible. No further individualistic digressions can be

tolerated. Anyone who is inclined by the Holy Ghost towards dissident opinions necessarily becomes a heretic, whose persecution and elimination take a turn very much to Satan's liking. On the other hand one must realize that if everybody had tried to thrust the intuitions of his own private Holy Ghost upon others for the improvement of the universal doctrine, Christianity would rapidly have perished in a Babylonian confusion of tongues—a fate that lay threateningly close for many centuries.

696   It is the task of the Paraclete, the "spirit of truth," to dwell and work in individual human beings, so as to remind them of Christ's teachings and lead them into the light. A good example of this activity is Paul, who knew not the Lord and received his gospel not from the apostles but through revelation. He is one of those people whose unconscious was disturbed and produced revelatory ecstasies. The life of the Holy Ghost reveals itself through its own activity, and through effects which not only confirm the things we all know, but go beyond them. In Christ's sayings there are already indications of ideas which go beyond the traditionally "Christian" morality—for instance the parable of the unjust steward, the moral of which agrees with the Logion of the Codex Bezae,[6] and betrays an ethical standard very different from what is expected. Here the moral criterion is *consciousness*, and not law or convention. One might also mention the strange fact that it is precisely Peter, who lacks self-control and is fickle in character, whom Christ wishes to make the rock and foundation of his Church. These seem to me to be ideas which point to the inclusion of evil in what I would call a *differential moral valuation*. For instance, it is good if evil is sensibly covered up, but to act unconsciously is evil. One might almost suppose that such views were intended for a time when consideration is given to evil as well as to good, or rather, when it is not suppressed below the threshold on the dubious assumption that we always know exactly what evil is.

697   Again, the expectation of the Antichrist is a far-reaching revelation or discovery, like the remarkable statement that despite his fall and exile the devil is still "prince of this world" and has his habitation in the all-surrounding air. In spite of his misdeeds and in spite of God's work of redemption for mankind, the devil still maintains a position of considerable power and holds all sublunary creatures under his sway. This situation can only be described as critical; at any rate it does not corre-

---

[6] An apocryphal insertion at Luke 6:4. ["Man, if indeed thou knowest what thou doest, thou art blessed; but if thou knowest not, thou art cursed, and a transgressor of the law" (trans. in James, *The Apocryphal New Testament*, p. 33).—TRANS.]

spond to what could reasonably have been expected from the "glad tidings." Evil is by no means fettered, even though its days are numbered. God still hesitates to use force against Satan. Presumably he still does not know how much his own dark side favours the evil angel. Naturally this situation could not remain indefinitely hidden from the "spirit of truth" who has taken up his abode in man. He therefore created a disturbance in man's unconscious and produced, at the beginning of the Christian era, another great revelation which, because of its obscurity, gave rise to numerous interpretations and misinterpretations in the centuries that followed. This is the Revelation of St. John.

*

698   One could hardly imagine a more suitable personality for the John of the Apocalypse than the author of the Epistles of John. It was he who declared that God is light and that "in him is no darkness at all."[1] (Who said there was any darkness in God?) Nevertheless, he knows that when we sin we need an "advocate with the Father," and this is Christ, "the expiation for our sins,"[2] even though for his sake our sins are already forgiven. (Why then do we need an advocate?) The Father has bestowed his great love upon us (though it had to be bought at the cost of a human sacrifice!), and we are the children of God. He who is begotten by God commits no sin.[3] (Who commits *no* sin?) John then preaches the message of love. God himself is love; perfect love casteth out fear. But he must warn against false prophets and teachers of false doctrines, and it is he who announces the coming of the Antichrist.[4] His conscious attitude is orthodox, but he has evil forebodings. He might easily have dreams that are not listed on his conscious programme. He talks as if he knew not only a sinless state but also a perfect love, unlike Paul, who was not lacking in the necessary self-reflection. John is a bit too sure, and therefore he runs the risk of a dissociation. Under these circumstances a counterposition is bound to grow up in the unconscious, which can then irrupt into consciousness in the form of a revelation. If this happens, the revelation will take the form of a more or less subjective myth, because, among other things, it compensates the one-sidedness of an individual consciousness. This contrasts with the visions of Ezekiel or Enoch, whose conscious situation was mainly characterized by an ignorance (for which they were not to blame) and was

[1] I John 1:5.
[2] 2:1-2.
[3] 3:9.
[4] 2:18f., 4:3.

therefore compensated by a more or less objective and universally valid configuration of archetypal material.

699   So far as we can see, the Apocalypse conforms to these conditions. Even in the initial vision a fear-inspiring, figure appears: Christ blended with the Ancient of Days, having the likeness of a man and the Son of Man. Out of his mouth goes a "sharp two-edged sword," which would seem more suitable for fighting and the shedding of blood than for demonstrating brotherly love. Since this Christ says to him, "Fear not," we must assume that John was not overcome by love when he fell "as though dead,"[5] but rather by fear. (What price now the perfect love which casts out fear?)

700   Christ commands him to write seven epistles to the churches in the province of Asia. The church in Ephesus is admonished to repent; otherwise it is threatened with deprivation of the light ("I will come . . . and remove your candlestick from its place").[6] We also learn from this letter that Christ "hates" the Nicolaitans. (How does this square with love of your neighbour?)

701   The church in Smyrna does not come off so badly. Its enemies supposedly are Jews, but they are "a synagogue of Satan," which does not sound too friendly.

702   Pergamum is censured because a teacher of false doctrines is making himself conspicuous there, and the place swarms with Nicolaitans. Therefore it must repent—"if not, I will come to you soon." This can only be interpreted as a threat.

703   Thyatira tolerates the preaching of "that woman Jezebel, who calls herself a prophetess." He will "throw her on a sick-bed" and "strike her children dead." But "he who . . . keeps my works until the end, I will give him power over the nations, and he shall rule them with a rod of iron, as when earthen pots are broken in pieces, even as I myself have received power from my Father; and I will give him the morning star."[7] Christ, as we know, teaches "Love your enemies," but here he threatens a massacre of children all too reminiscent of Bethlehem!

704   The works of the church in Sardis are not perfect before God. Therefore, "repent." Otherwise he will come like a thief, "and you will not know at what hour I will come upon you"[8]—a none too friendly warning.

705   In regard to Philadelphia, there is nothing to be censured. But

---

[5] Cf. Rev. 1:16–17.
[6] Rev. 2:5.
[7] 2:20f.
[8] 3:3.

Laodicea he will spew out of his mouth, because they are lukewarm. They too must repent. His explanation is characteristic: "Those whom I love, I reprove and chasten."[9] It would be quite understandable if the Laodiceans did not want too much of this "love."

706   Five of the seven churches get bad reports. This apocalyptic "Christ" behaves rather like a bad-tempered, power-conscious "boss" who very much resembles the "shadow" of a love-preaching bishop.

707   As if in confirmation of what I have said, there now follows a vision in the style of Ezekiel. But he who sat upon the throne did not look like a man, but was to look upon "like jasper and carnelian."[10] Before him was "a sea of glass, like crystal"; around the throne, four "living creatures" (ζῷα), which were "full of eyes in front and behind . . . all round and within."[11] The symbol of Ezekiel appears here strangely modified: stone, glass, crystal—dead and rigid things deriving from the inorganic realm—characterize the Deity. One is inevitably reminded of the preoccupation of the alchemists during the following centuries, when the mysterious "Man," the *homo altus*, was named λίθος οὐ λίθος, 'the stone that is no stone,' and multiple eyes gleamed in the ocean of the unconscious.[12] At any rate, something of John's psychology comes in here, which has caught a glimpse of things beyond the Christian cosmos.

708   Hereupon follows the opening of the Book with Seven Seals by the "Lamb." The latter has put off the human features of the "Ancient of Days" and now appears in purely theriomorphic but monstrous form, like one of the many other horned animals in the Book of Revelation. It has seven eyes and seven horns, and is therefore more like a ram than a lamb. Altogether it must have looked pretty awful. Although it is described as "standing, as though it had been slain,"[13] it does not behave at all like an innocent victim, but in a very lively manner indeed. From the first four seals it lets loose the four sinister apocalyptic horsemen. With the opening of the fifth seal, we hear the martyrs crying for vengeance ("O sovereign Lord, holy and true, how long before thou wilt judge and avenge our blood on those who dwell upon the earth?").[14] The sixth seal brings a cosmic catastrophe, and everything hides from

[9] 3:19.
[10] 4:3.
[11] 4:6f.
[12] This refers to the "luminosity" of the archetypes. [Cf. Jung, "On the Nature of the Psyche," pp. 190ff.—EDITORS.]
[13] Rev. 5:6.
[14] 6:10.

the "wrath of the Lamb," "for the great day of his wrath is come."[15] We no longer recognize the meek Lamb who lets himself be led unresistingly to the slaughter; there is only the aggressive and irascible ram whose rage can at last be vented. In all this I see less a metaphysical mystery than the outburst of long pent-up negative feelings such as can frequently be observed in people who strive for perfection. We can take it as certain that the author of the Epistles of John made every effort to practise what he preached to his fellow Christians. For this purpose he had to shut out all negative feelings, and, thanks to a helpful lack of self-reflection, he was able to forget them. But though they disappeared from the conscious level they continued to rankle beneath the surface, and in the course of time spun an elaborate web of resentments and vengeful thoughts which then burst upon consciousness in the form of a revelation. From this there grew up a terrifying picture that blatantly contradicts all ideas of Christian humility, tolerance, love of your neighbour and your enemies, and makes nonsense of a loving father in heaven and rescuer of mankind. A veritable orgy of hatred, wrath, vindictiveness, and blind destructive fury that revels in fantastic images of terror breaks out and with blood and fire overwhelms a world which Christ had just endeavoured to restore to the original state of innocence and loving communion with God.

709   The opening of the seventh seal naturally brings a new flood of miseries which threaten to exhaust even St. John's unholy imagination. As if to fortify himself, he must now eat a "little scroll" in order to go on with his "prophesying."

710   When the seventh angel had finally ceased blowing his trumpet, there appeared in heaven, after the destruction of Jerusalem, a vision of the *sun-woman*, "with the moon under her feet, and on her head a crown of twelve stars."[16] She was in the pangs of birth, and before her stood a great red dragon that wanted to devour her child.

711   This vision is altogether out of context. Whereas with the previous visions one has the impression that they were afterwards revised, rearranged, and embellished, one feels that this image is original and not intended for any educational purpose. The vision is introduced by the opening of the temple in heaven and the sight of the Ark of the Covenant.[17] This is probably a prelude to the descent of the heavenly bride, Jerusalem, an equivalent of Sophia, for it is all part of the heavenly

---

[15] 6:17 (AV).
[16] Rev. 12:1.
[17] Rev. 11:19. The *arca foederis* is an *allegoria Mariae*.

hieros gamos, whose fruit is a divine man-child. He is threatened with the fate of Apollo, the son of Leto, who was likewise pursued by a dragon. But here we must dwell for a moment on the figure of the mother. She is "a woman clothed with the sun." Note the simple statement "a woman"—an ordinary woman, not a goddess and not an eternal virgin immaculately conceived. No special precautions exempting her from complete womanhood are noticeable, except the cosmic and naturalistic attributes which mark her as an *anima mundi* and peer of the primordial cosmic man, or Anthropos. She is the feminine Anthropos, the counterpart of the masculine principle. The pagan Leto motif is eminently suited to illustrate this, for in Greek mythology matriarchal and patriarchal elements are about equally mixed. The stars above, the moon below, in the middle the sun, the rising Horus and the setting Osiris, and the maternal night all round, οὐρανὸς ἄνω, οὐρανὸς κάτω[18] —this symbolism reveals the whole mystery of the "woman": she contains in her darkness the sun of "masculine" consciousness, which rises as a child out of the nocturnal sea of the unconscious, and as an old man sinks into it again. She adds the dark to the light, symbolizes the hierogamy of opposites, and reconciles nature with spirit.

712   The son who is born of these heavenly nuptials is perforce a *complexio oppositorum,* a uniting symbol, a totality of life. John's unconscious, certainly not without reason, borrowed from Greek mythology in order to describe this strange eschatological experience, for it was not on any account to be confused with the birth of the Christ-child which had occurred long before under quite different circumstances. Though obviously the allusion is to the "wrathful Lamb," i.e., the apocalyptic Christ, the newborn man-child is represented as his duplicate, as one who will "rule the nations with a rod of iron."[19] He is thus assimilated to the predominant feelings of hatred and vengeance, so that it looks as if he will needlessly continue to wreak his judgment even in the distant future. This interpretation does not seem consistent, because the Lamb is already charged with this task and, in the course of the revelation, carries it to an end without the newborn man-child ever having an opportunity to act on his own. He never reappears afterwards. I am therefore inclined to believe that the depiction of him as a son of vengeance, if it is not an interpretative interpolation, must have been a familiar phrase to John and that it slipped out as the obvious interpretation. This is the more probable in that the intermezzo could not at the time have been understood in any other way, even though this

[18] "Heaven above, heaven below."
[19] Rev. 12:5; cf. 2:27.

interpretation is quite meaningless. As I have already pointed out, the sun-woman episode is a foreign body in the flow of the visions. There-fore, I believe, it is not too far-fetched to conjecture that the author of the Apocalypse, or perhaps a perplexed transcriber, felt the need to interpret this obvious parallel with Christ and somehow bring it into line with the text as a whole. This could easily be done by using the familiar image of the shepherd with the iron crook. I cannot see any other reason for this association.

713   The man-child is "caught up" to God, who is manifestly his father, and the mother is hidden in the wilderness. This would seem to indi-cate that the child-figure will remain latent for an indefinite time and that its activity is reserved for the future. The story of Hagar may be a prefiguration of this. The similarity between this story and the birth of Christ obviously means no more than that the birth of the man-child is an analogous event, like the previously mentioned enthronement of the Lamb in all his metaphysical glory, which must have taken place long before at the time of the ascension. In the same way the dragon, i.e., the devil, is described as being thrown down to earth,[20] although Christ had already observed the fall of Satan very much earlier. This strange repetition or duplication of the characteristic events in Christ's life gave rise to the conjecture that a second Messiah is to be expected at the end of the world. What is meant here cannot be the return of Christ himself, for we are told that he would come "in the clouds of heaven," but not be *born* a second time, and certainly not from a sun-moon conjunction. The epiphany at the end of the world corresponds more to the content of Revelation 1 and 19:11ff. The fact that John uses the myth of Leto and Apollo in describing the birth may be an indication that the vision, in contrast to the Christian tradition, is a product of the unconscious.[21] But in the unconscious is everything that has been rejected by consciousness, and the more Christian one's con-sciousness is, the more heathenishly does the unconscious behave, if in the rejected heathenism there are values which are important for life—if, that is to say, the baby has been thrown out with the bath water, as so often happens. The unconscious does not isolate or differentiate its objects as consciousness does. It does not think abstractly or apart from the subject: the person of the ecstatic or visionary is always drawn into the process and included in it. In this case it is John himself whose

[20] Rev. 12:9.
[21] It is very probable that John knew the Leto myth and used it consciously. What was unconscious and most unexpected, however, was the fact that his unconscious used this pagan myth to describe the birth of the second Messiah.

unconscious personality is more or less identified with Christ; that is to say, he is born like Christ, and born to a like destiny. John is so completely captivated by the archetype of the divine son that he sees its activity in the unconscious; in other words, he sees how God is born again in the (partly pagan) unconscious, indistinguishable from the self of John, since the "divine child" is a symbol of the one as much as the other, just as Christ is. Consciously, of course, John was very far from thinking of Christ as a symbol. For the believing Christian, Christ is everything but certainly not a symbol, which is an expression for something unknown or not yet knowable. And yet he is a symbol by his very nature. Christ would never have made the impression he did on his followers if he had not expressed something that was alive and at work in their unconscious. Christianity itself would never have spread through the pagan world with such astonishing rapidity had its ideas not found an analogous psychic readiness to receive them. It is this fact which also makes it possible to say that whoever believes in Christ is not only contained in him, but that Christ then dwells in the believer as the perfect man formed in the image of God, the second Adam. Psychologically, it is the same relationship as that in Indian philosophy between man's ego-consciousness and *purusha*, or *atman*. It is the ascendency of the "complete"—$\tau \acute{\epsilon} \lambda \epsilon \iota o \varsigma$—or total human being, consisting of the totality of the psyche, of conscious and unconscious, over the ego, which represents only consciousness and its contents and knows nothing of the unconscious, although in many respects it is dependent on the unconscious and is often decisively influenced by it. This relationship of the self to the ego is reflected in the relationship of Christ to man. Hence the unmistakable analogies between certain Indian and Christian ideas, which have given rise to conjectures of Indian influence on Christianity.

714   This parallelism, which has so far remained latent in John, now bursts into consciousness in the form of a vision. That this invasion is authentic can be seen from the use of pagan mythological material, a most improbable procedure for a Christian of that time, especially as it contains traces of astrological influence. That may explain the thoroughly pagan remark, "And the earth helped the woman."[22] Even though the consciousness of that age was exclusively filled with Christian ideas, earlier or contemporaneous pagan contents lay just below the surface, as for example in the case of St. Perpetua.[23] With a Judaeo-

---

[22] Rev. 12:16 (AV).
[23] [Cf. Marie-Louise von Franz, "Die Passio Perpetuae."—EDITORS.]

Christian—and the author of the Apocalypse was probably such—another possible model to be considered is the cosmic Sophia, to whom John refers on more than one occasion. She could easily be taken as the mother of the divine child,[24] since she is obviously a woman in heaven, i.e., a goddess or consort of a god. Sophia comes up to this definition, and so does the transfigured Mary. If the vision were a modern dream one would not hesitate to interpret the birth of the divine child as the coming to consciousness of the self. In John's case the conscious attitude of faith made it possible for the Christ-image to be received into the material of the unconscious; it activated the archetype of the divine virgin mother and of the birth of her son-lover, and brought it face to face with his Christian consciousness. As a result, John became personally involved in the divine drama.

715   His Christ-image, clouded by negative feelings, has turned into a savage avenger who no longer bears any real resemblance to a saviour. One is not at all sure whether this Christ-figure may not in the end have more of the human John in it, with his compensating shadow, than of the divine saviour who, as the *lumen de lumine*, contains "no darkness." The grotesque paradox of the "wrathful Lamb" should have been enough to arouse our suspicions in this respect. We can turn and twist it as we like, but, seen in the light of the gospel of love, the avenger and judge remains a most sinister figure. This, one suspects, may have been the reason which moved John to assimilate the newborn man-child to the figure of the avenger, thereby blurring his mythological character as the lovely and lovable divine youth whom we know so well in the figures of Tammuz, Adonis, and Balder. The enchanting springlike beauty of this divine youth is one of those pagan values which we miss so sorely in Christianity, and particularly in the sombre world of the apocalypse—the indescribable morning glory of a day in spring, which after the deathly stillness of winter causes the earth to put forth and blossom, gladdens the heart of man and makes him believe in a kind and loving God.

716   As a totality, the self is by definition always a *complexio oppositorum*, and the more consciousness insists on its own luminous nature and lays claim to moral authority, the more the self will appear as something dark and menacing. We may assume such a condition in John, since he was a shepherd of his flock and also a fallible human being. Had the apocalypse been a more or less personal affair of John's, and hence nothing but an outburst of personal resentment, the figure of the

---

[24] The son would then correspond to the *filius sapientiae* of medieval alchemy.

wrathful Lamb would have satisfied this need completely. Under those conditions the newborn man-child would have been bound to have a noticeably positive aspect, because, in accordance with his symbolic nature, he would have compensated the intolerable devastation wrought by the outburst of long pent-up passions, being the child of the conjunction of opposites, of the sunfilled day world and the moonlit night world. He would have acted as a mediator between the loving and the vengeful sides of John's nature, and would thus have become a beneficent saviour who restored the balance. This positive aspect, however, must have escaped John's notice, otherwise he could never have conceived of the child as standing on the same level as the avenging Christ.

717   But John's problem was not a personal one. It was not a question of his personal unconscious or of an outburst of ill humour, but of visions which came up from a far greater and more comprehensive depth, namely from the collective unconscious. His problem expresses itself far too much in collective and archetypal forms for us to reduce it to a merely personal situation. To do so would be altogether too easy as well as being wrong in theory and practice. As a Christian, John was seized by a collective, archetypal process, and he must therefore be explained first and foremost in that light. He certainly also had his personal psychology, into which we, if we may regard the author of the Epistles and the apocalyptist as one and the same person, have some insight. That the imitation of Christ creates a corresponding shadow in the unconscious hardly needs demonstrating. The fact that John had visions at all is evidence of an unusual tension between conscious and unconscious. If he is identical with the author of the Epistles, he must have been quite old when he wrote the Book of Revelation. *In confinio mortis* and in the evening of a long and eventful life a man will often see immense vistas of time stretching out before him. Such a man no longer lives in the everyday world and in the vicissitudes of personal relationships, but in the sight of many aeons and in the movement of ideas as they pass from century to century. The eye of John penetrates into the distant future of the Christian aeon and into the dark abyss of those forces which his Christianity kept in equilibrium. What burst upon him is the storm of the times, the premonition of a tremendous enantiodromia which he could only understand as the final annihilation of the darkness which had not comprehended the light that appeared in Christ. He failed to see that the power of destruction and vengeance is that very darkness from which God had split himself off when he became man. Therefore he could not understand, either, what that sun-moon-

child meant, and he could only interpret it as another figure of vengeance. The passion that breaks through in his revelation bears no trace of the feebleness or serenity of old age, because it is infinitely more than personal resentment: it is the spirit of God itself, which blows through the weak mortal frame and again demands man's *fear* of the unfathomable Godhead.

*

718   The torrent of negative feelings seems to be inexhaustible, and the dire events continue their course. Out of the sea come monsters "with horns" (i.e., endowed with power), the horrid progeny of the deep. Faced with all this darkness and destruction, man's terrified consciousness quite understandably looks round for a mountain of refuge, an island of peace and safety. John therefore weaves in a vision of the Lamb on Mount Zion, where the hundred and forty-four thousand elect and redeemed are gathered round the Lamb.[1] They are the παρθένοι, the male virgins, "which were not defiled with women."[2] They are the ones who, following in the footsteps of the young dying god, have never become complete human beings, but have voluntarily renounced their share in the human lot and have said no to the continuance of life on earth.[3] If everyone were converted to this point of view, man as a species would die out in a few decades. But of such preordained ones there are relatively few. John believed in predestination in accordance with higher authority. This is rank pessimism.

> Everything created
> Is worth being liquidated

says Mephisto.

719   This only moderately comforting prospect is immediately interrupted by the warning angels. The first angel proclaims an "everlasting gospel," the quintessence of which is "Fear God!" There is no more talk of God's love. What is feared can only be something fearful.[4]

---

[1] Rev. 14:1. It may be significant that there is no longer any talk of the "great multitude which no man could number, from every nation, from all tribes and peoples and tongues, standing before the throne and before the Lamb," who were mentioned in 7:9.
[2] 14:4 (AV).
[3] They really belong to the cult of the Great Mother, since they correspond to the emasculated Galli. Cf. the strange passage in Matthew 19:12, about the eunuchs "who have made themselves eunuchs for the sake of the kingdom of heaven," like the priests of Cybele who used to castrate themselves in honour of her son Attis.
[4] Cf. also Rev. 19:5.

720   The Son of Man now appears holding a sharp sickle in his hand, together with an auxiliary angel who also has a sickle.[5] But the grape harvest consists in an unparalleled blood-bath: the angel "gathered the vintage of the earth, and threw it into the great winepress of the wrath of God . . . and blood flowed from the winepress"—in which human beings were trodden!—"as high as a horse's bridle, for one thousand six hundred stadia."[6]

721   Seven angels then come out of the heavenly temple with the seven vials of wrath, which they proceed to pour out on the earth.[7] The *pièce de résistance* is the destruction of the Great Whore of Babylon, the counterpart of the heavenly Jerusalem. The Whore is the chthonic equivalent of the sun-woman Sophia, with, however, a reversal in moral character. If the elect turn themselves into "virgins" in honour of the Great Mother Sophia, a gruesome fantasy of fornication is spawned in the unconscious by way of compensation. The destruction of Babylon therefore represents not only the end of fornication, but the utter eradication of all life's joys and pleasures, as can be seen from 18:22–23:

> and the sound of harpers and minstrels, of flute players
> 　and trumpeters,
> 　shall be heard in thee no more;
>
> 　·　·　·　·　·　·　·　·　·　·　·　·
>
> and the light of a lamp
> 　shall shine in thee no more;
> and the voice of bridegroom and bride
> 　shall be heard in thee no more . . .

722   As we happen to be living at the end of the Christian aeon Pisces, one cannot help but recall the doom that has overtaken our modern art.

723   Symbols like Jerusalem, Babylon, etc. are always overdetermined, that is, they have several aspects of meaning and can therefore be interpreted in different ways. I am only concerned with the psychological aspect, and do not wish to express an opinion as to their possible connection with historical events.

724   The destruction of all beauty and of all life's joys, the unspeakable

---

[5] 14:14 and 17. The auxiliary angel might well be John himself.
[6] 14:19–20.
[7] 15:6–7 and 16:1ff.

suffering of the whole of creation that once sprang from the hand of a lavish Creator, would be, for a feeling heart, an occasion for deepest melancholy. But John cries: "Rejoice over her, thou heaven, ye holy apostles and prophets, for God hath avenged you on her [Babylon],"[8] from which we can see how far vindictiveness and lust for destruction can go, and what the "thorn in the flesh" means.

725   It is Christ who, leading the hosts of angels, treads "the winepress of the fierceness and wrath of Almighty God."[9] His robe "is dipped in blood."[10] He rides a *white horse*,[11] and with the sword which issues out of his mouth he kills the beast and the "false prophet," presumably his— or John's—dark counterpart, i.e., the shadow. Satan is locked up in the bottomless pit for a thousand years, and *Christ shall reign for the same length of time.* "After that he must be loosed a little season."[12] These thousand years correspond astrologically to the first half of the Pisces aeon. The setting free of Satan after this time must therefore corre- spond—one cannot imagine any other reason for it—to the enan- tiodromia of the Christian aeon, that is, to the reign of the Antichrist, whose coming could be predicted on astrological grounds. Finally, at the end of an unspecified period, the devil is thrown into the lake of fire and brimstone for ever and ever (but not completely destroyed as in Enoch), and the whole of the first creation disappears.[13]

726   The *hieros gamos*, the marriage of the Lamb with "his Bride," which had been announced earlier,[14] can now take place. The bride is the "new Jerusalem coming down out of heaven."[15] Her "radiance [was] like a most rare jewel, like a jasper, clear as crystal."[16] The city was built foursquare and was of pure gold, clear as glass, and so were its streets. The Lord God himself and the Lamb are its temple, and the source of never-ending light. There is no night in the city, and nothing unclean can enter in to defile it.[17] (This repeated assurance allays a doubt in

[8] Rev. 18:20 (AV).
[9] 19:15 (AV).
[10] 19:13.
[11] 19:11. Here again astrological speculations concerning the second half of the Chris- tian aeon may be implied, with Pegasus as paranatellon of Aquarius.
[12] Rev. 20:3 (AV).
[13] 20:10 and 21:1.
[14] 19:7.
[15] 21:2.
[16] 21:11.
[17] 21:16–27.

John that has never been quite silenced.) From the throne of God and the Lamb flows the river of the water of life, and beside it stands the tree of life, as a reminder of paradise and pleromatic pre-existence.[18]

727   This final vision, which is generally interpreted as referring to the relationship of Christ to his Church, has the meaning of a "uniting symbol" and is therefore a representation of perfection and wholeness: hence the quaternity, which expresses itself in the city as a quadrangle, in paradise as the four rivers, in Christ as the four evangelists, and in God as the four living creatures. While the circle signifies the round-ness of heaven and the all-embracing nature of the "pneumatic" deity, the square refers to the earth.[19] Heaven is masculine, but the earth is feminine. Therefore God has his throne in heaven, while Wisdom has hers on the earth, as she says in Ecclesiasticus: "Likewise in the beloved city he gave me rest, and in Jerusalem was my power." She is the "mother of fair love,"[20] and when John pictures Jerusalem as the bride he is probably following Ecclesiasticus. The city is Sophia, who was with God before time began, and at the end of time will be reunited with God through the sacred marriage. As a feminine being she coincides with the earth, from which, so a Church Father tells us, Christ was born,[21] and hence with the quaternity of the four living creatures in whom God manifests himself in Ezekiel. In the same way that Sophia signifies God's self-reflection, the four seraphim represent God's con-sciousness with its four functional aspects. The many perceiving eyes[22] which are concentrated in the four wheels point in the same direction. They represent a fourfold synthesis of unconscious luminosities, corre-sponding to the tetrameria of the *lapis philosophorum*, of which the de-scription of the heavenly city reminds us: everything sparkles with pre-cious gems, crystal, and glass, in complete accordance with Ezekiel's vision of God. And just as the *hieros gamos* unites Yahweh with Sophia (Shekinah in the Cabala), thus restoring the original pleromatic state, so the parallel description of God and city points to their common

---

[18] 22:1–2.

[19] In China, heaven is round and the earth square.

[20] Ecclesiasticus 24:11 and 18 (AV).

[21] Tertullian, *Adversus Judaeos*, XIII (Migne, *P.L.*, vol. 2, col. 635): ". . . illa terra virgo nondum pluviis rigata neo imbribus foecundata, ex qua homo tunc primum plasmatus est, ex qua nunc Christus secundum carnem ex virgine natus est" (. . . that virgin soil, not yet watered by the rains nor fertilized by the showers, from which man was originally formed [and] from which Christ is now born of a Virgin through the flesh).

[22] Ezekiel 1:18.

nature: they are originally one, a single hermaphroditic being, an archetype of the greatest universality.

728   No doubt this is meant as a final solution of the terrible conflict of existence. The solution, however, as here presented, does not consist in the reconciliation of the opposites, but in their final severance, by which means those whose destiny it is to be saved can save themselves by identifying with the bright pneumatic side of God. An indispensable condition for this seems to be the denial of propagation and of sexual life altogether.

*

729   The Book of Revelation is on the one hand so personal and on the other so archetypal and collective that one is obliged to consider both aspects. Our modern interest would certainly turn first to the person of John. As I have said before, it is possible that John the author of the Epistles is identical with the apocalyptist. The psychological findings speak in favour of such an assumption. The "revelation" was experienced by an early Christian who, as a leading light of the community, presumably had to live an exemplary life and demonstrate to his flock the Christian virtues of true faith, humility, patience, devotion, selfless love, and denial of all worldly desires. In the long run this can become too much, even for the most righteous. Irritability, bad moods, and outbursts of affect are the classic symptoms of chronic virtuousness.[1] In regard to his Christian attitude, his own words probably give us the best picture:

Beloved, let us love one another; for love is of God, and he who loves is born of God and knows God. He who does not love does not know God; for God is love. . . . In this is love, not that we loved God but that he loved us and sent his Son to be the expiation for our sins. Beloved, if God so loved us, we also ought to love one another. . . . So we know and believe the love God has for us. God is love, and he who abides in love abides in God, and God abides in him. . . . There is no fear in love, but perfect love casts out fear. For fear has to do with punishment, and he who fears is not perfected in love. . . . If any one says, "I love God," and hates his brother, he is a liar; for he who does not love his brother whom he has seen, cannot love God whom he has not seen. And this commandment we have from him, that he who loves God should love his brother also.[2]

[1] Not for nothing was the apostle John nicknamed "son of thunder" by Christ.
[2] I John 4:7–21.

253

730   But who hates the Nicolaitans? Who thirsts for vengeance and even wants to throw "that woman Jezebel" on a sickbed and strike her children dead? Who cannot have enough of bloodthirsty fantasies? Let us be psychologically correct, however: it is not the conscious mind of John that thinks up these fantasies, they come to him in a violent "revelation." They fall upon him involuntarily with an unexpected vehemence and with an intensity which, as said, far transcends anything we could expect as compensation of a somewhat one-sided attitude of consciousness.

731   I have seen many compensating dreams of believing Christians who deceived themselves about their real psychic constitution and imagined that they were in a different condition from what they were in reality. But I have seen nothing that even remotely resembles the brutal impact with which the opposites collide in John's visions, except in the case of severe psychosis. However, John gives us no grounds for such a diagnosis. His apocalyptic visions are not confused enough; they are too consistent, not subjective and scurrilous enough. Considering the nature of their subject, the accompanying affects are adequate. Their author need not necessarily be an unbalanced psychopath. It is sufficient that he is a passionately religious person with an otherwise well-ordered psyche. But he must have an intensive relationship to God which lays him open to an invasion far transcending anything personal. The really religious person, in whom the capacity for an unusual extension of consciousness is inborn, must be prepared for such dangers.

732   The purpose of the apocalyptic visions is not to tell John, as an ordinary human being, how much shadow he hides beneath his luminous nature, but to open the seer's eye to the immensity of God, for he who loves God will know God. We can say that just because John loved God and did his best to love his fellows also, this "gnosis," this knowledge of God, struck him. Like Job, he saw the fierce and terrible side of Yahweh. For this reason he felt his gospel of love to be one-sided, and he supplemented it with the gospel of fear: *God can be loved but must be feared.*

733   With this, the seer's range of vision extends far beyond the first half of the Christian aeon: he divines that the reign of Antichrist will begin after a thousand years, a clear indication that Christ was not an unqualified victor. John anticipated the alchemists and Jakob Böhme; maybe he even sensed his own personal implication in the divine drama, since he anticipated the possibility of God's birth in man, which the alchemists, Meister Eckhart, and Angelus Silesius also intuited. He thus outlined the programme for the whole aeon of Pisces, with its dramatic

254

enantiodromia, and its dark end which we have still to experience, and before whose—without exaggeration—truly apocalyptic possibilities mankind shudders. The four sinister horsemen, the threatening tumult of trumpets, and the brimming vials of wrath are still waiting; already the atom bomb hangs over us like the sword of Damocles, and behind that lurk the incomparably more terrible possibilities of chemical warfare, which would eclipse even the horrors described in the Apocalypse. *Luciferi vires accendit Aquarius acres*—"Aquarius sets aflame Lucifer's harsh forces." Could anyone in his right senses deny that John correctly foresaw at least some of the possible dangers which threaten our world in the final phase of the Christian aeon? He knew, also, that the fire in which the devil is tormented burns in the divine pleroma for ever. God has a terrible double aspect: a sea of grace is met by a seething lake of fire, and the light of love glows with a fierce dark heat of which it is said "ardet non lucet"—it burns but gives no light. That is the eternal, as distinct from the temporal, gospel: *one can love God but must fear him.*

*

734 The book of Revelation, rightly placed at the end of the New Testament, reaches beyond it into a future that is all too palpably close with its apocalyptic terrors. The decision of an ill-considered moment, made in some Herostratic head,[1] can suffice to unleash the world cataclysm. The thread by which our fate hangs is wearing thin. Not nature, but the "genius of mankind," has knotted the hangman's noose with which it can execute itself at any moment. This is simply another *façon de parler* for what John called the "wrath of God."

735 Unfortunately we have no means of envisaging how John—if, as I surmise, he is the same as the author of the Epistles—would have come to terms with the double aspect of God. It is possible, even probable, that he was not aware of any contrast. It is altogether amazing how little most people reflect on numinous objects and attempt to come to terms with them, and how laborious such an undertaking is once we have embarked upon it. The numinosity of the object makes it difficult to handle intellectually, since our affectivity is always involved. One always participates for or against, and "absolute objectivity" is more rarely achieved here than anywhere else. If one has positive religious convictions, i.e., if one believes, then doubt is felt as very disagreeable and

---

[1] [Herostratus, in order to make his name immortal, burned down the temple of Artemis in Ephesus, in 365 B.C.—EDITORS.]

also one fears it. For this reason, one prefers not to analyse the object of belief. If one has no religious beliefs, then one does not like to admit the feeling of deficit, but prates loudly about one's liberal-mindedness and pats oneself on the back for the noble frankness of one's agnosticism. From this standpoint, it is hardly possible to admit the numinosity of the religious object, and yet its very numinosity is just as great a hindrance to critical thinking, because the unpleasant possibility might then arise that one's faith in enlightenment or agnosticism would be shaken. Both types feel, without knowing it, the insufficiency of their argument. Enlightenment operates with an inadequate rationalistic concept of truth and points triumphantly to the fact that beliefs such as the virgin birth, divine filiation, the resurrection of the dead, transubstantiation, etc., are all moonshine. Agnosticism maintains that it does not possess any knowledge of God or of anything metaphysical, overlooking the fact that one never *possesses* a metaphysical belief but is *possessed by it.* Both are possessed by reason, which represents the supreme arbiter who cannot be argued with. But who or what is this "reason" and why should it be supreme? Is not something that *is* and has real existence for us an authority superior to any rational judgment, as has been shown over, and over again in the history of the human mind? Unfortunately the defenders of "faith" operate with the same futile arguments, only the other way about. The only thing which is beyond doubt is that there are metaphysical statements which are asserted or denied with considerable affect precisely because of their numinosity. This fact gives us a sure empirical basis from which to proceed. It is objectively real as a psychic phenomenon. The same applies naturally to all statements, even the most contradictory, that ever were or still are numinous. From now on we shall have to consider religious statements in their totality.

*

736   Let us turn back to the question of coming to terms with the paradoxical idea of God which the Apocalypse reveals to us. Evangelical Christianity, in the strict sense, has no need to bother with it, because it has as an essential doctrine an idea of God that, unlike Yahweh, coincides with the epitome of good. It would have been very different if the John of the Epistles had been obliged to discuss these matters with the John of Revelation. Later generations could afford to ignore the dark side of the Apocalypse, because the specifically Christian achievement was something that was not to be frivolously endangered. But for modern man the case is quite otherwise. We have experienced things so

unheard of and so staggering that the question of whether such things are in any way reconcilable with the idea of a good God has become burningly topical. It is no longer a problem for experts in theological seminaries, but a universal religious nightmare, to the solution of which even a layman in theology like myself can, or perhaps must, make a contribution.

737   I have tried to set forth above the inescapable conclusions which must, I believe, be reached if one looks at tradition with critical common sense. If, in this wise, one is confronted with a paradoxical idea of God, and if, as a religious person, one considers at the same time the full extent of the problem, one finds oneself in the situation of the author of Revelation, who we may suppose was a convinced Christian. His possible identity with the writer of the letters brings out the acuteness of the contradiction: What is the relationship of this man to God? How does he endure the intolerable contradiction in the nature of Deity? Although we know nothing of his conscious decision, we believe we may find some clue in the vision of the sun-woman in travail.

738   The paradoxical nature of God has a like effect on man: it tears him asunder into opposites and delivers him over to a seemingly insoluble conflict. What happens in such a condition? Here we must let psychology speak, for psychology represents the sum of all the observations and insights it has gained from the empirical study of severe states of conflict. There are, for example, conflicts of duty no one knows how to solve. Consciousness only knows: *tertium non datur!* The doctor therefore advises his patient to wait and see whether the unconscious will not produce a dream which proposes an irrational and therefore unexpected third thing as a solution. As experience shows, symbols of a reconciling and unitive nature do in fact turn up in dreams, the most frequent being the motif of the child-hero and the squaring of the circle, signifying the union of opposites. Those who have no access to these specifically medical experiences can derive practical instruction from fairy tales, and particularly from alchemy. The real subject of Hermetic philosophy is the *coniunctio oppositorum*. Alchemy characterizes its "child" on the one hand as the stone (e.g., the carbuncle), and on the other hand as the homunculus, or the *filius sapientiae* or even the *homo altus*. This is precisely the figure we meet in the Apocalypse as the son of the sun-woman, whose birth story seems like a paraphrase of the birth of Christ—paraphrase which was repeated in various forms by the alchemists. In fact, they posit their stone as a parallel to Christ (this, with one exception, without reference to the Book of Revelation). This motif appears again in corresponding form and in corresponding situa-

tions in the dreams of modern man, with no connection with alchemy, and always it has to do with the bringing together of the light and the dark, as though modern man, like the alchemists, had divined what the problem was that the Apocalypse set the future. It was this problem on which the alchemists laboured for nearly seventeen centuries, and it is the same problem that distresses modern man. Though in one respect he knows more, in another respect he knows less than the alchemists. The problem for him is no longer projected upon matter, as it was for them; but on the other hand it has become psychologically acute, so that the psychotherapist has more to say on these matters than the theologian, who has remained caught in his archaic figures of speech. The doctor, often very much against his will, is forced by the problems of psychoneurosis to look more closely at the religious problem. It is not without good reason that I myself have reached the age of seventy-six before venturing to catechize myself as to the nature of those "ruling ideas" which decide our ethical behaviour and have such an important influence on our practical life. They are in the last resort the principles which, spoken or unspoken, determine the moral decisions upon which our existence depends, for weal or woe. All these dominants culminate in the positive or negative concept of God.[1]

739   Ever since John the apocalyptist experienced for the first time (perhaps unconsciously) the conflict into which Christianity inevitably leads, mankind has groaned under this burden: *God wanted to become man, and still wants to.* That is probably why John experienced in his vision a second birth of a son from the mother Sophia, a divine birth which was characterized by a *coniunctio oppositorum* and which anticipated the *filius sapientiae*, the essence of the individuation process. This was the effect of Christianity on a Christian of early times, who had lived long and resolutely enough to be able to cast a glance into the distant future. The mediation between the opposites was already indicated in the symbolism of Christ's fate, in the crucifixion scene where the mediator hangs between two thieves, one of whom goes to paradise, the other down to hell. Inevitably, in the Christian view, the opposition had to lie between God and man, and man was always in danger of being identified with the dark side. This, and the predestinarian hints dropped by our Lord, influenced John strongly: only the few preordained from eternity shall be saved, while the great mass of mankind shall perish in the final catastrophe. The opposition between God and

---

[1] Psychologically the God-concept includes every idea of the ultimate, of the first or last, of the highest or lowest. The name makes no difference.

man in the Christian view may well be a Yahwistic legacy from olden times, when the metaphysical problem consisted solely in Yahweh's relations with his people. The fear of Yahweh was still too great for anybody to dare—despite Job's gnosis—to lodge the antinomy in Deity itself. But if you keep the opposition between God and man, then you finally arrive, whether you like it or not, at the Christian conclusion "omne bonum a Deo, omne malum ab homine," with the absurd result that the creature is placed in opposition to its creator and a positively cosmic or daemonic grandeur in evil is imputed to man. The terrible destructive will that breaks out in John's ecstasies gives some idea of what it means when man is placed in opposition to the God of goodness: it burdens him with the dark side of God, which in Job is still in its right place. But either way man is identified with evil, with the result that he sets his face against goodness or else tries to be as perfect as his father in heaven.

740   Yahweh's decision to become man is a symbol of the development that had to supervene when man becomes conscious of the sort of God-image he is confronted with.[2] God acts out of the unconscious of man and forces him to harmonize and unite the opposing influences to which his mind is exposed from the unconscious. The unconscious wants both: to divide and to unite. In his striving for unity, therefore, man may always count on the help of a metaphysical advocate, as Job clearly recognized. The unconscious wants to flow into consciousness in order to reach the light, but at the same time it continually thwarts itself, because it would rather remain unconscious. That is to say, God wants to become man, but not quite. The conflict in his nature is so great that the incarnation can only be bought by an expiatory self-sacrifice offered up to the wrath of God's dark side.

741   At first, God incarnated his good side in order, as we may suppose, to create the most durable basis for a later assimilation of the other side. From the promise of the Paraclete we may conclude that God wants to become *wholly* man; in other words, to reproduce himself in his own dark creature (man not redeemed from original sin). The author of Revelation has left us a testimony to the continued operation of the Holy Ghost in the sense of a continuing incarnation. He was a crea-

[2] The God-concept, as the idea of an all-embracing totality, also includes the unconscious, and hence, in contrast to consciousness, it includes the objective psyche, which so often frustrates the will and intentions of the conscious mind. Prayer, for instance, reinforces the potential of the unconscious, thus accounting for the sometimes unexpected effects of prayer.

turely man who was invaded by the dark God of wrath and vengeance—a *ventus urens*, a 'burning wind.' (This John was possibly the favourite disciple, who in old age was vouchsafed a premonition of future developments.) This disturbing invasion engendered in him the image of the divine child, of a future saviour, born of the divine consort whose reflection (the anima) lives in every man—that child whom Meister Eckhart also saw in a vision. It was he who knew that God alone in his Godhead is not in a state of bliss, but must be born in the human soul ("Gott ist selig in der Seele"). The incarnation in Christ is the prototype which is continually being transferred to the creature by the Holy Ghost.

742 Since our moral conduct can hardly be compared with that of an early Christian like John, all manner of good as well as evil can still break through in us, particularly in regard to love. A sheer will for destruction, such as was evident in John, is not to be expected in our case. In all my experience I have never observed anything like it, except in cases of severe psychoses and criminal insanity. As a result of the spiritual differentiation fostered by the Reformation, and by the growth of the sciences in particular (which were originally taught by the fallen angels), there is already a considerable admixture of darkness in us, so that, compared with the purity of the early Christian saints (and some of the later ones too), we do not show up in a very favourable light. Our comparative blackness naturally does not help us a bit. Though it mitigates the impact of evil forces, it makes us more vulnerable and less capable of resisting them. We therefore need more light, more goodness and moral strength, and must wash off as much of the obnoxious blackness as possible, otherwise we shall not be able to assimilate the dark God who also wants to become man, and at the same time endure him without perishing. For this all the Christian virtues are needed and something else besides, for the problem is not only moral: we also need the Wisdom that Job was seeking. But at that time she was still hidden in Yahweh, or rather, she was not yet remembered by him. That higher and "complete" ($\tau \acute{\epsilon} \lambda \epsilon \iota o \varsigma$) man is begotten by the "unknown" father and born from Wisdom, and it is he who, in the figure of the *puer aeternus*—"vultu mutabilis albus et ater"[3]—represents our totality, which transcends consciousness. It was this boy into whom Faust had to change, abandoning his inflated onesidedness which saw the devil only outside. Christ's "Except ye become as little children" prefigures this change, for in them the opposites lie close

[3] "Of changeful countenance, both white and black." Horace, *Epistulae*, II, 2.

together; but what is meant is the boy who is born from the maturity of the adult man, and not the unconscious child we would like to remain. Looking ahead, Christ also hinted, as I mentioned before, at a morality of evil.

743 Strangely, suddenly, as if it did not belong there, the sun-woman with her child appears in the stream of apocalyptic visions. He belongs to another, future world. Hence, like the Jewish Messiah, the child is "caught up" to God, and his mother must stay for a long time hidden in the wilderness, where she is nourished by God. For the immediate and urgent problem in those days was not the union of opposites, which lay in the future, but the incarnation of the light and the good, the subjugation of *concupiscentia*, the lust of this world, and the consolidation of the *civitas Dei* against the advent of the Antichrist, who would come after a thousand years to announce the horrors of the last days, the epiphany of the wrathful and avenging God. The Lamb, transformed into a demonic ram, reveals a new gospel, the *Evangelium Aeternum*, which, going right beyond the love of God, has the fear of God as its main ingredient. Therefore the Apocalypse closes, like the classical individuation process, with the symbol of the *hieros gamos*, the marriage of the son with the mother-bride. But the marriage takes place in heaven, where "nothing unclean" enters, high above the devastated world. Light consorts with light. That is the programme for the Christian aeon which must be fulfilled before God can incarnate in the creaturely man. Only in the last days will the vision of the sun-woman be fulfilled. In recognition of this truth, and evidently inspired by the workings of the Holy Ghost, the Pope has recently announced the dogma of the *Assumptio Mariae*, very much to the astonishment of all rationalists. Mary as the bride is united with the son in the heavenly bridal-chamber, and, as Sophia, with the Godhead.[4]

744 This dogma is in every respect timely. In the first place it is a symbolical fulfilment of John's vision.[5] Secondly, it contains an allusion to the

---

[4] *Apostolic Constitution* ("*Munificentissimus Deus*") of . . . *Pius XII*, §22: "Oportebat sponsam, quam Pater desponsaverat, in thalamis caelestibus habitare" (The place of the bride whom the Father had espoused was in the heavenly courts).—St. John Damascene, *Encomium in Dormitionem, etc.*, Homily II, 14 (cf. Migne, *P.G.*, vol. 96, col. 742). §30: Comparison with the Bride in the Song of Solomon. §33: ". . . ita pariter surrexit et Arca sanctificationis suae, cum in hac die Virgo Mater ad aethereum thalamum est assumpta" (. . . so in like manner arose the Ark which he had sanctified, when on this day the Virgin Mother was taken up to her heavenly bridal-chamber).—St. Anthony of Padua, *Sermones Dominicales, etc.* (ed. Locatelli, III, p. 730).

[5] *Apostolic Constitution*, §31: "Ac praeterea scholastici doctores non modo in variis Veteris

marriage of the Lamb at the end of time, and, thirdly, it repeats the Old Testament anamnesis of Sophia. These three references foretell the Incarnation of God. The second and third foretell the Incarnation in Christ,[6] but the first foretells the Incarnation in creaturely man.

*

745   Everything now depends on man: immense power of destruction is given into his hand, and the question is whether he can resist the will to use it, and can temper his will with the spirit of love and wisdom. He will hardly be capable of doing so on his own unaided resources. He needs the help of an "advocate" in heaven, that is, of the child who was caught up to God and who brings the "healing" and making whole of the hitherto fragmentary man. Whatever man's wholeness, or the self, may mean *per se*, empirically it is an image of the goal of life spontaneously produced by the unconscious, irrespective of the wishes and fears of the conscious mind. It stands for the goal of the total man, for the realization of his wholeness and individuality with or without the consent of his will. The dynamic of this process is instinct, which ensures that everything which belongs to an individual's life shall enter into it, whether he consents or not, or is conscious of what is happening to him or not. Obviously, it makes a great deal of difference subjectively whether he knows what he is living out, whether he understands what he is doing, and whether he accepts responsibility for what he proposes to do or has done. The difference between conscious realization and the lack of it has been roundly formulated in the saying of Christ already quoted: "Man, if indeed thou knowest what thou doest, thou art blessed: but if thou knowest not, thou art cursed, and a transgressor of the law."[1] Before the bar of nature and fate, unconsciousness is never accepted as an excuse; on the contrary there are very severe penalties for it. Hence all unconscious nature longs for the light of consciousness while frantically struggling against it at the same time.

746   The conscious realization of what is hidden and kept secret certainly

---

Testamenti figuris, sed in illa etiam Muliere amicta sole, quam Joannes Apostolus in insula Patmo [Rev. 12:1ff.] contemplatus est, Assumptionem Deiparae Virginis significatam viderunt" (Moreover, the Scholastic doctors saw the Assumption of the Virgin Mother of God signified not only in the various figures of the Old Testament, but also in the Woman clothed with the sun, whom the Apostle John contemplated on the island of Patmos).

[6] The marriage of the Lamb repeats the Annunciation and the Overshadowing of Mary.
[1] Codex Bezae, apocryphal insertion at Luke 6:4. [Trans. by James; see above, par. 696, n. 6.—TRANS.]

confronts us with an insoluble conflict; at least this is how it appears to the conscious mind. But the symbols that rise up out of the unconscious in dreams show it rather as a confrontation of opposites, and the images of the goal represent their successful reconciliation. Something empirically demonstrable comes to our aid from the depths of our unconscious nature. It is the task of the conscious mind to understand these hints. If this does not happen, the process of individuation will nevertheless continue. The only difference is that we become its victims and are dragged along by fate towards that inescapable goal which we might have reached walking upright, if only we had taken the trouble and been patient enough to understand in time the meaning of the numina that cross our path. The only thing that really matters now is whether man can climb up to a higher moral level, to a higher plane of consciousness, in order to be equal to the superhuman powers which the fallen angels have played into his hands. But he can make no progress with himself unless he becomes very much better acquainted with his own nature. Unfortunately, a terrifying ignorance prevails in this respect, and an equally great aversion to increasing the knowledge of his intrinsic character. However, in the most unexpected quarters nowadays we find people who can no longer blink the fact that something *ought* to be done with man in regard to his psychology. Unfortunately, the little word "ought" tells us that they do not know what to do, and do not know the way that leads to the goal. We can, of course, hope for the undeserved grace of God, who hears our prayers. But God, who also does *not* hear our prayers, wants to become man, and for that purpose he has chosen, through the Holy Ghost, the creaturely man filled with darkness—the natural man who is tainted with original sin and who learnt the divine arts and sciences from the fallen angels. The guilty man is eminently suitable and is therefore chosen to become the vessel for the continuing incarnation, not the guiltless one who holds aloof from the world and refuses to pay his tribute to life, for in him the dark God would find no room.

747   Since the Apocalypse we now know again that God is not only to be loved, but also to be feared. He fills us with evil as well as with good, otherwise he would not need to be feared; and because he wants to become man, the uniting of his antinomy must take place in man. This involves man in a new responsibility. He can no longer wriggle out of it on the plea of his littleness and nothingness, for the dark God has slipped the atom bomb and chemical weapons into his hands and given him the power to empty out the apocalyptic vials of wrath on his fellow creatures. Since he has been granted an almost godlike power,

he can no longer remain blind and unconscious. He must know something of God's nature and of metaphysical processes if he is to understand himself and thereby achieve gnosis of the Divine.

*

748   The promulgation of the new dogma of the Assumption of the Virgin Mary could, in itself, have been sufficient reason for examining the psychological background. It was interesting to note that, among the many articles published in the Catholic and Protestant press on the declaration of the dogma, there was not one, so far as I could see, which laid anything like the proper emphasis on what was undoubtedly the most powerful motive: namely, the popular movement and the psychological need behind it. Essentially, the writers of the articles were satisfied with learned considerations, dogmatic and historical, which have no bearing on the living religious process. But anyone who has followed with attention the visions of Mary which have been increasing in number over the last few decades, and has taken their psychological significance into account, might have known what was brewing. The fact, especially, that it was largely children who had the visions might have given pause for thought, for in such cases the collective unconscious is always at work. Incidentally, the Pope himself is rumoured to have had several visions of the Mother of God on the occasion of the declaration. One could have known for a long time that there was a deep longing in the masses for an intercessor and mediatrix who would at last take her place alongside the Holy Trinity and be received as the "Queen of Heaven and Bride at the heavenly court." For more than a thousand years it had been taken for granted that the Mother of God dwelt there, and we know from the Old Testament that Sophia was with God before the creation. From the ancient Egyptian theology of the divine Pharaohs we know that God wants to become man by means of a human mother, and it was recognized even in prehistoric times that the primordial divine being is both male and female. But such a truth eventuates in time only when it is solemnly proclaimed or rediscovered. It is psychologically significant for our day that in the year 1950 the heavenly bride was united with the bridegroom. In order to interpret this event, one has to consider not only the arguments adduced by the Papal Bull, but the prefigurations in the apocalyptic marriage of the Lamb and in the Old Testament anamnesis of Sophia. The nuptial union in the *thalamus* (bridal-chamber) signifies the *hieros gamos*, and this in turn is the first step towards incarnation, towards the birth of the saviour who, since antiquity, was thought of as the *filius solis et lunae,*

the *filius sapientiae*, and the equivalent of Christ. When, therefore, a longing for the exaltation of the Mother of God passes through the people, this tendency, if thought to its logical conclusion, means the desire for the birth of a saviour, a peacemaker, a "mediator pacem faciens inter inimicos."[1] Although he is already born in the pleroma, his birth in time can only be accomplished when it is perceived, recognized, and declared by man.

749   The motive and content of the popular movement which contributed to the Pope's decision solemnly to declare the new dogma consist not in the birth of a new god, but in the continuing incarnation of God which began with Christ. Arguments based on historical criticism will never do justice to the new dogma; on the contrary, they are as lamentably wide of the mark as are the unqualified fears to which the English archbishops have given expression. In the first place, the declaration of the dogma has changed nothing in principle in the Catholic ideology as it has existed for more than a thousand years; and in the second place, the failure to understand that God has eternally wanted to become man, and for that purpose continually incarnates through the Holy Ghost in the temporal sphere, is an alarming symptom and can only mean that the Protestant standpoint has lost ground by not understanding the signs of the times and by ignoring the continued operation of the Holy Ghost. It is obviously out of touch with the tremendous archetypal happenings in the psyche of the individual and the masses, and with the symbols which are intended to compensate the truly apocalyptic world situation today.[2] It seems to have succumbed to a species of rationalistic historicism and to have lost any understanding of the Holy Ghost who works in the hidden places of the soul. It can therefore neither understand nor admit a further revelation of the divine drama.

750   This circumstance has given me, a layman in things theological, cause to put forward my views on these dark matters. My attempt is

[1] "A mediator making peace between enemies."
[2] The papal rejection of psychological symbolism may be explained by the fact that the Pope is primarily concerned with the reality of metaphysical happenings. Owing to the undervaluation of the psyche that everywhere prevails, every attempt at adequate psychological understanding is immediately suspected of psychologism. It is understandable that dogma must be protected from this danger. If, in physics, one seeks to explain the nature of light, nobody expects that as a result there will be no light. But in the case of psychology everybody believes that what it explains is explained away. However, I cannot expect that my particular deviationist point of view could be known in any competent quarter.

based on the psychological experience I have harvested during the course of a long life. I do not underestimate the psyche in any respect whatsoever, nor do I imagine for a moment that psychic happenings vanish into thin air by being explained. Psychologism represents a still primitive mode of magical thinking, with the help of which one hopes to conjure the reality of the soul out of existence, after the manner of the "Proktophantasmist" in *Faust:*

> Are you still here? Nay, it's a thing unheard.
> Vanish at once! We've said the enlightening word.

751   One would be very ill advised to identify me with such a childish standpoint. However, I have been asked so often whether I believe in the existence of God or not that I am somewhat concerned lest I be taken for an adherent of "psychologism" far more commonly than I suspect. What most people overlook or seem unable to understand is the fact that I regard the psyche as *real.* They believe only in physical facts, and must consequently come to the conclusion that either the uranium itself or the laboratory equipment created the atom bomb. That is no less absurd than the assumption that a non-real psyche is responsible for it. God is an obvious psychic and non-physical fact, i.e., a fact that can be established psychically but not physically. Equally, these people have still not got it into their heads that the psychology of religion falls into two categories, which must be sharply distinguished from one another: firstly, the psychology of the religious person, and secondly, the psychology of religion proper, i.e., of religious contents.

752   It is chiefly my experiences in the latter field which have given me the courage to enter into the discussion of the religious question and especially into the pros and cons of the dogma of the Assumption— which, by the way, I consider to be the most important religious event since the Reformation. It is a *petra scandali* for the unpsychological mind: how can such an unfounded assertion as the bodily reception of the Virgin into heaven be put forward as worthy of belief? But the method which the Pope uses in order to demonstrate the truth of the dogma makes sense to the psychological mind, because it bases itself firstly on the necessary prefigurations, and secondly on a tradition of religious assertions reaching back for more than a thousand years. Clearly, the material evidence for the existence of this psychic phenomenon is more than sufficient. It does not matter at all that a physically impossible fact is asserted, because all religious assertions are physical impossibilities. If they were not so, they would, as I said earlier, necessarily be treated in the text-books of natural science. But religious state-

ments without exception have to do with the reality of the *psyche* and not with the reality of *physis*. What outrages the Protestant standpoint in particular is the boundless approximation of the Deipara to the Godhead and, in consequence, the endangered supremacy of Christ, from which Protestantism will not budge. In sticking to this point it has obviously failed to consider that its hymnology is full of references to the "heavenly bridegroom," who is now suddenly supposed not to have a bride with equal rights. Or has, perchance, the "bridegroom," in true psychologistic manner, been understood as a mere metaphor?

753   The logical consistency of the papal declaration cannot be surpassed, and it leaves Protestantism with the odium of being nothing but a *man's religion* which allows no metaphysical representation of woman. In this respect it is similar to Mithraism, and Mithraism found this prejudice very much to its detriment. Protestantism has obviously not given sufficient attention to the signs of the times which point to the equality of women. But this equality requires to be metaphysically anchored in the figure of a "divine" woman, the bride of Christ. Just as the person of Christ cannot be replaced by an organization, so the bride cannot be replaced by the Church. The feminine, like the masculine, demands an equally personal representation.

754   The dogmatizing of the Assumption does not, however, according to the dogmatic view, mean that Mary has attained the status of a goddess, although, as mistress of heaven (as opposed to the prince of the sublunary aerial realm, Satan) and mediatrix, she is functionally on a par with Christ, the king and mediator. At any rate her position satisfies the need of the archetype. The new dogma expresses a renewed hope for the fulfilment of that yearning for peace which stirs deep down in the soul, and for a resolution of the threatening tension between the opposites. Everyone shares this tension and everyone experiences it in his individual form of unrest, the more so the less he sees any possibility of getting rid of it by rational means. It is no wonder, therefore, that the hope, indeed the expectation of divine intervention arises in the collective unconscious and at the same time in the masses. The papal declaration has given comforting expression to this yearning. How could Protestantism so completely miss the point? This lack of understanding can only be explained by the fact that the dogmatic symbols and hermeneutic allegories have lost their meaning for Protestant rationalism. This is also true, in some measure, of the opposition to the new dogma within the Catholic Church itself, or rather to the dogmatization of the old doctrine. Naturally, a certain degree of rationalism is better suited to Protestantism than it is to the Catholic outlook. The

latter gives the archetypal symbolisms the necessary freedom and space in which to develop over the centuries while at the same time insisting on their original form, unperturbed by intellectual difficulties and the objections of rationalists. In this way the Catholic Church demonstrates her maternal character, because she allows the tree growing out of her matrix to develop according to its own laws. Protestantism, in contrast, is committed to the paternal spirit. Not only did it develop, at the outset, from an encounter with the worldly spirit of the times, but it continues this dialectic with the spiritual currents of every age; for the pneuma, in keeping with its original wind nature, is flexible, ever in living motion, comparable now to water, now to fire. It can desert its original haunts, can even go astray and get lost, if it succumbs too much to the spirit of the age. In order to fulfil its task, the Protestant spirit must be full of unrest and occasionally troublesome; it must even be revolutionary, so as to make sure that tradition has an influence on the change of contemporary values. The shocks it sustains during this encounter modify and at the same time enliven the tradition, which in its slow progress through the centuries would, without these disturbances, finally arrive at complete petrifaction and thus lose its effect. By merely criticizing and opposing certain developments within the Catholic Church, Protestantism would gain only a miserable bit of vitality, unless, mindful of the fact that Christianity consists of two separate camps, or rather, is a disunited brother-sister pair, it remembers that besides defending its own existence it must acknowledge Catholicism's right to exist too. A brother who for theological reasons wanted to cut the thread of his elder sister's life would rightly be called inhuman—to say nothing of Christian charity—and the converse is also true. Nothing is achieved by merely negative criticism. It is justified only to the degree that it is creative. Therefore it would seem profitable to me if, for example, Protestantism admitted that it is shocked by the new dogma not only because it throws a distressing light on the gulf between brother and sister, but because, for fundamental reasons, a situation has developed within Christianity which removes it further than ever from the sphere of worldly understanding. Protestantism knows, or could know, how much it owes its very existence to the Catholic Church. How much or how little does the Protestant still possess if he can no longer criticize or protest? In view of the intellectual *skandalon* which the new dogma represents, he should remind himself of his Christian responsibility—"Am I my brother's (or in this case, my sister's) keeper?"—and examine in all seriousness the reasons, explicit or otherwise, that decided the declaration of the new dogma. In so doing, he should guard against casting cheap aspersions and would do well to assume that there is more in it than papal arbitrariness. It would be desirable for the Protestant to understand that the new dogma has placed upon him a new responsibility toward the worldly spirit of our age, for he cannot simply deny his problematical sister before the eyes of the world. He must, even if he finds her antipathetic, be fair to her if he does not want to lose his self-respect. For instance, this is a favorable opportunity for him to ask himself, for a change, what is the meaning not only of the new dogma but of all more or less dogmatic assertions over and above their literal concretism. Considering the arbitrary and protean state of his own dogmas, and the precarious, schism-riven condition of his Church, he cannot afford to remain rigid and impervious to the spirit of the age. And since, in accordance with his obligations to the *Zeitgeist*, he is more concerned to come to terms with the world and its ideas than with God, it would seem clearly indicated that, on the occasion of the entry of the Mother of God into the heavenly bridal-chamber, he should bend to the great task of reinterpreting all the Christian traditions. If it is a question of truths which are anchored deep in the soul—and no one with the slightest insight can doubt this fact—then the solution of this task must be possible. For this we need the freedom of the spirit, which, as we know, is assured only in Protestantism. The dogma of the Assumption is a slap in the face for the historical and rationalistic view of the world, and would remain so for all time if one were to insist obstinately on the arguments of reason and history. This is a case, if ever there was one, where psychological understanding is needed, because the mythologem coming to light is so obvious that we must be deliberately blinding ourselves if we cannot see its symbolic nature and interpret it in symbolic terms.

755   The dogmatization of the *Assumptio Mariae* points to the *hieros gamos* in the pleroma, and this in turn implies, as we have said, the future birth of the divine child, who, in accordance with the divine trend towards incarnation, will choose as his birthplace the empirical man. The metaphysical process is known to the psychology of the unconscious as the individuation process. In so far as this process, as a rule, runs its course unconsciously as it has from time immemorial, it means no more than that the acorn becomes an oak, the calf a cow, and the child an adult. But if the individuation process is made conscious, consciousness must confront the unconscious and a balance between the opposites must be found. As this is not possible through logic, one is dependent on *symbols* which make the irrational union of opposites possible. They are produced spontaneously by the unconscious and are

269

amplified by the conscious mind. The central symbols of this process describe the self, which is man's totality, consisting on the one hand of that which is conscious to him, and on the other hand of the contents of the unconscious. The self is the τέλειος ἄνθρωπος, the whole man, whose symbols are the divine child and its synonyms. This is only a very summary sketch of the process, but it can be observed at any time in modern man, or one can read about it in the documents of Hermetic philosophy from the Middle Ages. The parallelism between the symbols is astonishing to anyone who knows both the psychology of the unconscious and alchemy.

756   The difference between the "natural" individuation process, which runs its course unconsciously, and the one which is consciously realized, is tremendous. In the first case consciousness nowhere intervenes; the end remains as dark as the beginning. In the second case so much darkness comes to light that the personality is permeated with light, and consciousness necessarily gains in scope and insight. The encounter between conscious and unconscious has to ensure that the light which shines in the darkness is not only comprehended by the darkness, but comprehends it. The *filius solis et lunae* is the symbol of the union of opposites as well as the catalyst of their union. It is the alpha and omega of the process, the mediator and intermedius. "It has a thousand names," say the alchemists, meaning that the source from which the individuation process rises and the goal towards which it aims is nameless, ineffable.

757   It is only through the psyche that we can establish that God acts upon us, but we are unable to distinguish whether these actions emanate from God or from the unconscious. We cannot tell whether God and the unconscious are two different entities. Both are border-line concepts for transcendental contents. But empirically it can be established, with a sufficient degree of probability, that there is in the unconscious an archetype of wholeness which manifests itself spontaneously in dreams, etc., and a tendency, independent of the conscious will, to relate other archetypes to this centre. Consequently, it does not seem improbable that the archetype of wholeness occupies as such a central position which approximates it to the God-image. The similarity is further borne out by the peculiar fact that the archetype produces a symbolism which has always characterized and expressed the Deity. These facts make possible a certain qualification of our above thesis concerning the indistinguishableness of God and the unconscious. Strictly speaking, the God-image does not coincide with the unconscious as such, but with a special content of it, namely the archetype of

the self. It is this archetype from which we can no longer distinguish the God-image empirically. We can arbitrarily postulate a difference between these two entities, but that does not help us at all. On the contrary, it only helps us to separate man from God, and prevents God from becoming man. Faith is certainly right when it impresses on man's mind and heart how infinitely far away and inaccessible God is; but it also teaches his nearness, his immediate presence, and it is just this nearness which has to be empirically real if it is not to lose all significance. Only that which acts upon me do I recognize as real and actual. But that which has no effect upon me might as well not exist. The religious need longs for wholeness, and therefore lays hold of the images of wholeness offered by the unconscious, which, independently of the conscious mind, rise up from the depths of our psychic nature.

*

758   It will probably have become clear to the reader that the account I have given of the development of symbolic entities corresponds to a process of differentiation of human consciousness. But since, as I showed in the introduction, the archetypes in question are not mere objects of the mind, but are also autonomous factors, i.e., living subjects, the differentiation of consciousness can be understood as the effect of the intervention of transcendentally conditioned dynamisms. In this case it would be the archetypes that accomplish the primary transformation. But since, in our experience, there are no psychic conditions which could be observed *through introspection* outside the human being, the behaviour of the archetypes cannot be investigated at all without the interaction of the observing consciousness. Therefore the question as to whether the process is initiated by consciousness or by the archetype can never be answered; unless, in contradiction to experience, one either robbed the archetype of its autonomy or degraded consciousness to a mere machine. We find ourselves in best agreement with psychological experience if we concede to the archetype a definite measure of independence, and to consciousness a degree of creative freedom proportionate to its scope. There then arises that reciprocal action between two relatively autonomous factors which compels us, when describing and explaining the processes, to present sometimes the one and sometimes the other factor as the acting subject, even when God becomes man. The Christian solution has hitherto avoided this difficulty by recognizing Christ as the one and only God-man. But the indwelling of the Holy Ghost, the third Divine Person, in man, brings about a Christification of many, and the question then arises

whether these many are all complete God-men. Such a transformation would lead to insufferable collisions between them, to say nothing of the unavoidable inflation to which the ordinary mortal, who is not freed from original sin, would instantly succumb. In these circumstances it is well to remind ourselves of St. Paul and his split consciousness: on one side he felt he was the apostle directly called and enlightened by God, and, on the other side, a sinful man who could not pluck out the "thorn in the flesh" and rid himself of the Satanic angel who plagued him. That is to say, even the enlightened person remains what he is, and is never more than his own limited ego before the One who dwells within him, whose form has no knowable boundaries, who encompasses him on all sides, fathomless as the abysms of the earth and vast as the sky.

4

THE MISSING ELEMENT IN
CHRISTIAN DOCTRINE

From *Letters*, vol. 2, pp. 6–9

Dear Dr. H.,   17 March 1951

To answer your long and meaty letter one must have time. My answer therefore comes a bit late.

Psychology as a natural science must reserve the right to treat all assertions that cannot be verified empirically as projections. This epistemological restriction says nothing either for or against the possibility of a transcendent Being. Projection is an unavoidable instrument of cognition. That the Christological projection remained attached to the "historical" man Jesus is of the greatest symbological significance, it seems to me. Attachment to the concrete man was necessary because otherwise the incarnation of God—most important!—could never have come about. The conception, already growing up on the Osiris tradition, of an Osiris belonging to the individual[1] is continued in the Judaeo-Christian idea of the *imago Dei* and in the Christian idea of the υἱότμς.[2] Docetism was a relapse into the pagan view of the world. Bultmann's attempt at demythologization[3] is a consequence of Protestant rationalism and leads to the progressive impoverishment of symbolism. What is left over does not suffice to express the prodigal (and dangerous) world of the unconscious, to join it to consciousness or, as the case may be, to hold it in check. As a result, Protestantism will become even more boring and penurious than it already is. It will also

(Handwritten.) Western Germany.
[1] Cf. Michaelis, 20 Jan. 39, n. 1.
[2] = sonship.
[3] Rudolf Karl Bultmann (b. 1884), German Protestant theologian, then professor at the U. of Marburg. He rejected the authenticity of large portions of the NT (e.g., the events on Good Friday and at Easter) as purely mythical and demanded the "demythologization of the Christian message."

continue, as before, to split up endlessly, which is actually the unconscious purpose of the whole exercise. With the Reformation it has lost one leg already, the essential ritual. Since then it has stood on the hypertrophied other leg, faith, which is beset with difficulties and gradually becoming inaccessible. Thanks to this defoliation of the symbolic tree religion will increasingly become a purely private affair, but the greater the spiritual poverty of the Protestant the more chance he has of discovering the treasure in his own psyche. At any rate he has better prospects in this regard than the Catholic, who still finds himself in full possession of a truly collective religion. His religion is developing by leaps and bounds. The Assumption of the B.V.M. is an eloquent example of this. It is the first step in Christianity towards wholeness, i.e., the quaternity.[4] We now have the old formula 3 + 1,[5] the 1 representing 98% a goddess and a mediatrix coordinated with the Trinity. Dreams referring to the Assumption are extremely interesting: they show that behind the *luna plena* or the sun woman[6] the dark new moon is rising up with its mystery of the *hierosgamos* and the chthonic world of darkness. That is why, as early as the 16th century, Gerardus Dorneus attacked the quaternity so fiercely,[7] because the acceptance of the *binarius*[8] (= devil) in the form of the feminine principle, represented by the even numbers 2 or 4, would break up the Trinity. The Pope probably did well to discourage the psychologizing tendency (chiefly among the French Jesuits). The Trojan horse should be kept hidden as long as possible. All in all, I consider the declaration of the Assumption the most important symbological event since the Reformation, and I find the arguments advanced by Protestant critics lamentable because they all overlook the prodigious significance of the new dogma. The symbol in the Catholic Church is alive and is nourished by the popular psyche and actually urged on by it. But in Protestantism it is dead. All that remains is to abolish the Trinity and the *homoousia*.[9]

Since the time of Clemens Romanus,[10] Jakob Boehme was the first to

---

[4] In Jung's view the Trinity is an incomplete quaternity, lacking the feminine element, earth, or body. Cf. *Psychology and Alchemy*, CW 12, pars. 26, 31, 319ff.; "Psychology and Religion," CW 11, par. 107.

[5] The quaternity is expressed by the formula 3 + 1, where 3 represents the Trinity and 1 the fourth person—be it the inferior function, the anima, the feminine element in the deity, or, in another context, the devil.

[6] Rev. 12:1. Cf. "Answer to Job," CW 11, pars. 710ff., 737f.

[7] "Psychology and Religion," pars. 103f. & n. 47, par. 120 & n. 11.

[8] Ibid.; cf. also "Dogma of the Trinity," CW 11, pars. 256, 262; *Mysterium Coniunctionis*, CW 14, par. 238.

[9] Cf. Niederer, 23 June 47, n. 6.

[10] Pope Clement I, *fl.* 96, apostolic Father, who is erroneously credited with the concep-

come to grips adequately with evil. I do not fight for a recognition of the "Fourth." Nowadays it doesn't need any recognizing—it's too obvious. I merely point to the existence of a problem which is of great importance in the history of symbols. I only fight *for* the reactivation of symbolic thinking, because of its therapeutic value, and *against* the presumptuous undervaluation of myth, which only a very few people have the least understanding of anyway.

I don't quite understand why you call a venture "faith."[11] A venture is a misnomer when you are convinced that it is going to turn out all right in the end anyhow. A venture is when you neither know nor believe. When her travelling carriage overturned, St. Teresa of Avila, lifting her arms to heaven, cried: "Now I know why you have so few friends."[12] It can also turn out like that.

I "believe" only when I have sufficient grounds for an assumption. The word "belief" means no more to me than that. Leaps into the dark I know very well. For me they have everything to do with courage and nothing with belief, but not a little with hope (i.e., that all will go well).

This summer a new work of mine will appear, which is concerned with Christian symbology (especially the figure of Christ), under the title *Aion*. Then I'll be ripe for an auto-da-fé. I can say with Tertullian: "*Novum testimonium advoco immo omni litteratura notius, omni doctrina agitatius . . . toto homine maius . . . Cansiste in medio anima!*"[13] But the soul is anathema to holy theology. "Demythologization"! What hybris! Reminiscent of the disinfection of heaven with sublimate of mercury by a crazy doctor who then declared God could [not] be found.[14] Yet God is the mythologem *kat 'exochen*. Christ was no doubt a moral philosopher—what else remains of him if he is not a mythologem? With best regards,

Yours sincerely, C. G. JUNG

tion of Christ as the right hand and the devil as the left hand of God (cf. "Foreword to Werblowsky's *Lucifer and Prometheus*," CW 11, par. 470). Actually it goes back to Pseudo-Clement, author of the Clementine Homilies, a collection of Gnostic-Christian writings dating from the middle of the 2nd cent. (cf. *Aion*, CW 9, ii, par. 99).

[11] In his letter to Jung of 29 Jan., Dr. H. wrote that in the most extreme situations of distress in life he would describe "the last leap into the depths, the venture of decision," as "faith."

[12] Cf. "Good and Evil in Analytical Psychology," CW 10, par. 883.

[13] "I summon a new witness, or rather a witness more known than any written monument, more debated than any doctrine . . . greater than the whole of man. . . . Approach then O my soul . . . !" Tertullian, *De Testimonie animae*, I. Full text in *Psychological Types*, CW 6, par. 18.

[14] The "not" is missing in the file copy, but has been inserted because Jung frequently told this anecdote in that sense. Cf. *Two Essays*, CW 7, par. 110.

INDEX

Abarbanel, Isaac, 215
Abraham ben Hiyya, 215
absence of good (*privatio boni*): as distortion (Jung), 18; human foundations of, 85; Jung's addressing of, 19; Jung's criticism of idea, 91; nullifies reality of evil, 84; Origen's doctrine of, 79–80; White's interpretation, 14–15
agnosticism, 256
Aion (Jung), 21, 37, 41
Albertus Magnus, 227
Albumasar, 216
alchemy: axioms of, 198; cosmic significance of *opus operatum* in, 153; cosmogonic symbols derived from, 201; in historical development of chemistry, 198; idea of washing in, 139; *lapis philosophorum* of, 78, 103–4, 227–28; Mercurius as name for the unconscious in, 137; numbers three and four in, 201; philosophical side of, 153, 227–28; role in history of philosophy and religion, 198–99; role of Mercurius in, 137–38; seed of unity in Christian and pagan, 201; significance of matter in, 102; symbolism expresses individuation process, 209; symbols pointing to one, 146; tree as symbol in, 204; union of natures as goal of, 130–31
allegories: common to Christ and the devil, 213
Amalric of Bene, 223
Answer to Job (Jung), 8–9, 20–21, 37–38, 64–65, 67
anthropomorphisms: images of God and Christ as, 103; metaphysical statements as (Jung), 65
Antichrist: in legend, 80; problem of, 81; as psychic complement and balance to Christ, 81, 97, 99–100

antichristian era, 225–26
Apelles, 216
apostolic authority principle, 175
Aquinas, Thomas, 88–89
archetype of the self: Christ as, 76, 104; recognition of, 105; responsive to Christian message, 110–11
archetypes: archetype of wholeness, 79; Christ and Satan in archetype of the self, 82; evolving images of God based on, 9; Jung's theory of, 14; psychological, 104; symbols representing circumambulation of a centre, 62–63 *See also* symbolism
Assumption of the Virgin Mary: dogma of, 166, 226–27, 264–69, 274
astrology: conjuction of Saturn and Jupiter in Pisces, 215, 217–18; effect on conscious mind, 208; Jupiter in medieval, 217; linking Christ to, 229–33; Mars during conjunction of Saturn and Jupiter in Pisces, 218; related to Christ's birth, 229–32; Saturn as abode of the devil, 216; as a source of fish symbol, 213–33
attritio, 204
autosuggestion, 59

Bacon, Roger, 227
Barth, Karl, 3, 11
Basil, 84–85, 98
Basilides: three sonships of God, 100–102
Benedictine order, 222–23
Böhme, Jakob, 59, 97, 274–75
Book of the Seven Seals, 242–43
Brunner, Emil, 3, 12

Cardan, Girolamo, 222
Catholic Church: attitude toward Manichaean dualism, 87; Jung's inability to

277

religion - a set of beliefs concerning the
cause, nature, and purpose of the
universe esp. when considered as the
creation of a superhuman agency or
agencies usually involving devotional &
ritual observances & often having a
moral code for human affairs.
   - institutionalized beliefs & practices

Theology - the field of study thought &
analysis that treats of God. His attributes,
His relations to the universe; the science
or study of divine things or religious
truth; divinity

Believe - To have confidence in the truth of
something as reliable without having
absolute proof - To have confidence in.